The Sociology of Modernization

The Sociology of Modernization

Studies on Its Historical and Theoretical Aspects
with Special Regard to the Latin American Case

Gino Germani

Transaction Books
New Brunswick (U.S.A.) and London (U.K.)

"Urbanization, Social Change, and the Great Transformation" reprinted from
Modernization, Urbanization, and the Urban Crisis, Gino Germani, ed. (Boston:
Little, Brown, 1973).

"Social and Political Consequences of Mobility" reprinted from *Social Structure
and Mobility in Economic Development*, Neil J. Smelser and Seymour Martin
Lipset, eds. (Chicago: Aldine Publishing Co., 1966).

Library of Congress Catalog Number: 79-64855
ISBN: 0-87855-268-5 (cloth)
Printed in the United States of America

Library of Congress Cataloging in Publication Data

Germani, Gino.
    Sociology of modernization.

    Includes index.
    1. Social change. 2. Industrialization.
3. Secularization. 4. Urbanization — Latin
America. I. Title.
HN18.G43   301.24   79-64855
ISBN 0-87855-268-5

Contents

Gino Germani: 1911-1979

Irving Louis Horowitz

Gino Germani is one of those figures in contemporary sociology of whom it is no exaggeration to say: understand the sociologist, understand the man. Just as truthfully, to understand the man is to understand the sociologist. The interaction between personal life history and social analysis could hardly be more evident than it is in this reluctant cosmopolitan.

Germani traversed three continents in his lifetime. He was born, raised, and initially educated in Italy. As a consequence of fascism he migrated in 1934 to Argentina, where he spent his middle years. In Buenos Aires he made his reputation as a sociologist of development. In the mid-sixties he moved to Harvard University and became Monroe Gutman Professor of Latin American Affairs and Sociology. Germani was not especially content at Harvard — not because of any lack of fame, recognition, or money, but because the ethnic riches with which he had grown up were hard to come by in the Harvard atmosphere. Even those select North Americans he had become close to, like myself, Joseph Kahl, Kalman Silvert, and Seymour Martin Lipset, represented in their own way an ethnic variety with which he could identify. That is why his last years, mostly spent in Naples and Rome, were perhaps his most content, if not necessarily his most triumphal period. As Gino was quick to point out, nothing in modern day Italy admits of triumphalism. No one easily accepts transplants. In a nation as profoundly hostile to the world of ideas and learning as contemporary Italy, a scholar like Germani had to carry the burdens of his fame even more lightly than he did in exile.

Germani's informal education also took place on three continents. In each instance he was a perennial exile, the outsider, someone for whom the world itself was a strange place. His wit, his skeptical manner, his style, professed an air of unconcern about external circumstances which proved disconcerting to many. Curiously enough, rarely has anyone been more concerned with these same external forces as they impinge upon individual careers.

Sociology as a profession has never meant much in a nation like Italy, with its strong belief that political rather than social forces dominate. The entire history of Italian social theory is largely enveloped by the history of

1

its political theory. Even its definition of class tends to derive from Vilfredo Pareto and Gaetano Mosca, and is linked not so much to an economic class or a social struggle, but to political classes and the struggles of parties, factions, or forces attempting to control the political arena. Between World Wars I and II, Italian social theorists from Giovanni Gentile, through Benedetto Croce, to Antonio Gramsci — that is from Right to Left — understood that the relationship between economics and politics is not a mechanical one where economics can be considered infrastructural and politics superstructural. Quite the contrary, twentieth-century politics tends to be *sub*structural and economics *super*structural.

Politicians allocate wealth, determine levels of production, influence rates of inflation, and define national boundaries. Germani's work evolved in this kind of world milieu. It is no accident that till the end of his life Germani was deeply concerned with problems of authoritarianism, totalitarianism, and above all, fascism; not simply as Italian national phenomena, but as the highest expression of state power, as a problem in the integration of societies and the integration of classes, masses, and elites.

The long sojourn from Italy to Argentina resulted in a curious blend of concerns: developmental interest in backwardness, modernization, and immigration — issues that can hardly be avoided in a nation like Argentina — coupled with political interest in mass society, party identification, and integrating mechanisms in a period of rapid change. Argentina was a veritable laboratory for such analyses. Not only did it exhibit problems of development, but it put on display the urban/rural, native/ethnic, and upper/lower-class dichotomies. It is hard to say whether this was a consequence of internal militarism, lack of system legitimacy, external colonialism, or the multinational imposition of a more advanced form of economy. Argentina was a part of the Third World that cried out for Germani's kind of modernization analysis; even though it was never clear whether Argentina was a model or an exception.

What Germani provided was not simply inherited from Italian political theory. He established a more intimate relationship with the works of scholars such as Weber, Simmel, and Mannheim. Even during the years of Peronism, Argentina was not simply another part of Latin America, but was very much an extension of the European migratory processes. In Buenos Aires Germani first absorbed the complete works of Weber, Simmel, Mannheim, and other classic German social theorists. Even before these were well known in North America, relatively complete works were available to sociologists in Argentina. In a singularly creative way, Germani united the Italian school of power with the German school of authority.

This fusion accounts for what superficially appears to be Germani's indebtedness to Talcott Parsons. This superficial connection linked Germani's work to the grand theorists of North America. To be sure, it made

Germani's works intellectually meaningful to an important sector of sociological opinion at Harvard, namely Parsons himself. Parsons's estimate was reinforced by scholars such as Seymour Martin Lipset, who first knew Germani in South America. Germani developed an imposing intellectual fusion of traditions, not unlike that found in the Parsonian theory of social action. But in Germani's case, this came about not through a migration to Europe, but rather *from* Europe. If that fusion of traditions made Parsons the premier sociologist on return from Germany to the New World, Germani's movement from Italy to the New World made him the foremost political sociologist who entered into exile.

His later movement to North America and to Harvard University led not so much to reorientation as crystallization of concepts that he was already widely using: modernization, mobilization, urbanization, immigration. His conceptual fusion of development and modernization characterizes Germani's work after he entered the United States. It represented not so much a philosophical change as a realization of the need to reconsider work he had suspended in earlier stages. The supreme merit of the American experience was that it allowed him time and freedom. America offered an intellectually dispassionate and humanly compassionate climate that provided him with material assets to complete his task.

By the end of his life Germani, poetically enough, did complete his life's work. His three major volumes: the first *Authoritarianism, Fascism, and National Populism,* a second *Marginality,* and a third *The Sociology of Modernization* in many ways represent the main pivots of his theory of social stratification and political class. They amplify and clarify his earlier works and essays, especially *Política y Sociedad en una Epoca de Transición* and *Sociología de la Modernización,* and provide a systematic basis on which to evaluate his work. These latter works enable us to appreciate the systematic nature of his thought rather than forcing us to infer it from his earlier writings.

From a theoretical point of view, what were the main pivots of Germani's work? Germani's "big three" were modernization, mobilization, and marginality. These key notions in terms of a theory render Germani's world view of political psychology and political sociology.

His third and most advanced work is on modernization. Germani sees modernization as the touchstone of the twentieth century. But modernization is not reducible simply to high levels of communication and transportation, nor is it the rapidity with which messages are translated from elites to masses, nor for that matter is it a purely consuming theory of automobile production as the highest expression of economic culture. Germani's notion of modernization is much more ample — and political. It has to do with how a society can harness technology for distinctly political ends and link science to distinctly economic ends. In Germani's view, modernization is in sharp contrast with other theories that heavily emphasize factors such as internal migration of the poor from country to city, overseas migration from Europe to America, unionization of the Argentine as well as the American working class, the growth of a middle sector that is unconnected and often in opposition to the old aristocracy, and the expansion of a communication network as a form of political legitimation.

Many of Germani's concepts of modernization were developed under the crazy-quilt system of Peronism. If Marx was right that the first Napoleon represented tragedy and the second comedy or farce, it could be said with equal vigor that Italy's Mussolini represented a comic figure, followed by Argentina's Perón who was tragic in himself and for Argentine political mythology. But whether Peronism emerged as comedy, tragedy, or neither, the notion of bureaucratic authoritarianism linking arms with modernization gave Germani a special insight into the Third World, as a whole.

Modernization for Germani was a problem of political systems, not economic backwardness. Argentina had in common with Italy the mobilization of a political system for modernizing ends. Mussolini harnessed futurism as an ideology of early fascism. Perón harnessed folklorism as a belief that to lead was the unique destiny of Argentina in a hemisphere of backwardness. The development impulse provided Argentina with countervailing hemispheric power. That Argentina failed to develop hemispheric power does not invalidate Germani's notion of modernization. However, it does call attention to the special context of a modern society suffering stagnation, not to be confused with the kinds of modernization typical in the Middle East or typical, in the 1960s, of the rest of Latin America and parts of Asia and Africa.

The notion of mobilization is equally important in Germani's work. It, too, derives in large measure from conditions prevalent in Italy and Argentina, or at least developed there to a peak because these were modernizing as well as mobilizing societies. Large numbers of people were involved in vitalizing the political system. Unlike Brazil and Germany, mass mobilization in Italy and Argentina was and remains at a high level. How modernization feeds mobilization, and in turn, how mobilization provides stimulus to the modernizing process, is the basic interaction at the core of political sociology; it is the fundamental characteristic of Germani's work.

Mobilization is such a Latin concept that it sometimes comes as a rough shock to those who live in purely authoritarian societies or in those in which representationalism without mass participation has become a norm. A European concern about mobilization became the prevalent style in nations like Argentina. This concern helps to explain the Perón phenomenon: leadership not simply as a function of elites in its classic sense, but also the role of the masses in a less classic model of leadership. There are widespread notions of the mass as part of a socialist vanguard, no less than definitions of a class conscious proletarian. But Italy and Argentina represented phenomena of a conservative mass inspiring innovating elites. Germani looks at this process carefully, indeed cautiously, because mobilization leads not simply to a theory of revolutionary socialism, but just as much helps explain reactionary fascism. Mobilization theory cuts across social formations; hence it is an important variable in its own right. It helps to account for much of the twentieth century: the totaliarian political experience in a variety of economic guises.

The third element, marginality, is a function of the fragmentation of social classes in the modern world. Germani offers a concept widely used among Latin American scholars before and after him, but he uses it in a very special way. Marginality not only has to do with the notion of being outside the primary classes; it is a main feature of the stratification system within a total society with no center. In this respect marginality characterizes the Third World societal framework, where alienation and anomie become collectivized.

Marginality not only defines individuals who are outside the main occupational activities of industrial urban civilization, but more to the point, it is a general characteristic of many people within a social system. Germani provides a political psychology to go along with his political sociology. His lifelong fascination with the psychoanalytical movement, particularly scholars like Freud, Horney, and Fromm — each of whom were translated into Spanish — was not typical of sociologists. Nor was his fascination with Marcuse, who attempted to link Marxian and Freudian elements to a larger theory of love, death, and civilization. Concepts like eros and thanatos hardly appear in Germani's writings. He uses the psychoanalytic approach to show that the structure of authority is often rooted in the parental framework and the need for shared security.

Marginality became typical of modern society, typical of the way postindustrial people survive. Mobilization became the public expression of the authoritarian syndrome and conversely, its private expression. The private element in marginality is closely linked to the psychiatric condition. Marginality became the general theory of alienated social classes, the way mobilization yielded its private self to public control. Privatization became the opposite of socialization: both expressed ways in which the public and private are opposite. The modernizing sensibility is not simply concerned with innovation, or new things for the sake of a novel aesthetic, but rather a mechanism for integrating marginal social classes on one hand, and mobilizing large social sectors for political ends on the other.

This brief intellectual biography prefaces the completion of a trilogy that represents the most ambitious of Germani's English-language writings. It is always sad to lose someone, but Germani had a full life, living to nearly seventy. He lived long enough to realize, if not his life's ambition, then at least to see his major works completed. Like most liberal antitotalitarians who have suffered dictatorships of a varied and sundry type, he was suspicious of grand theory and resistant to a metaphysical world view that reified and polarized the social world. Germani's greatest sociological curse words were *reification* and *polarization*. Intellectual reification, especially in the name of synthetic grand theory, was for him not the essence of the sociological imagination, but its metaphysical corruption. Scheler, Rickert, and Dilthey, the German metaphysical tradition in social thought, were particularly unappealing to him as he grew older. Germani became increasingly familiar with the vagaries of human affairs and the impotence of neat abstractions to explain events.

Germani was not a master methodologist. He never made such a claim. But like any good social scientist, he had great respect for data: an appreciation of the degree to which all theories are falsified by reality. He understood reality as a series of data about the world. But he also viewed data as an ultimate act of faith. The sociological experience of reality became a risk for him when it limited new observations. Perhaps this is why he turned toward anthropology and culture at the end of his life.

In a Latin American context Gino Germani was not viewed as a radical, but in the context of North American thought, even of postwar European thought, he was indeed a man of the Left. Like other critics and crusaders in social science, Germani was a synthetic figure, attempting to link Northern and Southern European intellectual traditions, and ultimately to wed them to the uniqueness of the American experience in politics and society. He contributed eloquently to the *festchrift* honoring C. Wright Mills in *The New Sociology*. He participated in a wide variety of intellectual publications, not just mainline sociological journals. He steered a broad intellectual course rather well, perhaps better than most systems builders.

This panoramic vision gave Germani's work freshness whether or not his estimates were always correct. He may not have always been right. For example, the migration movement from European to American centers was not the same in cause or consequence as that from rural to urban areas. His general underestimation of racial and religious tensions can be considered valid only where nationalism is triumphant. But in a world in which sociology needs more figures who not only attempt middle-range but upper-range theory using the full panoply of available data, Gino Germani made a particularly vibrant and vital contribution. His loss is tempered by an appreciation of the degree to which his professional tasks were achieved, and also by the degree to which his personal aims were given institutional forms. He was able to return to his beloved Italy where he was born and where he died.

This trilogy began in 1963 when Germani first came to the United States. He had a full professorship at Harvard, but he was keenly aware of the system of "publish or perish." Nowhere has that system been cultivated with the same ferocity as in the United States. We worked out an arrangement whereby I would serve as editor of a volume of his major writings, well known in Argentina, on the social structure of Argentina. His work in this field was undoubtedly his highest claim to fame prior to the publication of this trilogy. But it was dated, in part because the data base was limited to what was available during the Perón era and prior to the post-Perón census system. Also Germani's theories evolved; by the mid-sixties, he no longer felt that he would be well served by a translation of his basic work of the late fifties. Nonetheless, we did sign an agreement with Prentice-Hall for a translation, update, and expansion of that work. This project never came to pass. In part, Gino continually rethought his earlier work. Thus despite my cajoling, my concerns, my insistence that he would have to return the modest advance to the publisher, he decided to push ahead with a final synthesis.

Whatever the specific cause, the volume on Argentine social structure remained untranslated. Instead Gino first issued a series of essays that modified this earlier work, three of which were published during my tenure as editor of *Studies in Comparative International Development*. A fourth essay, the basic framework on modernization, appeared in *The New Sociology*. It became clear to me that behind these fragments on fascism and social class, and mobilization and immigration, a larger corpus of work was in the making. However, it was difficult to convince a publisher of this in the absence of a decent "track record." As a result, over the years, Prentice-Hall lost interest in the translation project entirely. As is characteristic of many large publishing houses, by the time any interest could be rekindled, not one of the original Prentice-Hall editors remained tied to the project, which, as a result, never got off the ground. I maintained close contact with Germani over the years. In the summer of 1974 he indicated he had completed a trilogy which needed "only" several more years of polishing and editing, before he would be interested in seeing it published.

The next five years were occupied with internal editing and copyediting. Also Gino began his dual academic life, sharing time between Harvard and Naples. In the interim, editor, copyeditor, and author worked hard to produce the final trilogy of manuscripts. One day in 1978 Gino asked me to see him. I stopped by his office, and he presented me with three huge (or so it seemed at the time) volumes, and asked me if Transaction would be interested in publishing them. If we would be interested in publishing them as a trilogy, he in turn would be willing to make such an agreement. We contracted for all three volumes on the condition that each would be edited one additional time, and that their publication would be separated by at least one year, so that the full impact of each volume could be appropriately realized. The first volume, *Authoritarianism, Fascism, and National Populism*, had already been published in Italian. It came out while he was doing the final editing on the remaining two. Transaction began publication of the trilogy and it also assumed the publishing role of an edited volume that Germani had done earlier for Little, Brown: *Modernization, Urbanization, and the Urban Crisis*. Transaction had also published a significant volume by Joseph A. Kahl on *Modernization, Exploitation, and Dependence in Latin America*, in which the work of Germani's "middle period" in Argentina figured prominently.

I am a deep admirer of Germani's work; moreover I have been profoundly influenced by his character and say so unabashedly. His kind of political sociology, his linkages between state and society represent the best of the modern sociological era. Toward the very end he was turning his attention to the relationship of state to individuals — an early concern rekindled by his acute awareness that whimsy in the hands of leaders may turn out to be mayhem against masses.

My indebtedness to this extraordinary man — as knowledgeable about Antonio Vivaldi and Paul Klee as he was about Pareto and Weber — can never be fully discharged. This is the inevitable relationship of novice with respect to mentor. But with the publication of *The Sociology of Modernization* and the completion of this trilogy, the full scope of Gino Germani's powerful intellect can be revealed for all to see, and for many to learn from. This trilogy will also make it painfully clear what an extraordinary scholar graced our midst during this long and somber century.

1.
Industrialization and Modernization

The Nature of Modernization

Modernization, Westernization, Industrialization

We are living through one of the great transformations of mankind. The first was the emergence of the human group itself (the primitive community) with the dawn of consciousness. The second was the appearance of civilization (the historical societies), and the third the crystallization of modern (or industrial) society and its spread throughout the planet. The three "revolutions" are usually viewed as occurring in an evolutionary sequence. However, they do not necessarily represent a deterministic sequence, as seen in the fact that primitive and "civilized-nonmodern" societies have survived to our day. We do not know why several primitive communities mutated into civilizations, or why the Western culture (classical and premodern) was the only, or at least the first, one to generate the "modern-industrial" cultural complex. We also lack universally accepted criteria to evaluate these three societal forms and their numerous varieties. In fact, the superiority or desirability of modernity, progress and even civilization remains an open question. For, even if we think that the transition from "primitivism" to "civilization" created new and immensely richer potentialities for alternate orientations of human evolution, their development was deeply affected once the modern-industrial complex crystallized in the West. Its tremendous material power and inner expansiveness, coupled with its great attraction to different cultures, gave it an irresistible thrust, transformed all societies and inaugurated the era of universal history. Because of its origins, and the cultural, economic, political and military domination exercised by the "first comers" to modernity, the whole process was initially regarded as one of Westernization or Europeization. Political and military events, new trends appearing in the transitional process itself, a different ideological climate and advances in the social sciences, have substantially altered this view. Among the main factors in the adoption of the new perspective are changes among the dominated as well as among the dominant peoples. These include struggles for independence, nationalism, decolonization and "new nations" building, the continuing transformation of the initial model of modern society (industrial capitalism), the rise of new models (like socialist and other forms of centrally planned economies), the fusion of Western and non-Western components in modernized and modernizing

9

societies, and consequently the strengthening of a more universalistic, and less ethnocentric consciousness among the intellectuals and the public. Modernization cannot be perceived as the mere transplant of European institutions, nor as a transition toward a unique and fixed societal type. From the perspective of the contemporary observer, modernization involves a variety of models, all of which are in permanent flux. It is also clear that there are many paths towards modernity. Perhaps the powerful trend toward planetary unification, triggered by modernization itself, will finally bring an increasing social and cultural homogeneity. Surely it will be a new world civilization, an heir to both Western and non-Western cultures. Yet modernity cannot be conceived of as a final goal, one relatively static once reached. Since its first emergence, modernity has not ceased to change. We may already distinguish a "paleomodern," a "transitional" and a "neomodern" society, and the contemporary scene reveals the first glimpses of the "postmodern." Modernization is permanent revolution. It is not an end of history but an acceleration of it.

The Components of Modernization

Modernization is a total process affecting the economic, the political and the social organization — all the subsystems of society. Economic development is modernization in the field of economy. Because of its central function in self-sustained growth and its historical role in the birth of the first industrial society, particularly the British industrial revolution, industry symbolizes modern economy. Since industrial techniques and mentality permeate most areas of human activity, while agriculture predominated and characterized most institutions of nonmodern civilizations, industrialization and industrial society are commonly used as synonyms for modernization and modern society. Political modernization (also called political development) has often been identified with democratic-constitutional regimes because this was the first form it assumed in modern society. It is now recognized that many different types of political systems are compatible with the institutions and functioning of a modern society. In the most general sense, any political system may be considered as modern which has the capacity to promote, or at least to maintain, self-sustained economic and social growth with a type of "stability" (which may assume contrasting forms) compatible with a degree of integration sufficient to adjust to continuous change, without "excessive" disruption. Finally social modernization includes changes in all sectors of society at every level: personality, norms, social relations and institutions. Various forms of social organization are compatible with a modern society. The three subsystems involved in the total process of modernization are closely interconnected, but they must be maintained as analytically distinct, since their respective rates of change, and the sequence in which they occur, vary a great deal under the different historical conditions characterizing the transition of each society towards modernity.

Secularization: Three Basic Principles of Modernization

The difficulty in formulating a satisfactory definition of modernization lies not only in its manifold aspects but in the diversity of forms it assumes and their inherent change. Another source of confusion is that we must always keep separate the historical process leading to the crystallization of the "modern-industrial" cultural complex, what we call primordial modernization, from the many transitions through which modernity is spreading everywhere and may become the definitive modernization of the planet. Nonetheless, we can still conceptualize a meaningful notion of modernization and define modern society as a general category which comprises many different types, but is endowed with common traits peculiar to all of them and radically different from the societies of the past, as well as from other surviving primitive communities and civilizations.

At the more visible level we find the continuous and accelerated expansion of knowledge and its deliberate application to technology in the production of goods and services, with the use of ever new and higher forms of energy, and the goal of maximizing efficiency. Underlying these traits it is possible to detect a particular structural configuration characterizing all modern societies, whatever their form be. Philosophies of history, analyses of progress and social evolution as well as general theories of society and social change coincide on the existence of this common core, although descriptions and definitions may vary a great deal. The notion of secularization reflects the essential meaning of the modern as perceived by a wide range of theoretical perspectives: from the nineteenth century evolutionists, to Marx, Tönnies, Durkheim, Weber, and most of the present social sciences. It presents, however, some differences with the current "traditional" versus "modern" dichotomy, insofar as secularization is not coterminous with modernization or industrialization. In fact it must be emphasized that a certain degree and different types of secularization are also common to any historical civilization while only its rudiments may be found in the primitive world. What makes modernity distinctive is not only its extreme degree (at least in certain aspects of the sociocultural structure), but also the peculiar orientation it assumed. Within these limits it should be regarded as a set of interrelated basic principles summarizing the necessary (although not the sufficient) conditions for the rise and maintenance of any modern society. As such it is valid both for "primordial" and for "definitive" modernization. These principles may be expressed in terms of extreme "ideal type" poles of three dimensions, a conceptual construct not to be found anywhere in its pure form, concerning the nature of social action, orientation toward change and the degree of differentiation and specificity of institutions.

Let us first distinguish two opposed types of social action: prescription and choice of elective action. Both, as all human behavior, are socially and culturally patterned. Such regulation operates at two levels: internal and external. At the former, the individual internalizes during his lifetime the attitudes, motivations and knowledge, required, approved, or tolerated by the society, in any or most circumstances he is likely to confront. This learned behavior tends to become an integral part of the personality, although it may remain rather superficial (and changeable), or get deeply rooted in the self (and unchangeable), according to areas of action, types of situation and conditions of the internalization process. At the external level the regulation is enforced with a variety of controls through psychological, social and physical punishments or rewards. The two kinds of action differ in terms of the normative framework (and its internalized counterpart) regulating them. In the case of prescription, a specific course of action is required, while in elective behavior the individual selects his own course of action, and what is prescribed are general rules and criteria which must be followed in performing the choice. Occupational or matrimonial choices provide illustrations of both types of action. In most nonmodern societies the individual must follow the occupation of the father, or marry either according to traditional prescriptions or the family's decision. In modern society the expectation is to choose one's spouse or occupation, but the choice is bound to follow certain criteria: vocation, aptitudes, opportunities for the occupational choice; feelings, psychological and cultural compatibility and the like, in the case of marriage. Furthermore, while choice requires a fully individualized self, prescription is the individual expression of a collective act. Rational action, generally considered a hallmark of modernity, is a particular kind of action by choice, in which the guiding criterion is rationality, or the optimum choice of means to a given end, since instrumental rationality (and not necessarily other forms of it), is one of the basic requirements of modern society.

Both types of action may be found in all societies, but the number of areas and range of behavior, kind of groups and proportion of people in the population is virtually nonexistent in primitive communities, severely restricted in civilized societies and very much enlarged and increasing in modern societies.

Although it may be extremely slow, or interrupted by prolonged stagnation, or limited to particular sociocultural areas, change is universal. Societies differ in their orientation toward change. Primitive communities and civilizations do not accept nor legitimize change in all or most of their institutions. The opposite occurs in modern societies, in which change is expected or even required. The latter institutionalizes tradition; the former institutionalizes change. But as in the case of social action, not all changes are legitimized in modern societies, but only those changes occurring in given areas, and according to certain rules.

All societies accomplish a series of functions: maintenance of life through the production of goods and services, replacement of its own members through reproduction as well as their proper rearing and education, regulation of individual and collective behavior, defense from external human or environmental attacks and satisfaction of religious, esthetic, recreational and other needs. They vary, however, in the number and nature of the institutions devoted to the performance of these functions. At one extreme we find the primitive community which, even when endowed with a rather complex structure, presents a general embedment of all functions. Civilizations show a qualitatively and quantitatively distinct level of differentiation. Still, the primitive community diverges in two aspects from the modern one. First, differentiation affects only a tiny minority of the population, usually the elite and part of the urbanite. Secondly, all institutions, in fact the whole society, are pervaded and dominated by the same values and norms. In modern society institutional differentiation and the division of labor reach an unprecedented level and possess an inner tendency toward seemingly limitless increase. Institutions become more and more autonomous. All human activities are fragmented by increasing specialization and the unity of the person itself runs a risk of being lost in a multiplicity of roles. This process is gradually expanded to include the entire population. Here again, as in the case of the other dimensions of secularization, there is a limit defined by the interdependence of the various institutions and differentiated roles. No matter how autonomous the former, and how specialized the latter, they must still work together and maintain a minimum of compatibility.

The three principles of secularization are not independent of one another: institutionalization of change and increasing institutional and role differentiation are made possible by elective action. Both involve innovation, purposeful deviation from the established pattern which can take place only through choice. This brings us to the central meaning of secularization: choice, as a deliberate act, requires persons endowed with sufficiently individualized consciousness. Individuation, a complex psychological and historical process which may vary not only in degree but also in nature, underlies the transition from primitivism to civilization, both Western and non-Western. The former generated a particular kind of civilization, the modern-industrial complex, and this change was characterized not only by an exceptional growth of individuation, in terms of intensity and relative diffusion within society, but also by a specific orientation, a different way for the individual to relate to his own self, to society, to nature and to the fundamental problems of human existence.

Because the conquest, control and use of the material world is one of the central components of modern civilization, its rise, as well as the maintenance and universal spread of any model of modern society, requires a high degree of secularization in knowledge, technology and economy.

Secularization and Stability

High secularization cannot remain isolated. The three areas mentioned above are part of a total social context and since change is circular ("effects" have reprecussions on their "causes"), their secularization is preceded, accompanied and succeeded by many social transformations. Secularization has a tendency to increase in degree, and spread in range, once it reaches a sufficient level to generate self-sustained growth in knowledge, technology and economy. Increasing secularization extremely accentuates pluralism in values. Thus an inherent imbalance is introduced in any secularizing society through the erosion of the very foundation of an integrated social system: a "common core" of shared values and norms. We will find many expressions of this imbalance in our discussion. Many of the problems of our age have their ultimate origins in such contradictions.

Nonmodern and Premodern Societies: Their General Characteristics in Relation to Modernization

Primitive and Civilized Societies

The well known dichotomy "traditional versus modern" has often been criticized or rejected as a gross, or even misleading, simplification. Its merits or demerits must be judged according to the specific purpose of the comparison. It is sufficient, or perhaps necessary, when the emphasis lies on the peculiarity of modernity vis-a-vis all other cultures, but beyond this first step we need further distinctions. This is particularly true when considering modernization as a process whose nature and outcome is deeply affected by the "starting point," by the characteristics of each society prior to the initiation of the transition. But a typology of nonmodern societies based on a generally accepted theory of modernization is still lacking. Another difficulty lies in the immense variety of societal organizations and cultural orientations, and the multiplicity of criteria which could be adopted. The distinctions between primitive and civilized levels are pretty clear. In the first place, the immense cleavage existing between both categories in terms of population and territory is noted. Primitive societies (both nomadic and sedentary) are restricted from a few hundred to a few thousand individuals living in a small territory. Civilizations may reach hundreds of millions and occupy a continental area, with the subsocieties belonging to them varying a great deal in size, from small scale societies, like the "city-state," to large scale ones, such as the empire. This is the phenomenon of "universal states" which, in the opinion of some scholars, constitutes a specific stage in the normal evolution of any civilization. The difference in scale stems from their respective capacity to control the environment, the use of natural resources and the type of social organization. A well established agriculture and technological innovation (like metallurgy, irrigation, animal husbandry or the wheel), the existence of an economic surplus which makes possible the appearance of the city, and written language are usually considered essential to the material and nonmaterial culture of any civilized society with its higher differentiated social organization. Also, great differences in social change have been emphasized. Primitive communities are not static. In fact, they brought the predecessors of man to a real human level, and some of them generated the innovations which made possible the rise of civilizations. Still, once this level is reached, the rate and especially the nature of change are altered. The time scale is shortened from tens of millennia to millennia, or centuries, and the social-cultural transformations acquire new meanings: cycles, rises and falls, stages, directionality, are all the very hallmark of history. Historicity in this sense, and not the mere availability of written records (though important), gives meaning to the distinction between historic and prehistoric (and surviving nonhistoric) societies. Civilizations, represent an essential step in secularization and its psychological correlate of individuation. In primitive man, ego functions, self-objectification and some potentiality for self-awareness have already emerged through biological and "protocultural" evolution, since this is the universal condition for any kind of sociocultural order (Hallowell). But the subjective experience of the self, its extension, limits and nature in relation to the object — world, including other human beings, society, nature and the supernatural (religion), acquire new dimensions in civilization. This mutation, variously described as the "dawn of consciousness" (Breadsted), transition from "shame to guilt culture" (Dodds), decreasing strength of collective consciousness (Durkheim) and individualization of man out of "tribal consciousness" (Marx), represents the psychological counterpart of the structural change and the qualitative leap from primitive to civilized societies. Deliberate elective action is now extended to the point of opening an entirely different and larger scope of cultural creativity, hence the peculiar attributes of civilization: the level of differentiation and specialization, the (relative) acceleration of change, the diversity of cultural orientations and its "historicity." Differentiation in primitive society is essentially biological and social organization coincides with kinship through which all the essential societal functions are performed. What from a contemporary perspective are identified as economic, familial, political, military, religious, esthetic, recreational and other functions originating from delimited roles are performed, at the primitive level, as part of a single interrelated web of norms, attitudes, behavior patterns. Division of labor barely transcends age and sex categories. Hierarchization remains at a minimum and the kin group, from the nuclear family to the larger but close knit descent group, coincides with the total community. Religion, magic and myth permeate and give meaning to the whole life. In civilization the division of labor marks an entirely new step not only at the artisanal level but also with a decisive growth in local specializations, above all with the separation of agriculture from trade and craft industry, of town from country, "the greatest division of material and mental labour" (Marx), the emergence of new forms of property, and the differentiation of lower and higher classes, the basic universal of social evolution (Marx) or at least one of them (Parsons). Family and kinship, religion, law and politics, military, education, as well as other institutions acquire distinctiveness and assume diverse organizational patterns and forms of reciprocal relationship. A higher stage in religion and the appearance of writing should be stressed as being particularly strategic in infusing dynamicity to civilizations. Civilized religions, particularly the great historical religions, are universalistic and express for the first time "a clear structured conception of the self" (Bellah), both important prerequisites of the rise of modernity. Finally, written language operates as a purposeful cultural and social multiplier in terms of differentiation and complexity, acceleration of innovation, extension of influence, communication and interaction in space and time. In fact it is because of this role that the terms literate-nonliterate are commonly used as synonyms for civilized-primitive. The new horizons opened by such an expansion of human potentialities generated the rich array of structural arrangements and cultural orientations exhibited by civilized societies, and provided the broad basis from which the particular evolutionary orientation towards modernity could take place. Other general features must be added to the common characteristics of civilized societies which distinguish them from the primitive level. Although industry (in its artisanal form), and commerce (including long distance and overseas trade) did exist and achieved some importance, agriculture remained the fundamental basis of their economy. It absorbed the largest proportion of the population, perhaps from ninety to ninety-five percent of the total, hence the term agrarian society, which is often applied to nonmodern civilizations. In all of them, economic activity and institutions enjoy a lower status than other human activities. Economy is only partially differentiated and still lacks autonomy in values and norms. Technology was "empirical" and "organic" (Sombart) (that is, not founded on science) being "routed in the sphere of living nature." Furthermore, it suffered several basic limitations (Ellul): in time, since its change was extremely slow; in space, being local and peculiar to each civilization; in range of application, since it affected only a few narrow areas. Population growth was extremely low in all nonmodern and premodern civilizations. Although all of them had some means of controlling fertility, population balance was maintained through high mortality. The cemetary located in the center of the village or town symbolized the omnipresence of death. According to the most common descriptions, stratification tended to be rigid, highly hierarchical, with large discontinuities and cleavages between strata in terms of various dimensions: wealth, income, politics, civic, social rights, prestige and consumption, as well as the asymmetry and inequality in interpersonal relations. Mobility was not legitimized by the legally formalized or customary norms and values. In any case, the real chances of moving upward or downward were usually scarce. A two strata system (a tiny elite or upper stratum at the top, and a large minority of commoners at the bottom) also tended to prevail. While this picture is an oversimplification deforming the highly diversified complexity of civilized societies, it helps to stress some features of nonmodern stratification. Two provisos must be added. First, the two main strata were usually subdivided in several internal horizontal and vertical differentiations, often based on distinct hierarchies (military or religious) and on a variety of groups and associations sometimes endowed with functional meaning. Merchant and artisan guilds and cultural, religious and recreational associations can be found in all civilized societies. Further internal differentiation came from the fact that the same group could be located in different positions along the various hierarchies. Although the superior strata, elites, aristocracies, oligarchies or ruling groups normally ranked equally high in all dimensions, certain categories — in general economic ones, like merchants and artisans — remained low in power and prestige, even when rich, while others, such as religious or cultural elites, could enjoy high prestige despite low power or wealth. These discrepancies were usually legitimized in terms of the predominant societal values, customs or law. Finally caste stratification was common and generated various internal inequalities and excluded, in particular, segregated outcasts or enslaved categories. Second, the rigidity of the system could vary: social mobility could be higher in some societies, in one or more dimensions during certain epochs, particularly in times of political or social troubles, for given areas of activity (military, religious or cultural ones). In many cases it was a de facto mobility, sometimes followed by legitimization in terms of the predominant societal values. But this relatively higher flexibility was almost always limited to the cities, thus a general degree of higher rigidity, as compared with modern societies, did prevail, and economic mobility was not likely to be legitimized as such. The extended family and the predominance of kinship structures have been emphasized as typical traits of nonmodern civilizations. Here again great variations may be found among societies and in the various strata, with the extended family and large household prevailing in the upper strata and more reduced kinship units in the lower ones and among the outcasts. The political systems of civilized societies also present great forms of diversity, such as cities, states, feudal systems, patrimonial and bureaucratic empires and others. By oversimplifying a rather complex matter, one may suggest five dimensions accounting for this diversity. The first is centralization. Civilized polities diverged from the extremely decentralized "feudal" systems, to highly centralized bureaucratic societies, while many partimonial states stood in intermediate positions, and the city-state at a somewhat different level. Relative differentiation (and relative autonomy) of the political system, connected with differentiation in the social structure, is another important variable to which we must add at least three factors: types of legitimation, degree of participation and degree of bureaucratization. Although legitimation was usually "traditional," that is founded on inheritance or religious beliefs, in some cases other forms, including choices by collective bodies, could be found. Participation was restricted either to the ruler and a small circle of aides, or it tended to coincide with the higher class. The extent of participation depended also on the degree and forms of centralization. In some societies larger participation, comprising a category of "citizens," did exist. But, even in these cases, such extension was restricted to part of the city dwellers, that is it remained minimal, since it excluded the peasant (the immense majority of the population), the outcasts and other lower groups. Bureaucratization, finally, could vary considerably from nonexistence, to a considerably organized and autonomous level. The social organization of all civilized including choices by collective bodies, could be found. Participation was nonmodern society, in its various institutional spheres and areas of activity may be characterized as a mix of secularized and nonsecularized structures, with relatively large variations according to each society, epoch of development, types of institutions and kind of activity. But in any case it is the nonsecularized which predominates over the secularized aspects. Applying the principles of electivity, specialization and change to types of social relationships, it is noted that ascription is more frequent than achievement (that is, relations depend more on what the person is, in terms of nonelective characteristics such as sex, age, social and ethnical origins or family, than on his capability and efficiency and relevance to the role or relationship). Particularism tends to prevail over universalism (relations and roles refer to specific persons, more than to formally defined categories on the basis of general criteria). Finally, roles and relationships tend to be more diffuse (that is, covering a wide range of undifferentiated aspects) than specific, and more expressive than instrumental (more oriented toward emotional or esthetic manifestations than tasks).

Western and Non-Western Civilizations

Civilized nonmodern societies are not easily classified according to evolutionary criteria. When this is attempted it is usually conducted in terms of affinity with the modern societal type, usually corresponding to what has been defined here as secularization, and also on the basis of a single general factor reputed more relevant for evolution, such as "enhancement of adaptative capacity" (White, etc.), technological advances, "mode of production" (Marx), "growth in rationality" (Weber, Ginsberg) and "growth in freedom" (Hegel). As could be expected, Western societies, including those of classical antiquity tend to be placed in a prominent position in the evolutionary sequence. This preference in part reflects Western ethnocentrism, but it is also founded on historical process, at least to the extent that modernity was generated mostly by the Western line of social evolution. As it happens, the very distinction of Western societies from non-Western ones belongs to a theoretical framework antithetical to, or at least quite divergent from, evolutionism. These conceptions of history assume as a "significant unit" the "civilization," a vast cultural entity which may include one or more societies of quite different size and is characterized by peculiar "styles" in its cultural achievements, or even by a central paramount configuration of values, giving it a specific individuality. Each civilization, according to these theories, follows the same succession of cycles, stages or fluctuations, which, once they achieve their full course, bring the civilization itself to an end (Spengler) though not necessarily causing the disappearance of their cultural heritage, since this may be received and incorporated by other civilizations or even accomplish a major role in generating a new one (Toynbee, Kroeber, Sorokin). The "cyclical" (also called "fluctuating") theories of history can be partially reconciled with evolutionism taking into account that first, the transition from "primitive" to "civilized" may be considered implicitly evolutionary even by those who emphasize the uniqueness of each civilization, and second, Western civilization has generated the particular cultural configuration able to generate a qualitative leap at least in some components of culture and social organization (science, technology and economy). This leap is replacing the "parallel histories" of multiple civilizations by the "universal history" of a single one, a new civilization still in the making. It must be stressed that in the opinion of many scholars such components are perhaps the only evolutionary (or cumulative) ones, while many of the others, particularly the esthetic and the ethical, are nonevolutionary (noncumulative), a distinction dramatically expressed in the contemporary dilemma of "material" versus "moral" progress.

Stability and Survival in Non-Modern Societies

The most common notion underlying old and new evolutionism is adaptation. If adaptation is defined as the ability to survive while confronting the challenge of natural environment or internal stresses, then primitive communities seem to show higher survival potential than civilizations. We don't know the "average" life of single primitive communities, but the slow change and other traits observed in the contemporary primitive, suggest high longevity, perhaps of the order of millennia. This contrasts with civilizations. Although more adapted to face environmental, and external sociocultural factors (they usually prevail over the primitive), they seem to show a shorter life span, and much higher vulnerability to internal stresses. History indicates that civilizations are destroyed by war, by cultural contacts, or by internal events. In any case, (the cyclical theories insist), there will be an end: either they become "petrified" or "die." It is relevant to our present purpose to note that practically all these theories recognize a stage in which "secularization" is intensified, marking the final "breakdown" and the end of the civilization. While this agreement is an expression of the pessimistic ideology predominant in this theoretical orientation, it may also underline an important point: that while intensified secularization increases creativity, it also produces higher stresses, and higher vulnerability. The "schism in the soul" (Toynbee) which is secularization, involves the risk of disintegration.

Primordial Modernization — The First Historical Pattern

The Problem of the Genesis of Modernity

We have already introduced the distinction between the unique historical process leading to "modern civilization" and the multiplicity of the subsequent transitions involving successively, or simultaneously, the rest of the world. The former, the great transition (Polanyi), may be conceived as a series of separate but often associate trends, whose confluence finally created a qualitatively new synthesis. To a great extent they represent increasing secularization that is oriented toward certain values. Secularization may generate cumulative processes. In fact we have imputed to it the two main identifiable evolutionary steps: the emergency of the civilized level and the birth of the modern industrial complex. It should be noted that these steps seem different. Although the role of cultural contacts and diffusion was certainly very important, the cumulative growth in secularization leading to the new "civilized" stage occurred to a great extent out of several independent primitive sociocultural backgrounds and generated various qualitatively distinct "primary" and "secondary" or "affiliated" civilizations (to distinguish the "first comers" from the "seconds" and "late comers" to the civilized level, that is, those civilizations whose origins are to be found in previous or contemporary ones). The process of primordial modernization took place, instead, mostly within a single cultural tradition (that is within two closely "affiliated" secondary civilizations, "Western Classic" and the "Western-Premodern"). Certainly it received significant contributions from other civilizations — the Arabic, the Hindu, the Chinese. Nonetheless it was unique in creating a capacity for self-sustained growth. In fact, science, technology and economy became really cumulative only under the particular form they acquired in the West, while in other "higher" civilizations they assumed different patterns. Only in the West did knowledge take the form of logico-experimental science; technology was developed as scientific technology and economy, as a production oriented economy. May these "peculiarities" be imputed to the central values or the "spirit" of Western tradition? May they be imputed to its particular form of secularization and especially to its peculiar type of individuality, its pattern of relating the self and the world? This approach, pursued mainly by the cyclical theories (and also by some schools in the history of science, economy and technique), certainly offers meaningful insights, but has failed so far to generate adequate explanations. Analogous shortcomings may be found in the "socioeconomic" approach, which focuses its attention on some characteristics of the Western social organization and its evolution from the ancient city-state to the beginnings of the modern era. In any case at the present state of knowledge the historical origins of the modern industrial civilization still remains an open question. Now, after Western modernity has deeply affected all the coexisting and surviving civilized and primitive societies, it is hard or impossible to ascertain if these could have independently reached a similar "modern" stage, remained "nonevolutionary" or "cyclic," or perhaps discovered some other social and cultural orientation enabling it to evolve in terms of those components presently reputed to be "noncumulative." Nonetheless there are certain aspects to be considered. The general level out of which modern science and mathematics began to grow was far from being higher than the state of scientific knowledge reached in the classical West. Nor was technology, despite some important advances during medieval times, at a significantly lower or less developed stage. All to the contrary, some crucial inventions, as illustrated by the famous example of Heron's steam engine, has been available since the Hellenistic era. Equally puzzling was the case of Chinese science and technology which maintained between the third and the thirteenth centuries a "level of scientific knowledge unapproached in the West" (Needham), and produced many technological innovations including the three discoveries — printing, gun powder and the magnet — which Bacon thought had "changed the whole face and state of things of the world." But in both cases science was arrested and technological innovations failed to be applied. No single and simple answers may be given. If, as it is reasonable to assume, basic value orientations did intervene, they should be explained within the context of the total fabric of the society, in a reciprocal or circular casual relationship with the forms of social organization. On this aspect the social sciences formulated highly suggestive hypotheses concerning certain special features in the development of the political and economic structures in the West.

Modern Traits in the Classic Western Societies

In the first place let us present the nature of the differentiation of the economic subsystem out of the general matrix of primitive economy. While a differentiation of some sort has occurred in all civilizations it would seem that nowhere, except in the West, has the economy acquired such distinctiveness and prominence. No civilized society could be called an "economic society" as is the case of the Occident. However it took a relatively long time to develop from the quite rudimentary forms of the controversial ancient capitalism to the already clearly defined commercial capitalism of medieval Europe, the immediate predecessor of industrial capitalism. It is possible to detect some significant coincidences which underlie the many theoretical disagreements. Most anthropologists, economic historians and sociologists stress the fact that only in the West did the economy cease to be consumption, prestige or power oriented, and to assume an increasing emphasis on production per se. Sombart's and Weber's distinction between "natural" and "economic man" (the bourgeois), may be rejected by Marxists and others as too "idealistic," but they remain nonetheless a good description of the cultural mutation which occurred in Europe at a certain epoch. No other civilization could create the model of the *Homo Oeconomicus,* and assume it as the faithful image of "human nature" itself. This mutation involved a redirection in the use of the economic surplus from higher consumption, or political, military, religious, esthetic purposes, to purely economic functions, to reinvestment for further production.

The change did not occur suddenly. The basic preconditions for the rise of the modern economic system had to be created. Let us consider two of them: the market and private property. Trade and exchange already existed before civilization, and are still found in contemporary primitive communities. But at this level, as well as in the historic civilized societies, the market was not primarily an economic institution. To be sure it accomplished the economic function of exchange, but it did not operate on the basis of the impersonal, universalistic, purely economic mechanism of supply and demand. As Polanyi and others have shown, it was based on "equivalencies" traditionally fixed or disguised under the form of reciprocity, even when it took place between distant places and involved the exchange of goods in relatively substantial quantity and value. At the civilized level, this type of "nonmarket trade," served other than purely economic purposes, while at the same time it was the necessary complement to satisfy the additional economic needs for the mainly self-sufficient economic units which predominated even in the urban centers. Reciprocity (which could be defined as reciprocal gift giving, with latent economic functions) continued to take place, under various forms, between units larger than the kinship and tribal groups of the primitive community. It was also underlying the exchange operations within and between political entities such as city-states or even empires. From the late European Middle Ages up to the beginnings of the modern era it can be detected under the form of the doctrine of the "just price," and it continues to our day, within the family and other primary groups. But already in fifth-century Athens, or in late Republican Rome, the market as an economic mechanism had begun to emerge, and the kind of dualistic economy produced by the co-existence of these two entirely different modes of exchange may help in understanding the ambiguity of "Ancient Capitalism," the strange mixture of "modern" and "archaic" economic traits which generated the famous controversy among economic historians. The "abortive" capitalism of Classical Antiquity has still other fundamental meanings. The market, as an economic institution, could not emerge without the dissolution of the "communal" property, without private property. Such dissolution began at the civilized level, particularly with the rise of the city. But, as Marx and Engels stressed, not any city could serve this purpose. The great capitals of military empires, the societies based on what they called the "Asiatic mode of production," could not. These, according to the Marxian thesis failed to develop, insofar as they maintained the primitive communities, with their "biological" division of labor, common property, and low individuation. Those cities were essentially "parasitic," to use Hoselitz' term, and the military, political or religious functions lacked the dynamic drive required by a commercial economy. Only the classical city of the West was able to dissolve the bonds of the primitive community, to release the individual, to achieve for the first time the full privatization of property, to generate a commercial, quasi-capitalistic economy and an urban bourgeoisie which approached in many respects the forms they assumed in premodern Europe. The classical heritage which directly or indirectly contributed to the crystallization of modernity is not confined to intellectual development, beginnings of science, and economic innovations. Another crucial aspect is to be found in the political system. If Marx saw in the "Asiatic" mode of production the principal obstacle which blocked its further development, Weber emphasized certain aspects of social and political structure of the Eastern city: only the Western city-state established a real citizenry, as an association of equals, as a military and political sovereign corporation. What Durkheim would call the "segmental" nature of primitive society, preventing the dynamic density (frequency of contacts and the creative factor determining higher forms of differentiation and the growth of secularization), characterized, according to Weber, the Oriental city.

> In China, the magic closure of clans, in India the closure of castes, eliminated the possibility of civic confederations. In China the clans as bearer of the ancestors were indestructible. In India the castes were carriers of particular styles of life upon the observance of which salvation and reincarnation depended. Ritualistically thus, the castes were mutually exclusive.

Only the Western city, both in antiquity until the late Roman empire and in the Middle Ages, counted on a "self-equipped army . . . whether it was a peasant militia, an army of knights or a burgher militia." The urban army was composed of individuals who enjoyed military independence. The "military associations" of self-equipped soldiers "were also a fundamental component in the origin of the corporate, autonomous urban community." In the East the army depended on the centralized authority of the bureau-cratic-military empire, and was far removed from the control of the commoners. Weber also recognized the role of antiquity in the creation of an economy which was already, in its most advanced sectors, beyond the self-sufficient economic order of the "oikos."

This brief inventory of the legacy of Western antiquity and its relevance to the rise of modernity cannot omit the contribution of Roman rational and universalistic law, the influence of Rome's relatively advanced political organization and its role in the diffusion and the "Westerniza-tion" of the Judeo-Christian tradition. This was an essential component in the emergence of the new cultural complex, particularly because of its universalistic emphasis. Thus the "Greek Miracle" and the ancient classic societies did initiate the line evolution took leading to modern society. Their main failure was the incapacity to develop their strong potentiality for scientific development and its application to technology with the consequent creation of a technologically expansive economy and self-sustained growth. It is reasonable to suggest that this failure was part of a complex causal chain, in which socioeconomic factors did intervene. Needham imputes the scientific arrest in China to its agrarian-bureaucratic organization, while Farrington and other Marxists attribute it to the slavish mode of production of ancient society. Many others point to the low status of manual work, of economic activities in general, and to the consequent lack of institutionalization of science. But religious and intellectual traditions and the peculiar basic values of the culture closely interacting with "structural" factors cannot be ruled out. These include a lack of faith in a universal law of nature, as it is said of the Chinese, or the predominance of "Apollonian" as against the "Faustic" ideals as Spengler suggested, or perhaps the orientation of human strength and will towards the domination of the inner self, instead of the outer world, the thrust to control passions, and not atoms, or to emphasize the "esthetic" instead of the "theoretical" aspects of the human potentialities.

Premodern West and the Birth of Modern Civilization

This "failure" did not prevent the "affiliate" civilization of premodern Europe to build onto the classic heritage what was to become the background of the final crystallization of modernity. Here again we find in Weber an admirable synthesis of the main differences which prevented the European cities of the Middle Ages from following the dead-end of their classical predecessor and providing the preconditions for uninterrupted social development. Weber enumerates several of these differences. First is the "guild character of the Middle Ages city, which helped to create a specific town economy," and "made the surrounding country subservient to the town interests." None of this can be found in the ancient city where the guilds had a different character. Second, "the typical citizen of the medieval guild city is a merchant or craftsman . . . . in antiquity on the contrary the full citizen is the land holder." This fact also has consequences for the exercise of citizenship rights, which are more equalitarian, at the legal level, in the Middle Ages city. Next, as a consequence of these two differences, social cleavages within the city are different. In the ancient city the major opposition is between the land owner and the landless. In the Middle Ages city the conflict approaches the class type of modern capitalism: it is the forerunner of the conflict between capitalists and proletarians. Fourth, the basis of the wealth in the ancient city was the land and the major source of new wealth, the war. In the Middle Ages city it was trade and craft industry. Fifth, although the ancient city had a considerable development of trade and ndustry, both were subordinated to military interests. Finally, as a consequence of this "the city democracy of antiquity is a political guild." This trait, together with the great military strength of the city (the greatest in its time), explains "the form and direction of industry in antiquity, with relation to profit through war and other advantages to be attained by purely political means. Over against the citizen stands the 'low-bred': anyone is low-bred who follows the peaceful quest of profit in the sense of today." In this urban setting a new class, the bourgeoisie, created the modern order. In its birth we find first of all the highest peak in secularization recorded in premodern times. Most historical civilizations have known periods of growth in intensity of secularization. It was particularly prominent in fifth-century Athens and in Augustan Rome. But it reached a much higher level in terms of geographical and institutional influence during the European Renaissance. Most important, it was able to create in conjunction with the other great religious and political changes a stable basis for permanent growth, if not in its original setting in the southern and central European cities then in the first nation-states of the continent. As Burckhardt noted long ago, the new wave of individuation at a far higher degree than in its expression in the classical epoch and the correlated ideology of individualism, generated, along with the other deep transformations of the social and cultural context, the outburst of human creativity needed to provide the preconditions of modern industrial capitalism, modern science, modern politics and modern technique. As in all the great cultural revolutions of mankind it was a global change whose multiform aspects appear to be inextricably interwoven. Let us give a few examples in terms of the previous discussions. "One of the most striking innovations in medieval cities was the emergence of a new attitude towards manual labor. For the first time in history of Western civilization the stigma placed on manual labor was obliterated" (Gerschenkron). Was not this psychosocial change a turning point in the birth of a knowledge founded both in "pure" thinking and the manipulation of "brute" matter, as required by experimentation? Was not the growth of a money economy reciprocally connected with quantification, which was in turn an essential element in the new science, in the perception of time, and in conjunction with the spread of "elective action," in the deliberate, "rational" use of it? Money, as Simmel maintained, could be taken as one of the more apt symbols of the dynamic character of the emerging new world. It was a kind of universal dissolvent of the premodern bonds, rigidities and immobility. The rise of the money economy, with universal commercialization, and the transformation of all the products of work into merchandise is also reciprocally related to that other basic form of dissolution: the separation of the workers from the means of production, the creation of "free labor" the transformation of work itself into a merchandise and the emergence of the new dynamic class of capital-goods owners. This was a change unanimously regarded as one of the essential traits of modern industrial economy in its capitalistic version.

Any enumeration of the scientific, technological and social changes, or the intellectual and religious transformations which took place in the four centuries preceding the first industrial "take off" are clearly beyond our purposes. Let us remember some aspects particularly relevant not only to the emergence of modern society, but also to its universalization. At the psychological level we find a new type of personality with the capacity to translate into normal behavior patterns the three principles of secularization. This had to be directed first toward productive economic activities, and all indications are that the reevaluation of work which emerged in the Middle Age city did not suffice. It required another powerful impulse to produce the tremendous concentration of efforts necessary to create the basis of an industrial economy and its organizational and material basis.

The famous Weberian "Protestant Ethic Thesis," however controversial, provides the type of explanation required to understand how the energies of man could be channeled in such a way towards purely economic productive purposes, an attitude which seems rather "unnatural" in the light of what we know about the economic behavior of nonmodern civilizations and primitive communities. At the structural level a new political unit, and a different political system had to be created. Both the city-state and the feudal-patrimonial organization had to be replaced by the centralized bureaucratic state. This state was first rooted in the territorial basis of the absolute monarchy, and later founded on the principle of nationality, with its connotations of citizenship, universalistic, rational legitimation of power, and potentially universal participation. All of this certainly was based on the institutions developed in classic and premodern civilization; nonetheless they involved yet another qualitative change in the long course towards modernity.

All this and much more led the emergence of the first industrial society. Trends and innovations do not correspond obviously to successive stages. They must be conceived of as long term historical processes, taking place to some extent along parallel lines but discontinuously and asynchronically. In fact, although endowed with certain evolutionary directionality, they appeared in different forms and intensity, developed, and sometimes decayed, decreased and even faded away only to reemerge later in another historical context. They certainly evidenced a tendency to be associated among themselves, to form clusters. However, in several concrete historical cases, during the history of Western Culture, these clusters were incomplete (some component was lacking), or their development was insufficient to generate the definitive crystallization of the "modern cultural complex." We lack, for the moment, a satisfactory explanation of these "failures," or why the "stages" of secularization which also appeared in non-Western civilizations did not generate a similar evolution. But it is reasonable to accept that the notion of secularization, used as a set of basic principles underlying modernity, at the systemic level, as a static construct common to any modern society, can also be perceived as a comparative dynamic construct useful for the description of concrete historical processes, occurring at different times and places, with varying intensity and extension, particularly within the western world since the classical era. Let us finally note that both in terms of logical consistency and in terms of empirical convergence, these concrete historical processes of secularization have been associated to different extents with other trends and innovations, whose confluence finally led to the emergence of the "modern-industrial complex." This is their meaning as basic components of the primordial modernization.

Modern Societies: Their General Characteristics

Diversity, Change and Conflicting Models

Any description of modern society as a category is controversial, except at a rather high level of generality. There are two reasons for this, both rooted in the very nature of modernity: its continuous and rapid change and the fact that our own times are characterized precisely by the ideological and military struggles around conflicting models of modernity. The diversity of presently existing modern and modernizing societies presents another problem. But this difficulty is also confronted with regard to non-modern civilizations, and probably is less pronounced, given the universality of modernization and the powerful trends towards homogeneization. Such tendencies are both internal and external. The former stems from scientific, economic and technological "imperatives" imposed by modernization and the universal traits of secularization. The latter are generated by the increasing unification of the planet because of intense communications and close interdependence. At the present state of knowledge there is no possible verification of the "convergence" hypothesis nor of its opposite. Any general description of modern civilization is bound to be based on the already mentioned universalizing trends of secularization, modern "imperatives," their sociocultural consequences and requirements, and the expansiveness of the more powerful cultural models of modernity. In the following discussion we have stressed the traits of the more advanced (or "neomodern") models rather than the "Paleomodern"characteristics.

Science and Technology

Scientific knowledge is the central dynamic component of modern society, its "prime mover." The three principles of secularization — choice, on the basis of instrumental rationality, change and specificity — should be applied virtually without any limitations. Science should be sharply differentiated from all other intellectual activities or forms of knowledge not based on logico-empirical procedures (i.e., theology or philosophy). This distinction not only affects its content and methods but also its material and social organization in teaching and research as well. The principle of continuous institutionalized change is built into the very methodology of science. All scientific propositions are provisional *ex definitione,* being submitted to permanent control, and the "scientific community," the human agent of science, will exist as long as it accepts this principle and the rules according to which it must take place. Likewise, the principle of autonomy, in terms of values and norms, cannot be curtailed without destroying its dynamic creativity. This autonomy, however, does not eliminate the ethical and social implications of science, and here we find one of the main sources of tensions inherent in modern civilization. Technology obeys the same principles, which makes it sharply different from premodern techniques described in a previous section. An important trait of modern technology which has wide repercussions on the whole society is its centralizing tendencies, which, through specialization, interdependence, central coordination, economies of scale, require or make possible increasing concentration in decision making in every sphere of life and in larger geographical areas. Permanent change takes the form in science and technology (as in economy) of self-sustained growth, a process almost entirely based on quasi-automatic, purely organizational, impersonal mechanisms. At the present turning point reached by the most advanced societies, the organizational coordination of individual rational action has initiated the collectivization and automatization of choice and change, except, perhaps, for the great scientific and technological revolutions. This unexpected outcome of the extreme individualism which generated modernity is yet another inherent contradiction of modern civilization.

The Economic System

The highest differentiation, specificity and autonomy of economic institutions is the hallmark of any modern economy. It must be free from religious, ethical, aesthetic and prestige connotations and exclusively oriented towards maximizing efficiency. Whichever the type of social, political or economic order, all the aspects of the economy must obey these principles. Its essential characteristics are a capacity for self-sustained growth, and the automatization of such process. A developed modern (ideal-typical) economy should possess all or most of the following traits:

- existence of appropriate mechanisms (institutional and human resources) for the permanent creation and/or absorption of technological and organizational innovations. Such mechanisms should insure the continuous rise of new dynamic sectors, to compensate for, or replace, those whose dynamic role in the economy is decreasing or have reached their maximum capacity for expansion.
- use of increasingly higher forms of energy and higher efficiency technologies in all branches of economic activities.
- predominance (with some exceptions) of the industrial, and later the service, sectors over agriculture (in terms of their respective shares in the total gross national product (GNP) and proportion of active population employed in them, but always with high per capita productivity in all sectors.
- increasing predominance of capital intensive over labor intensive activities.
- increasing concentration and size of units at the technological and at the economic level in all economic activities, accompanied by increasing technological specialization and coordination within larger economic units.
- savings and capital investment increasingly achieved by and through public and/or private corporate organizations.
- increasing separation of the legal property from the effective control of the economic units, with the predominance of corporate (public and/or private) management of the economy; from overall state ownership ("state capitalism" or

"socialist economy"), to a different "mix" of public and private ownership and control.
- increasing national planning from state controlled and compulsive planning to a varying "mix" of public and private (corporations, unions, and other organized interests), implicit or explicit planning.
- generalization and intensification of technological and economic interdependence both within each nation, and at the international level.
- "normal" increase of per capital GNP and a (probable) tendency towards a more equalitarian distribution of it, in terms of socio-occupational strata, and (to a lesser extent) sectorial activities and geographical areas within each nation (equalization supported mainly through deliberate state planning, more than by the spontaneous operation of the market).

The same tendencies seen in science and technology may be observed in advanced economies: the replacement of individual entrepreneurship typical of paleomodern society by the "organization man" and collective management of "neomodern" society. Also, once self-sustained growth in production is achieved, a shift towards consumption takes place. Although probably for different reasons, this trend towards "mass consumption" is common to "neocapitalist," advanced "socialist" and "mixed" societies. The newly emerging "consumer society" presents its own structural and psychosocial problems.

The Political System

Pye has aptly synthesized the main traits of any modern polity. They involve first, with respect to the population as a whole, a change from widespread subject status of an increasing number of contributing citizens, to a spread of mass participation, a greater sensitivity to the principles of equality and a wider acceptance of universalistic laws. Second, with respect to governmental and general systemic performance, political development involves an increase in the capacity of the political system to manage public affairs, control controversy, and cope with popular demands. Finally with respect to the organization of the polity, political development implies greater structural differentiation, greater functional specificity, and greater integration of all participating institutions and organizations. There are some highly controversial problems regarding the universal features of modern political systems. What does "political participation" mean in a modern advanced totalitarian state, as against a pluralistic democracy characterized by elective action in politics? The answer may be found in the fact that the position of a person under totalitarian rule is very different from the "subject" status of nonmodern polities. In the latter the ruled classes are outside the political system proper; they are nonpoliticized. In terms of secularization they are not requested to make any politial choice either in terms of political ideas (since they are spontaneously socialized into traditional beliefs, beyond any possible controversial or alternative "opinions"), or legitimation of authority (which is traditional or prescribed). In the totalitarian system, the individuals must be highly politicized; they are required to have an ideology and are expected to be convinced through a deliberate rational (or pseudo-rational) choice. The totalitarian "election" is highly symbolic of this expected participation. The role of the party, the unions and many other organizations, as well as the political meetings, mass rallies and discussion groups, all point in the same direction: they exist in order to satisfy the requirement of political mobilization of the "citizen," and legitimation of authority, even if choice and participation are forced or greatly restricted. Furthermore there are other forms of participation, at different levels, which may effectively function even in totalitarian or limitedly pluralistic regimes.

Another difficult question confronted by any political system regards its capacity to promote and absorb change. This is a requirement imposed by the dynamic nature of the social and the economic system. But change usually means conflict. Institutionalization of change, in politics as in other spheres, does not mean absence of conflict. The capacity of a modern system for conflict resolution must be high. Nonetheless all advanced societies include at least some area in which change may result in too much conflict, in some cases to the extent of causing disintegration or severe disruption of the social order. Causes of deep conflict are inherent in the modern structure itself, and, among them, the norms regulating change, the so-called "rules of the game," may become highly controversial. There are other sources of serious conflicts in sectors specific to each society. As indicated, a central core of shared values, must be maintained even in modern society. In part this is what Laski called "agreement on fundamentals." When these are really threatened, modern mechanisms for conflict resolution may fail. The existence of this "central core" leads us to consider another essential component of any modern political system: the national basis of the state. The principle of nationality in the process of primordial modernization, in already advanced societies, and in modernizing ones is essential precisely as the supreme mechanism of social integration. It may express at the same time the "agreement on fundamentals," the mobilization and participation of all members of the society, and the "prescriptive" principle, beyond arbitrary change, which maintains the unity and identity of the society by replacing the primitive bonds of the tribe or the religious-traditional loyalties. Historically, in presently advanced countries, the acquisition of a national identity proceeded from the bourgeousie to the middle and, finally, to the lower classes, and it coincided with the extension of civil, political and social rights to all the members of the nation. In modernizing societies nationalism and national identity comprise the main driving force which focusses all energies towards development, one of the functional substitutes of the "Protestant Ethic."

Social Organization

Secularization characterizes modern society at all levels: at the sociocultural level transforming values, norms, roles, institutions and groups, as well as at the psychosocial, changing motivations, attitudes, personality, social relations and behavior. Societies or social groups in which prescriptive action and particularistic, diffuse, ascribed roles predominate will require a type of personality very different from the personality structure which is adjusted to social environments dominated by choice, achievement, instrumentalism, universalism and specificity. The latter must internalize mechanisms adequate for self-guidance, self-made decisions with a propensity for change, or at least some capacity for confrontation. In the "ideal-typical" traditional man, unexpected situations, or change, are likely to produce anomie or personal disorganization. This danger exists, for "modern" man, too, not only in transitional situations but also because of the stresses inherent in the modern structure itself: its rate of change, the contrasting demands of pluralistic and often conflicting systems of values and norms, and the particular difficulties confronted by any modern and modernizing society in replacing the old mechanisms of socialization, and creating new, and continuously changing ones. In fact the type of personality found in the more advanced countries already seems different from the one typical of "paleomodernity." Most interpersonal relations are transformed. Achievement, universalism, specificity and instrumentality are extended well beyond the sphere of knowledge, technology and economy. In other words, primary ties (based on intimate personal contacts, in which the individual is involved in his uniqueness) are replaced in many areas by secondary relationships, comprising only segmental roles, whose character is impersonal, and in which the individual is interchangeable, in a way typical of rational-bureaucratic organization. However, primary bonds do not and cannot disappear in modern society, but they tend to function at a level compatible with the minimum requirements of modernity. Particularistic, expressive and diffuse relations cannot decrease below the threshold required by the psychological adjustment of the individual. From one side industrial society emphasizes impersonal roles according to the principle of maximum efficiency. But on the other such instrumentalization confronts insurmountable limits, since each person needs an intimate circle in which he can be socialized, develop his personality and find emotional support. This sets the conditions, highly variable according to each cultural and social setting, in which the family, kinship networks, friendships, and other forms of primary groups, roles and relations are maintained. The family may be restricted to the nuclear family, and the kinship network may be likewise reduced, but it is never suppressed. Also many other primary ties are maintained or recreated, transformed and fused with modern traits, and often turn out to be compatible, or even functional, with the requirements of modern institutions. Developed, advanced societies both within the Western and the non-Western cultures show peculiar and diverse combinations of this type, such as ascriptive persistence in Japanese enterprises, the familistic adaptations and the frequent intrusion of expressive behavior in instrumental roles, which is common in advanced Latin societies.

It must be noted that this adaptability does not eliminate the structural tensions caused by the conflicting requirements mentioned above which are a part of any modern society. Drastic transformations in the size, growth, composition and ecological distribution of the population are important aspects of social modernization. The demographic transition is the process through which a modernizing society passes from a stage of high to one of low demographic potential. In the former both fertility and mortality rates are high, while in the latter both are low. Since the decrease in mortality precedes by many decades the lowering in fertility, between the first and the last stages, there is an intermediate phase of high population growth. Besides, even at the low potential stage, the rate of natural growth is higher than in premodern times. This is the well-known population explosion, which in presently developing countries has reached an unprecedented level. Modernization, medical knowledge, improvements in hygienic and sanitary conditions and in the level of living reduce mortality dramatically, while modern attitudes towards family planning (that is deliberate choices in the number and spacing of children) reduce the fertility. The psychological innovation takes more time since the new attitudes spread slowly from high and middle urban strata to the lower urban and rural population. Through changes in vital rates the age structure is also drastically modified. The agricultural revolution which usually accompanies or precedes the industrial take-off (and the international division of labor, which in early modernization displaced the agricultural sector to countries specializing in food producing and raw material), coupled with the expanding demand for industrial labor first, and for modern services later, produces spectacular population movements from rural to urban areas. This is the urban explosion (which again acquires a new character in contemporary less developed countries). This transformation reverses the rural predominance existing since prehistory: in advanced countries the large majority live in urban areas (and the remaining ecologically rural follow an urbanized way of life). Once the population is mobilized into the modern structures (mostly through internal and international rural to urban migrations), all local roots, be they the place of birth or of living, tend to disappear. People cease to be really located in a specific city, town or village. They are instead placed in an occupational or organizational network covering the whole nation (or increasingly larger international areas), and move within it according to individual choices, as regulated by economic, educational and other goals and opportunities.

Ecological mobility expresses the dynamic nature of modern society and derives from the need to maximize the efficiency of human resources through population redistribution. The same requirement exercises powerful effects on the occupational structure and through it, on education and stratification. Technological, organizational and economic innovations (the prime mover of self-sustained growth) continuously replace old occupations for new ones. Their number and types, furthermore, are incessantly expanded through increasing specialization and the opening of new areas of activity. Modern occupations, as well as all aspects of modern life, not only require universal literacy (again for the first time in history) but also increasing education levels. In a paleomodern society a few years of primary school (or even none) were sufficient for most jobs; in advanced nations high school is a universal requirement, and college education follows a similar course. But the most striking change is taking place in the timing and forms of education. The present system is already becoming obsolete. First, education ceases to be a limited stage in the life cycle of an individual and becomes a permanent need. Continuing education is required by the permanent revolution in occupations. Second, continuing education itself needs the reformulation of educational goals to foster the highest plasticity and potentiality for change. Third, mass or universal and continuing higher education demands new institutional and pedagogical mechanisms.

Besides these economical and technological imperatives, new cultural needs are rising, which soon may exercise strong pressures and demands to be satisfied in one way or another. This dynamism in occupations, education and other causes has a strong impact on social classes. The stratification system in modern society tends to be shaped by the requirement of maximizing efficiency in role allocation to individuals and in the use and distribution of human resources. Further and powerful sources of continuous transformation are originated by four orders of closely interrelated factors: by the productive system, because of the changing occupational structure; by education, because of the renewal of educational requirements; by the distributive system because of rising GNP, income redistribution, and the increasing diversification, quality and quantity of consumption; and by the political system and by ideological trends, and because of pressures towards the extension of social rights and higher participation into the material and immaterial culture of modern society.

Under the impact of these factors (and reacting on them at the same time), modern stratification tends to acquire a visible pattern which may be summarized as follows: first, the stratification profile has a rhomboidal shape, with most of the population in the middle positions, and minorities at the top and at the bottom; second, the discontinuity and hierarchization between strata, in terms of income, consumption, style of life, education, symmetry or equality of interpersonal relations, manners, social distance, and prestige tends to be greatly reduced; in consequence, instead of the deep cleavages and differentials, characteristic of most nonmodern societies, discrete classes are transformed into a stratification continuum; third, vertical social mobility (upward, but also in lower degree, downward), is much higher and, finally, values, attitudes, ideologies, motivations and expectations concerning classes and mobility are modified: equalitarianism, not hierarchization, is proclaimed, and social mobility is expected and institutionalized in terms of equality of opportunities and achievement.

This description cannot be accepted without essential qualifications, since it gives only the visible pattern, the image of modern stratification. It requires some consideration of its latent structure. In this area, as in others, there is a built-in tension in modern society between the achievement criteria demanded by the principle of efficiency and the maintenance of ascription as rooted in the prescriptive units, particularly the family, and, in many societies, having ethnic and regional origins. Distribution of power is another strong factor in limiting achievement criteria. This occurs mainly through differential opportunities in education, differentials in early socialization (deeply affecting each individual's intellectual development, attitudes and personality), and also through direct allocation of positions more on the basis of particularism, or ascription, than of achievement. This is possible without appreciably diminishing efficiency in role performance, since most tasks, even those high in the social hierarchy, may be adequately accomplished by the average individual. Certainly it is a fact that income and wealth distribution is more concentrated in premodern and less developed societies than in the more advanced ones. It is also true that all or most stratification differentials are larger in the former, than in the latter. Nonetheless the degree of equalitarianism really existing in the class structure of modern societies is lower than commonly perceived and is emphasized by the established values and predominant ideologies. On the other hand, power may tend to be more concentrated in advanced societies than in premodern ones. Concerning this, we must remember the consequences of the centralizing nature of technology, which are both economic and political. Although insufficient data and the nature of the matter introduce considerable uncertainty, these statements are gaining increasing acceptance among scholars (particularly regarding the higher rigidity and differentials of the cleavages at the top and at the bottom of the system). If real, which is the cause of this discrepancy between the image and the reality of stratification? This image, we must add, is quite strategic in giving legitimacy to the social order. In part the reason may be found in the predominant values and ideologies which obviously affect the perception of a vast majority.

To a greater extent such perception is reinforced by a number of real processes directly impinging on the material and psychological experience of the individual. First there is the external uniformation of life syles. Differences in them are more concealed than publicly exhibited (a reversal from premodern situations). Also mass recreation and mass media provide many areas of interests and activities in which all strata find a common ground. Second, equalitarianism in interpersonal relations and manners has a strong psychological impact on individuals' self-respect and personal life. Third, given the organizational complexity of society the exercise of authority is shared by many people up and down the hierarchy. Even if big decisions are taken by the ruling elite, many middle range and small decisions are delegated. An entire category, the "service" class is devoted to it (Dahrendorf). Fourth, and most important of all, there is a completely novel trait which characterizes modern stratification. This is what we may call the process of self-sustained mobility, similar, and closely connected to the other types of self-sustained changes already noted. From one side the educational and skill requirements do introduce a greater fluidity in the system, by allowing more downward (and equivalent upward) mobility. But this type of "exchange" mobility would be insufficient to satisfy the expectations of the great majority. The mass experience of moving up is produced by three factors. In the first place, occupational upgrading through the continuous replacing of lower tasks by the machine (and/or by the flow of newcomers and immigrants from peripheric regions or groups within or outside the nation). To this we must add educational upgrading and, finally, the consumption upgrading, produced not only by the general increase in real incomes, but also by the continuous creation of new types of goods and services which are usually introduced from the top of the social hierarchy and circulated downward, particularly within the huge middle portion of stratification (depending on the nature of the product, this downward distribution may be achieved sometimes in externally imitative forms). The three kinds of upgrading involve an incessant circulation of status symbols from top to bottom. Since the symbols tend to retain their prestige for a certain period (a property similar to price's viscosity, in economics), the subjective experience is one of moving up the social ladder, not of a downward distribution of objects which in the higher echelons has already been replaced by new ones. This complex process may help to explain why each individual experiences personal mobility while remaining at the same relative position in the social hierarchy, since it is the whole system which is being moved upward, in terms of the various forms of consumption.

The maintenance of self-sustained mobility, probably the key foundation of the legitimacy of the social order and the acceptance of the modern cultural model, depends on the continuity of technological and economic innovations. Even so, it may well be a transitional process. The viscosity of prestige is likely to decrease over time, so that downward circulation must be increasingly accelerated. Also the succeeding generations cease to believe in or be satisfied by it. This is precisely one of the meanings of the current criticism against the "consumer society." It remains to be said that existing types of neomodern systems — nocapitalist and poststalinist socialist societies — fail to show essential differences with regard to their stratification. Certainly the legal property of wealth is more equalitarian in socialist countries, but effective control of the means of production is even more concentrated. Income may be somewhat more evenly distributed, but power is monopolized by a small elite. A significant difference between the two systems is perhaps the role of political power as an influential factor in stratification and mobility chances in socialist countries.

Many aspects of modern social organization have not been considered. We may mention among others organized religion, its specialized functions and structure, the rise of spontaneous cults, the multiplicity of voluntary formal associations, and informal groups, the recreational institutions, mass media, popular and higher cultural activities in art and literature, the new conditions under which intellectual and other elites are formed, and achieve their functions, the shaping and reshaping of a multiplicity of subcultures, the changing conditions of the various generations: childhood, adolescence, youth, adulthood and old age. An analysis of these and many other sectors of the complex modern sociocultural world would reveal the same pattern of accelerated secularization we have underlined in the foregoing discussion.

Definitive Modernization: Patterns of Transition Toward Modernity

A Universal Condition of Modernizing Patterns

Primordial modernization was unique. The modernization of the world is diverse. No two countries follow the same transitions towards a modern sociocultural structure. A typology of transitions is not yet possible. But there are common factors underlying the individual paths of each nation.

Our first generalization is that modernization or development is never balanced. Change is asynchronous: the many components of the sociocultural structure do not initiate their transformation simultaneously, proceed at the same speed, nor do the various processes follow identical sequences. At the geographical level, some countries initiated their modernization before others, and the same type of geographical imbalance occurred within each country. This is why we can speak of underdevelopment at all. The differentiation between a center, and a periphery, is an essential international as well as internal (national) phenomenon. At the institutional and at the psychosocial levels, as well as at the level of social groups, strata, classes and other sectors of the population, change is equally asynchronous. There is an imbalance also within individual personalities: modern and archaic attitudes, values, motivations coexist. The three components of modernization — economic, social, political — are initiated at different epochs, take place at different rates, and occur in different sequences, within each transition. Each of the main components, furthermore, consists of a multiplicity of similarly asynchronous subprocesses. The total transition, resulting from the acceleration or deceleration of given processes or subprocesses, or peculiar retardations or anticipations in their sequence, is a highly determining factor in modernization. Anticipation of a given process may in one case speed up the whole transition, while in another it may create blockage, even cause a "breakdown" of modernization. Because of the consequences of asynchronism, and the impact of the determinants of modernization discussed below, it is very difficult to formulate a universally valid sequence of stages. Their usefulness is limited, as shown by the criticism against all such attempts, including Rostow's *Stages of Economic Growth,* and others. As further discussed below, the internal and external conditions of modernization are changing permanently, and this reduces the validity of generalizations.

Main Determinants of Modernization Patterns

We will assume two main categories of independent variables: the "starting point," and the "international system." The starting point is the sum of the characteristics of each society at the beginning of the transition. Several multidimensional factors or variables are included in this category, the first being levels and forms of secularization. This variable corresponds to the types of societal forms described in previous sections, and are taken in decreasing order of primordial modernization, and civilized secularization. (This evolutionary sequence is an oversimplification and the partially nonevolutionary nature of historical change must be remembered.) This factor is the main determinant of the order of priority in the initiation of the transition and of the internal or external challenge of modernity. Both exercise deep effects on all other determinants and on the transition. (Black's modernization patterns, though based on different criteria, roughly correspond to the classification suggested by this factor.) We may distinguish several groups of countries: Western (European),

Westernized (from European origins and/or submitted to prolonged European influence), civilized, and primitive societies.

Type I, the Western first comer, both in terms of political and economic modernization, was Great Britain. France is a political but not an economic first comer. Second Western comers (type IIA) are the central and northern European countries, such as Holland, Switzerland, the Scandinavian nations, the German states, the Austrian-Hungarian empire, and others. The Westernized second comers, (type IIB) correspond to the "offshoots" of France and Great Britain overseas: the former colonies which developed into the United States, Canada, Australia, and New Zealand. Western third comers (type IIIA) may be considered the southern and eastern European countries. Russia is classified in this group because of its related origins and its previous process of Westernization, but it includes Non-Western and even primitive cultures. The Westernized third comers (type IIIB) are the Latin American nations. The first civilized non-Western comer (type IV) is Japan; the next category, the civilized non-Western comers (type V), is composed mostly of Asian countries, many classified as higher civilizations (like India or China), with some African countries such as Egypt, Morocco, Algeria and Ethiopia. For the majority of this category the political transition was initiated at the earliest at the turn of the century, and mostly before the World War II. In many cases they remained for a period under colonial rule. Finally we have the surviving primitive societies (type VI). Most of them are located in Africa, and their transition may be considered as dated in the second half of the present century, with postwar decolonization.

It must be noted that many of the Westernized areas overseas included archaic civilizations and primitive societies. This is particularly important in the Americas. Mexico, Peru, and part of the Caribbean had large populations that had reached a civilized level when they submitted to colonial domination. The pre-Western, more precisely pre-Hispanic, civilizations had a strong influence in colonial times and are contributing powerfully today to shape the new nations which emerged after independence. Less important was the social, political and cultural influence of the local primitive communities, since they were practically destroyed by the contact with the premodern and modern West as it occurred in the United States, Canada, Argentina and Uruguay (what may be called the "final" solution of the indigenous problem). An analogous situation can be found in the "offshoot" nations in Oceania. To the local primitive communities we must add the imported population from primitive areas: the Africans, in the United States, Brazil and other Latin American countries. These imported, and uprooted, "primitives" do exercise an impact on the shape of the transition and in the problems it creates in the receiving nations. Finally, in all the Western nations, at the "starting point," the great majority, especially the peasantry, lived in premodern, and sometimes in precivilized sociocultural forms. "Pockets" or even relatively large areas, or specific categories of the population, persisted in a relatively unmodernized level for a long time and even now may be found within the most advanced societies. This effect of asynchronism (the "contemporaneity of the noncontemporaneous") is particularly strong among the Western third comers. On the other hand structural dualism is typical of all non-Western modernizing countries.

Next we must consider three closely interrelated variables: the existence (or not) of a centralized-bureaucratic territorial state coextensive (or not) with prenational ethnical cultural homogeneity; ethnical cultural homogeneity, as a basis for nationality and possibly the beginnings of a national identity; and, finally, the self-governing or (on the contrary) the externally dominated condition of part or all the territory of the rising modern country (such as the dominated regions of a plurinational territorial state in Europe, and of colonies elsewhere). The duration of the colonial rule is an important dimension of this variable. All three variables, variously combined, exercise a strong impact on the transition. The more favorable configuration is the presence at the "starting point" of a self-governing centralized bureaucratic territorial state that is nationally homogeneous. This was the case of the Western first and some of the second and third comers, of Japan (except in the degree of bureaucratization), China and a few others. In the great majority of the remaining countries, one, two or all the traits were lacking. This deficiency varied from very low to very high: minimum among the Western comers and their Westernized "off-shoots" (even if it involved prolonged conflicts and delays); higher and more frequent among the non-Western civilizations, attaining its maximum among the recently decolonized states of Africa: nation-building there starts from detribalization; millennia must be reduced to decades.

Another factor is the nature and availability of resources. As suggested by Hoselitz, this variable may stimulate two different types of development: expansionist or intrinsic. This is a version of the old "man-land ratio." The contrast is between high human resources and low natural ones, and vice versa. The United States, Canada, Australia, Argentina, and other Latin American countries could start economic development with an extensive employment of labor. This is the expansionistic pattern. Many old and low-resouces nations — Switzerland, Holland and others — had to choose the intensive application of labor, the intrinsic pattern. The expansionistic pattern involves also the so-called "economy of the open spaces." But this pattern, as in the case of Argentina, Uruguay, or Brazil, has contributed to the delay in industrialization. Also the acceleration in population growth, with its increasing burden on investment, modifies the meaning of this variable. However, it is important in explaining diversities in the economic development of the Western and Westernized countries.

The era of world history began with modern civilization. The rise of the first modern-industrial society generated immediate effects on the rest of the world which increased at a fast rate during the nineteenth century and were multiplied by technological innovation and economic growth. The rise of an international system at all levels, technological, economic, intellectual, ideological, political and military, was unavoidable and implicit in the "logic" of the modern-industrial civilization. Certainly, power, in its various forms, was essential. But no less important was the requirement to expand more and more the space range for maximization of efficiency in production, and the increasing specialization, centralization and interdependence, the three technoeconomic imperatives of modernization. An international stratification of countries based on many dimensions — among them, political, economic, military power—was essential. A world center and a world periphery were increasingly differentiated. The center exercised the leadership over the periphery, in most cases as formal or "informal" colonization.

An essential feature of the international system (both center and periphery) is its continuous change. There are two orders of causes: changes in the modern-industrial civilization itself and the repercussions of international events, usually military and other conflicts between the hegemonic members of the center, modifications in the center's "membership," revolutionary changes, economic crises and social movements in the center and in the periphery). Three phases may be distinguished in the transformation of the international system: a first phase, from the early nineteenth century to World War I and the Great Depression; a second phase, from World War II to the 1970s and a third phase, emerging since the Vietnam crisis. Because the international system is continually transformed, its "state" (in every aspect), at the epoch in which each individual transition is initiated and its subsequent changes during the transition, are major determinants of the transition itself.

The description of the system includes several multidimensional aspects, and only a few will be considered here. The first aspect is the degree and nature of centralization. This is a very complex factor and an essential one in determining the dominant or satellitic pattern of development and modernization, since it results from the synthesis of the economic, political and military aspects of the center's domination. According to a general trend in modern civilization, the degree of world interdependence and centralization have increased while the forms assumed by the domination, have changed. In the nineteenth-century revolution in transportation, particularly the advent of the steamship and the railroad, coupled with the high productivity of the industrial center (mostly Great Britain, but followed by the Western second comers), initiated the integration of the world market. This meant the transference of the primary sector production (agriculture and foodstuff, mining and other raw materials), to undeveloped areas of the planet, endowed with the proper resources.

At the same time it involved the "conquest of the markets." With some exceptions most peripheric areas initiated their economic modernization and their integration into the world system through some form of primary export economy. Usually this type of production became an essential factor in shaping the whole social structure, in conjunction with the characteristics of the "starting point." Transportation systems, structural dualism, stratification, urbanization, political leadership, delay in industrialization, and the form and pace of other modernizing processes were affected by dependent development. Primary export economy and extensive private investments were the first expressions of the center's economic domination, during the first phase (which corresponds roughly to the paleomodern and transitional stages of the societies composing the center). Politically and militarily it tended to assume the form of direct colonization affecting mostly non-Western civilizations and Africa. Only a few large civilized societies like Japan or China escaped it, but even they suffered strong pressures and interference. Latin America was a typical "informal colony." In this phase the center was composed of Great Britain and a few other Western second and third comers, with the exception of their offshoots overseas. The United States was culturally, but much less economically, dependent. Its power was growing, but at first it was only exercised on the bordering Latin American nations in the Caribbean. The struggle among Western powers within the center produced the delayed territorial imperialism of formerly dominated countries, like Italy, or newly unified ones, like Germany. The contrast between the "have" and "have not" or the "plutocratic versus the proletarian nations" was first created in Italy, and later in Germany. With World War I and decisively with the WWII, the international system stepped into a second phase. The composition of the center was deeply modified: the United States, Russia, the European Common Market countries, and later China, became part of it. In the economic sphere (not in the politico-military sense), other Westernized "offshoots" were also included (this was an important case of successful "dependent modernization and development"). But the center became bifurcated, and the same occurred in the periphery.

At the same time the form of satellitism changed. Direct colonization disappeared and practically all areas of the world became organized (at least formally) under the "nation-state" model. Under the impact of two traumatic events, the Great Depression and World War II, but also because of the "neomodern" economic system in the center, economic dependence changed too. The periphery began its industrialization, and the primary export economy decreased its importance. In the "neomodern" society, the internationalization of the economy took the form of "common markets," and "multinational corporations" (under different but quasi-parallel forms in the so-called "capitalist" and "socialist" worlds). Since the beginning of the 1970s and late 1960s, a third phase has appeared, seemingly characterized by polycentrism, instead of bicentrism, and by an increasing trend towards more autonomous growth in the periphery to be observed in its three main sectors: "Western," "socialist" (already split in two, Russian and Chinese), and "unaligned." The transformation of the periphery into the "Third World" and the internal competition among the members of the "multicenter" (with its various versions of "neomodern" systems), may turn out to define the nature of the new coming stage of the international system.

The second aspect of the system is the state of science, technology, and organizational innovations. Each major advance imposes new conditions on the individual transitions: from the means of transportation and communications, to the discovery and use of new raw materials, to their substitution by synthetics, to the increasing capital-intensive technologies, and new forms of energy. The overwhelming weight of science and technology means increasing dependence for the periphery. This factor, more than any other is now supporting the hegemony of the center. The so-called "advantages of backwardness' may be cancelled by the higher investments required by the monopoly exercised by the center and by the fact that the technology is being created in response to the demands of advanced societies, which often make it unadapted to the developing countries. The same considerations apply to organizational innovations, at all levels: public, private, economic and educational. An intervening factor here, as well as in the case of technology, is the impact of the demonstration effect: the imitative tendencies stemming from psychological and cultural dependence.

The third descriptive aspect involves the changing internal structure of central and of peripheric countries. The transformations of the center, from "paleomodern" to "transitional" to "neomodern," the appearance of new models (various forms of socialist and centrally planned systems), the changes in the periphery, because of advancing modernization, creation of new solutions, and shifting areas of satellitism, or higher degrees of autonomy involve a continuous ongoing global modification of the impact of the international system on the individual transitions. The impact has operated mostly at two levels. The first modifies the actual concrete conditions impinging on modernization, both external and internal (to each country). The second creates successively different global ideological climates, and consciousness of the problems of modernization. The two levels cannot be easily differentiated. Both were decisively affected by key world events, mostly the same ones which affected the changing phases of the international system. A few examples will be given. With the techno-economic transformation of the central economies their reciprocal relations and the relations with the periphery changed. The two World Wars and the Great Depression drastically modified the composition, orientation and relative size of foreign trade in the central countries. Its size, although higher in absolute volume, decreased in percentage of GNP. The proportion of industrial goods greatly increased in its composition, and a great part of foreign trade occurred between the industrialized countries themselves. At the same time internal expanding markets, voluntary (or unintended) protectionism, and ideological changes stimulated industrialization in the more advanced peripheral countries. The fact and the ideology of the "international division of labor" came to an end and was replaced by new forms of relations between center and periphery. Foreign investment turned to industrial, not primary production (or infrastructural social capital, as the prewar British), and it tended to be oriented much more towards other central countries than towards the periphery. Its effects on both types of countries became increasingly controversial, particularly because ideological and political issues as well as power struggles were involved in it. The changing and increasing intervention of the state, the universalization of some kinds of planning, the consolidation of "corporate" capitalism, together with the growth of "socialist" economies and partially nationalized ones, all combined to destroy or greatly diminish the belief in the automatic operation of the market and private enterprise. The extension of civil, political and social rights to an increasing proportion of the population in central countries, and the universal diffusion of mass communication accelerated similar demands in many peripheral countries, particularly since the second phase of the international system. This change in the ideological climate occurred at the level of the masses (which to some extent became available for social and political mobilization) and, most important, at the level of the modernizing elites, favoring the conditions for drastic social reform, or revolutionary changes. Mass consumption in central countries generated new aspirations in peripheral nations. Underdeveloped economies clashed with modernized consumption models. The only defense for the status quo remained the persisting barrier created by the center and the periphery, internal to each country, with the marginalization of the peripheral population (sometimes more than fifty percent of the total, even in relatively advanced nations of the Third World), and the attempts to coopt or to integrate, in one way or another, the popular strata located in the center.

Some Combined Consequences of Asynchronism, Starting Points and the Changing State of the International System on the Modernization Patterns

We have already discussed several effects of the impact of these three basic conditions on the individual transitions. Other important generalizations may be advanced. (In this, as in the previous discussion, the variables or factors are dealt with as continuous: there is always a different "mix" of modern preconditioning, and archaic traits, or of external and internal challenges of modernity.)

Our component of the starting point, "levels and forms of secularization," not only is important in determining the order of priority in modernization and the extent of modern preconditioning (hence the particular "mix" of exogenous on endogenous components in the drive to modernize), but also under which phase of the international system the transition is initiated. An illustration of the type of leadership and elites at the initiation of the process, and the changes likely to occur during its course, may highlight the consequences of a particular combination of these and other variables. In Great Britain, France, Central and Northern European States, and their overseas offshoot, the elite was to a great extent the bourgeoisie (that is the new class created by primordial modernization), with the "conflicting cooperation" of other sectors of the ruling classes. But already we find in Germany a different situation, with the "Bismarckian" model of development, revolution "from above" and "weak bourgeoisie." Germany and the former members of the Austrian-Hungarian empire confronted additional complications — lack of one or more of the three factors (territorial state, nationality, independence) which are also an aspect of the above mentioned "weakness." The next two groups (the Western third comers and the Westernized third comers) show increasing "deficiency" in these factors. Comparing nineteenth-century development of European countries such as England, Germany, Austria, Hungary, and Russia, Gerschenron suggests a typology of "agents" of development: "factory" in the first comer; "bank" and factory, in the second comers; "state, bank and factory in the third comers (such as Italy or prerevolutionary Russia). In the Westernized third comers group the delay in formation of the national bourgeoisie, its permanent weakness, was still more pronounced, since insufficient preconditions (Hispanic heritage), lack of autonomy, territoriality and nationality, were decisively reinforced by the state of the international system at the initiation and during the transition. In fact this involved the adoption of the "primary export economy," high satellitism, delay or incapacity in industrialization and in solving the problem of incorporating large proportions of the population and establishing a viable political system.

A similar pattern is reproduced in a much more extreme degree in the societies of the civilized non-Western comers and the primitive societies, characterized by a configuration of factors in which the already mentioned "deficiencies" are much more accentuated. In this respect the generalization could be advanced that the lower the "primordial modernization preconditionings," the later the initiation of the transition, the higher the dependence on the center, and the more likely that the modernizing élite initiating, or assuming the leadership later on, will be of the "intellectual revolutionary" or "military nationalistic" type. This happened in Russia and in Cuba (both under the impact of strong traumatic situations). Significantly a similar revolution in Mexico, but initiated in a different ideological climate and under a different international system, turned out to become a "sui generis" middle class regime. A temporary, but prolonged, "breakdown" of modernization and delay occurred in European countries (Western third comers plus Germany) during the interwar periods. The same was true of Japan, which nonetheless is the only case of successful modernization under "established" leadership.

Contrasts in rates and sequences of component processes of modernization, particularly between the Western first comers, Western and Westernized second comers and Western third comers, and all the others (roughly the present Third World) illustrate the impact of different configuration of factors on the course of the transition. Let us first examine the demographic transition. In the Third World a decrease of mortality is anticipated, and a decrease in fertility (at the "starting point" higher than in the West) which is delayed in comparison with the first three groups. As a consequence the population explosion is much higher, and anticipated with regard to economic development (also in comparison with the Western experience). In urbanization the same acceleration is occurring. This means urbanization without industrialization. The third transition involves the persistence of duality and marginality, stronger contrasts between levels of modernization within countries, with the highest proportion in excluded or nonparticipant sectors and an accentuation over time of internal disequilibria. These delays are much more serious to confront in the changed ideological climate: higher aspirations and widespread demand for social rights. Overtertiarization is another transition characterized by growth of public and private bureaucracies beyond the "historical" level in the West and the appearance of a "pseudo-tertiary" really composed by an urban marginal population. In most urban areas there is a "higher" proportion of urban middle strata than at the "historical" level. There is a simultaneous occurrence of processes which in the first three groups occurred successively and with great "spacing in time": urban "mass" society coexisting with "traditional" marginality; political and social mobilization in the "center"; and insufficient political and economic development. These are a few examples of the considerable differences among the various modernization patterns of relatively "earlier" and relatively "later" comers.

Modern Civilization: Problems and Prospects

Transitional and Structural Problems

Many of the problems of modern society have been mentioned when dealing with the nature of modernity, its rise and diffusion. They may be classified into four main categories, always remembering that concrete occurrences often participate in more than just one category. Transitional problems are those created by the transformation from nonmodern to modern. By and large they are similar in primordial as in definitive modernization, with only one great difference: total resistance to modernization as such has decreased steadily, until it has almost disappeared (except for the "Neo Luddism" of the youth culture). What was important and still remains so, is partial resistance to specific aspects of it. There are no societies which reject modernity but all or most want a special kind of it. The divergence takes the form of conflicting ideologies, and often is based on the defense of those traits of the status quo whose elimination is perceived as threatening. It is not a mere question of interests or power. Values, attitudes, habits and intellectual convictions play an equal role. Increasingly in recent times, the "dark" side of modernity is becoming a driving force in this rejection of given aspects. This brings us to consider the structural, internal and international contradictions of modernization. Secularization introduces an inherent imbalance, namely how to reconcile the extreme ethical, esthetical, ideological pluralism, with the maintenance of common basic bonds holding society together. This has several consequences: how is the individual to be socialized to have an autonomous capacity to choose and change values? How is he to learn how to control conflicts, or reduce role incompatibility? Some of the features of modern society tend to impede the operation of mechanisms required to respond to these demands. Centralizing technology and organizational patterns generate countertrends towards massification, atomization and suppression of autonomous individual choice. The terrifying prospect of total control of individuals, through scientific, technological and organizational means is not science-fiction imagination, but a concrete possibility. In another aspect, the prescriptive requirements of any society clash with the principles of universalism and achievement. Instrumentalism in most human activities destroys the need for authentic emotional and esthetic expressions.

Modernization and Conflict

All theories of modernization coincide in that the transition toward "modernity" is highly conflictual and often revolutionary and violent. But they disagree on the importance and the type of conflict. According to Marxism the prime mover in history is class conflict, class being mainly defined by control (or not) of the means of production. Others do not assign such total importance to conflict, in general, nor to class conflict in particular. Both Marxism and most other theories coincide in expecting a decrease or the disappearance of conflict at the "most advanced stage" of modernity: "communism" for Marxism, some form of "neomodern" or "postmodern" society for others. For the latter, conflicts would become more and more institutionalized and contained in "civilized" patterns. There is no scientific answer to these questions, so far. A plausible guess on the basis of the previous discussion, would be that in primitive and civilized non-modern societies conflicts cannot be reduced to class conflicts. During "primordial modernization" and more after the rise of modernity, the differentiation and the predominance of the "economic society" tend to convert most (by no means all) relevant conflicts into class-conflicts (in the Marxian sense). But with present "neomodern" and the (eventual) "postmodern" society, as far as we can see, the meaning of (Marxian) class is greatly reduced and new significant cleavages appear. However, the contradictions inherent in modern civilization, as well as those inherited by its historical formation, do not suggest a decrease in violent conflicts. On the contrary, unless a "mutation" occurs, conflicts, violent and otherwise, are likely to reach new unprecedented heights.

The Global Problems: Survival

The most serious contradictions are found at the global, planetary level. A fast growing "external proletariat" is threatening modern civilization, and the gap between advanced and "developing" countries increases more and more. The premodern international game, of conflicts between states competing for power and hegemony, continues in its fullest expression. Uncontrolled technology is destroying the environment. For the first time in history man has the power to destroy himself. All this points in a single direction: modern civilization is intrinsically planetary and can survive only through global, long range rational planning guided by universalistic values, on the behalf of mankind as a unity. But the historical form of organization assumed by modernity so far is the nation-state, and the nation has turned out to be so far the main, or the only, nucleus able to hold together modern societies.

Modern civilization, which has opened immense horizons to human creativity, has also created the actual possibility of ultimate catastrophe. If modern man is to survive, he must be able to grow emotionally and socially, to invent and consolidate the social order required by the scientific and technological civilization he created. He must be able to reconcile moral with material progress.

2.

Urbanization, Social Change and the Great Transformation

Definitions of Urbanization

Not only are the terms "urbanization" and "modernization" frequently used in contemporary social science but, since they are thought to represent aspects of the "revolution of our time," these words have been taken up by politicians, journalists, and others in a variety of social contexts. Such diffusion, however, does not guarantee clarity or an unambiguous meaning. On the contrary, as so often happens with social science concepts, several definitions of them are possible and, in fact, are currently employed.

The two meanings of urbanization in which I am interested here are the demographic and the sociological. The former seems less complex and controversial than the latter. It requires only two criteria — space and population (that is, the size and density of a human settlement). "Urban" is defined in terms of an agglomeration of population of a given size, within a certain area. Demographic urbanization, then, proceeds in two ways: "The multiplication of the points of concentration and the increase in size of individual concentrations."[1] It must be remembered, however, that even this relatively simple statement generates different interpretations and applications. For instance, although official statistics and census reports usually adopt demographic definitions, they vary with regard to the dividing line (in terms of size) between urban and nonurban. A common procedure is to define as "urban" those places with 2000 or more inhabitants; but the numbers 5000, 10,000, or 20,000 have sometimes been used instead to define minimum size.

On occasion, demographers and official statisticians have adopted entirely different criteria to define "urban," such as the type of politico-administrative organization of an area or, as was suggested in the past by the International Institute of Statistics, the preponderance of agricultural or nonagricultural occupations among the inhabitants.[2] Economic, legal, or political criteria are clearly related to a sociological definition rather than to a purely demographic conception of urbanization. A sociological definition of "urban" should take social structure and psychosocial and behavioral patterns into account, postulating that urban society differs from nonurban society in some significant way.

51

To try to endow a definition of this type with universal validity — that is, to cover all possible types of urbanization (and cities) — may turn out to be incomplete and insufficient for many scientific purposes. The reason lies in the fact that the nature of the "urban" or the "nonurban" changes according to the type of society. These concepts, like many others in the social sciences, are best dealt with by taking into consideration specific historical conditions. Except perhaps in the case of very general and highly abstract theorizing, the study of urbanization requires a lower level of generality, more concrete concepts, definitions carefully fitted to actual historical and cultural conditions. Obviously, different problems may require diverse levels of generality and abstraction. The objective should be to choose the most appropriate level in each case and to avoid the extension of the application of a given concept beyond the sociohistorical area in relation to which it was constructed.

Louis Wirth's classic definition of the city as "a relatively large, dense, and permanent settlement of socially heterogeneous individuals" and his psychosocial analysis of "urbanism as a way of life" certainly constitute one of the best attempts to formulate a theoretical framework for the study of urbanization and the city.[3] Wirth incorporates the essentials of the existing sociological tradition on this subject, to which I will refer later. Volume, density, and heterogeneity may be considered the structural independent variables in the definition. The remaining traits, mostly psychosocial in nature, are dealt with as dependent variables characterizing urbanism: predominance of secondary over primary groups, individualism, tolerance, segmental roles, propensity for change, social and ecological mobility, abstract thinking, universalism, achievement, instrumentality and so forth, along with other traits regarded as the "dark" side of urbanism, such as anomie, social disorganization, loss of identity, and other aspects largely analyzed in the usual critique of "mass society."[4]

Notice that Wirth's analysis corresponds to a given historical phase of urban history and perhaps to a specific cultural tradition and socioeconomic setting. Many of the psychosocial traits included are precisely those usually attributed to "industrial society" in the commonly used dichotomies (or continua) opposing "traditional" (or sacred) to "modern" (or secular) society. Wirth's formulation therefore cannot be regarded as a universally valid definition of urbanization. It pertains essentially to "modern" urbanization or even more particularly to one of its different types.[5] Analogous limitations and qualifications have been applied to other conceptions of the urban — such as the "folk-urban" continuum.

Two points deserve emphasis here. Methodological criticism of this sort is correct. Yet such criticism should not lead us to forget two well-known facts: that modern society is an urban society par excellence and that the city has played an essential role in the rise of modernity.

Typologies and distinctions are the usual available procedures to overcome the difficulties and limitations of universal definitions or the improper extension of historically or culturally limited ones. Max Weber's distinction between the occidental and the oriental city is crucial in the historical analysis of the rise of modernity in the West.[6] Similarly, the typology presented by Redfield and Singer, contrasting "folk" society, "primary" urbanization (and cities of "orthogenetic transformation") with "secondary" urbanization (and cities of "heterogenetic transformation"), not only answers some of the criticisms addressed to the "folk urban" continuum construct but also provides an excellent basis for the analysis of the relation between urbanization (the city of "heterogenetic" transformation) and the process of secularization, one of the central processes of modernization.[7] An analogous analytic function is achieved by the three types of urbanization identified by Pizzorno.[8]

In the same vein, the evolutionist typologies developed by several authors may be fruitful for analytic and descriptive purposes. Sjoberg's *Pre-Industrial City* and the "phases" of urbanization suggested by Eric Lampard may be cited as good illustrations.[9] "Primordial urbanization," according to Lampard, is defined as "the first achievement of incipient urban organization as an additional and more productive mode of collective adaptation to physical and social environment." Definitive urbanization for him is the "culmination of primordial tendencies in the additional and alternative forms of social organization." Because of its new capacities, the "definitive city artifact is now capable of transplanting itself from its native uterine environments." Definitive urbanization is then distinguished in two substages, "classic urbanization" (preindustrial civilization) and "industrial urbanization."

In this chapter a variety of definitions will crop up. Perhaps the best solution for the study of urbanization would be the combination of demographic and sociological definitions, the former being constructed or selected according to the nature of the problem at hand.

Secularization, Civilization, Modernization

Definitions of modernization are much more controversial, and I will not discuss them. Instead I will use the notion of secularization, a concept associated both with the city and with the two great changes in the history of mankind: the transition from "primitive" to "civilized" society and the emergence of modernity through a sociocultural mutation occurring within a particular "civilization." Secularization is defined here as a set of three closely interrelated aspects concerning: (1) type of social action; (2) differentiation and specialization of institutions; and (3) institutionalization of change.[10]

1. Two main types of social action may be found in any society; action by prescription, in which in any given situation a specific course of action is required, and action by choice, in which the individual selects his or her own course of action. In both cases the action is regulated by sociocultural norms and internalized attitudes and motivations; but while in the former the individual must execute the particular act prescribed for each situation, in the latter he must exercise a choice, according to given criteria. Thus elective action is still regulated action, but what is prescribed are the norms, and criteria of choice, not a specific act. Societies vary a great deal in terms of extension and areas of life regulated by choice or by prescription.

2. All societies must accomplish functions, but they are widely different in the number of functions and in the degree of differentiation, specialization, and autonomy of the institutions performing the functions.

3. All societies change, but whereas most of them reject it and institutionalize tradition (with regard to many or all aspects of the social structure), others may tolerate or even expect and institutionalize change.

Secularization is at its minimum level in "primitive" (or "folk") society: most or all areas of life are regulated by prescription, a general "embedment"[11] or indifferentiation of all institutions characterizes its organization, and tradition is institutionalized. However, such "ideal typical" rigidity does not correspond necessarily to all concrete or empirical folk societies. From some primitive cultures civilization emerged. Innovation ("choice"), differentiation, and change did take place in the folk setting, though it remained very limited in range, rare in occurrence, and extremely slow in pace. In any case, in a few primitive cultural areas the preconditions for civilization were created.

Social and technological innovations, closely interrelated, mark the transition to the civilized level and define it: an established agriculture, metallurgy, irrigation, animal husbandry, and the like are the "material culture" counterpart of a new type of social organization in which secularization has reached a higher degree. At least for certain groups there is now a limited area regulated by "elective action." The division of labor transcends the age and sex categories of primitive societies, crafts are differentiated, social strata appear, and relatively separate institutions and roles replace the kinship groupings through which all societal functions are carried on in primitive societies. Tradition is still institutionalized, and change, with few exceptions, strongly resisted — but even if not legitimized or expected, change acquires a faster rate (its time scale shrinks from tens of millennia to millennia or even centuries) and a new nature, since sociocultural transformations with their higher visibility and directionality (cycles, rises and falls, stages) become history. In conjunction with written language, the city is the universal hallmark of civilization. Cities can be found in all the "primary" civilizations (those which emerged, probably independently, out of a "primitive" setting after approximately 3500 B.C.). (Mayan civilization constitutes a partial exception in that its major "cities" were only great ceremonial centers without permanent population.) Because of the new technological and social potential acquired at the civilized level (through the existence of an economic surplus and the more rapid accumulation of knowledge), the city became the most powerful multiplier for the expansion of civilization itself. Finally it must be noted that the extension of elective action involves a higher degree of individuation. Though "primitive" man has acquired, through what Hallowell calls "protocultural" evolution, a potential for self-awareness, his subjective experience of the self and his identity are still submerged in the group. Civilization requires an increase in the number of more highly individuated persons, even if this characteristic remains restricted to segments of the elite. The urban social setting is the necessary (although not always the sufficient) condition for this extension of individuation. With civilizations human creativity is enormously enhanced: new horizons are now open, which make possible the diversity of cultural orientations so richly expressed in the historical civilizations.

The emergence of modernity reflects one particular expression of such creativity, a specific sociocultural orientation more than a relatively generalized evolutionary tendency, as seems to be the case with regard to the transition toward civilization. Historically the first emergence of the "modern industrial-cultural complex" was the result of a unique process taking place within Western culture as selectively influenced by classical antiquity and contacts with other civilized societies. Although we don't know whether other historical civilizations could have independently developed along a similar line, it would seem that their predominant values and types of social structure were not particularly conducive to the kind of "techno-economic" society characteristic of "modern civilization."[12] The "peculiarity" of classical antiquity and the premodern West is attributable to three main sets of factors: (1) the high degree and the relative spread (in dominant and strategic groups) reached by secularization at certain epochs in the two civilizations; (2) the feedback between attitudes toward economic production and control of the external world, on the one hand, and structural developments such as the complete dissolution of the communal "property" typical of primitive society, on the other hand; and (3) the confluence at a certain epoch of high secularization and a series of other trends and innovations which stablized secularization itself, transforming it into the basic structural configuration of society. The nature, intensity, and degree of secularization gave to the new civilization an inherent dynamism: from one side it provided a mechanism for continuous "self-sustained" change, a kind of "permanent revolution"; from the other side it promised a seemingly boundless geographic expansion through direct or indirect domination and/or imitation. The latter was common in all civilizations — in fact the cyclical theories of history have identified the establishment of a "universal state" as a particular stage in the "normal life cycle" of a civilization (incidentally the "last" one). But only modern civilization could actually reach a planetary level, thus replacing the parallel histories of the great historical civilizations (always spatially limited and relatively isolated) by a truly universal history. Nobody could prove that this feat was the result of any ethical or aesthetic superiority of the new society. Modern secularism succeeded because of its power — economic, political, and military — based on science and technology. It imposed itself, and it enticed millions with the promise of satisfying all man's material needs. Only in modern society knowledge took the form of logico-experimental science; economy became oriented toward production per se, ceasing to be directly related to consumption or to be overshadowed by considerations of prestige or by moral and social values. Only modern society (under the "paleocapitalist" form in which it first crystalized) could become an "economic society," and only in that society could "economic man," a construct of early industrial economics, be assumed to reflect an intrinsic and basic aspect of "human nature" itself.

These few indications may provide a useful criterion to distinguish "industrial-modern society" as a generic category comprising many possible specific types from other societal forms originating in different civilizations. Secularization in the spheres of knowledge, technology, and economy (as well as in the institutions and behavior closely related to them) is the minimum necessary requirement for the existence of any industrial society. Alone it is not sufficient, since there are other possible requirements that will vary according to the sociocultural setting, historical epoch, and other conditions. Yet in every industrial society secularization must be present to make efficiency in all aspects of production the overriding goal. With secularization comes increasing use of diversified energy sources and continuous technological innovation.

Secularization reaches its highest level in modern society, achieving greatest intensity there, affecting most areas of behavior, and spreading among the population. Whereas at the purely civilized level (including Western premodern civilization) secularization remained restricted to the elite (and in some epochs to larger segments of the urban population), the vast majority of individuals continued to live in social settings dominated by prescription and traditionalism. In fact, secularization until recently was an urban phenomenon, and we must remember that the proportion of urban population remained quite small until our own time (Table 1).[13]

TABLE 1
Percentage of World Population Living in Cities

Year	World population (millions)	Percentage in cities 5,000 and over	100,000 and over
1800	27.2	3.0	1.7
1850	74.9	6.4	2.3
1900	218.7	13.6	5.5
1950	716.7	29.8	13.1
1960	948.4	31.6	20.1

Moreover, in many nonmodern cities secularization not only remained restricted to a very small elite but also confined itself to the elaboration and the development of the dominant values of the society — the transformation of the small traditions into the "great tradition" — without transcending the traditional values or generating pluralism and heterodox change (that is, they were the cities of orthogenetic change). The properties of heterodox change are typical of secularization in modern society. The expansion of choice and individuation tends to become cumulative, and generates increasing institutional and role differentiation, increasing pluralism in values and attitudes, and increasing acceleration of change.

The level, range, and nature of secularization produce several consequences. If on the one hand the new dynamism creates new unprecedented possibilities, on the other hand it threatens the very foundation of society: it shakes the common core of shared values and norms, the rules of change, what Laski called the "agreement on fundamentals," without which the existence of any collectivity of "individuals" becomes impossible. This tension between the need to maintain a minimum prescriptive framework and the extension of action by choice introduces an inherent instability in modern society, at least under the different concrete types known until now. No wonder that in the cyclical theories of history the epochs of higher secularization are perceived as the beginnings of the "breakdown" of a civilization, to be followed by a contrary trend of strictly regulated autocratic (usually militaristic) regimes.[14] Until now the answer of modern society to the Hobbesian problem has been the adoption of the nation-state as the basic political, social, and economic organization, one capable of generating a deeply internalized identification with the total community. But this "solution" clashes with the universalistic tendencies in modern culture. It likewise conflicts with the powerful economic and technological requirements of a civilization based on centralization and interdependence on a planetary scale.

Similar tensions are created by the discontinuities in the process of modernization: the unevenness of change and the resulting coexistence, in all aspects of society, of "modern" and "nonmodern" social structures; from the contrasts between developed and underdeveloped areas (within and among nations), to the conflicts between "archaic" and "modern" attitudes, values, and institutions. Another key source of tensions concerns the particular orientation under which modern civilization itself crystallized: "economic society" as an ideal, or at least as "the natural" society, and "instrumental rationality" as the prescribed criterion for choice, at least in the realm of knowledge, economy, and technology. The maximization of effiency demands instrumental rationality, a rationality which does not discuss ends but is solely concerned with the more efficient means to achieve them. In the "economic society" maximization of production tends to become the end — through the operation of the "profit motive" of paleo-capitalism, through the "corporate organization building" of neo-capitalism, or through the "construction of socialism" as applied in the USSR and other countries. It is no chance that GNP, the gross national product, turned out to be not a mere indicator of economic development but also a sort of supreme goal for most nations. Instrumental rationality, it must be added, makes little distinction between the production of the "instruments of life" and the "instruments of death," as tragically illustrated by the Nazi policy of "rational genocide" or the present accumulation of nuclear weapons.

Certainly the dynamism of secularization provides an appropriate mechanism to turn the blind instrumental ends of the society (or its hegemonic sectors) into controversial issues and eventually demote them. But despite the "institutionalization of change," further modifications of central values may destroy the "agreement on fundamentals" to the point where revolutionary change will be necessary. As noted long ago, though modern civilization brought about cumulative growth in the natural sciences, in technology, and in economic output, it has failed so far to induce a similar growth in the field of ethics and to reconcile material with moral progress, to use a rather outdated expression. Finally even material progress may cease to be a certainty under the growing contradictions between technological and economic "imperatives" and lagging social structures, such as the viability of the nation-state, or the economy (be this one of the various forms of "neocapitalism,"or "socialism"), or, to return to our main subject, the viability of the city, a sociocultural and material structure inherited from a distant past and essential in the birth of modernity, but one that may turn out to be unadaptable to the demands of the new era. Again, in confronting these dilemmas modern society finds the unresolved "Hobbesian" problem, the seemingly irreconcilable conflicts stemming not only from opposite particularistic interests, but also from contrasting values and ideologies, or alternate models of "postmodern" society.

The "urban crisis" of contemporary advanced nations and the problems of Third World cities are expressions of both the inherent and the transitional contradictions of modern society and modernization as a process. It is a truism to say that the city is part of the total society, but it is worthwhile to repeat it, since too often the perspective of "urban sociology" disguises this obvious truth. In modern civilization, where urbanization in its double meaning — demographic and sociological — is expanded to the whole society, the adoption of a global perspective is even more necessary for a realistic perception of the "urban crisis."

Currently the term modernization is used with reference to the spread of the modern industrial civilization, and not to the unique historical process which led to its crystallization in the West. Following the terminology used by Lampard in relation to the city, we could refer to the emergence of industrial societies in the West as primordial modernization and label the subsequent spread of industrialism over the planet definitive modernization. It is important to emphasize that the latter not only comprises many individual transitions but also that they represent present wide variations among themselves and cannot even be compared with the Great Transformation, Karl Polanyi's term for the specific process that created the modern West.[15] The advent of the new industrial era triggered a process of universal and rapid change, since both the early modernizing countries (the first comers) and the successive waves of late comers were involved in continuous transformations. Successive modifications of the first "model" of industrial society have appeared. Especially among the late comers, new types of socioeconomic structures have appeared also, oriented toward different models and rationalized in terms of diverging ideologies. All the forms and types, however, may be classified within the modern-industrial complex, conceived as a broad category distinct from all nonindustrial civilizations and cultures.

The general principle I have summarized under the label of secularization underlies both primodial modernization and definitive modernization. The reasons for the difference between the two processes are quite clear. In the first place, the Great Transformation occurred within a specific culture, whereas the diffusion of industrialism over the world affected entirely different cultural traditions. Second, the very emergence of the first industrial societies modified substantially the modern international system, or more precisely established it for the first time through interdependence and the possibility of world control and domination. Third, the international system and the single societies composing it underwent a process of continuous and rapid transformation. Consequently, under the ever-changing contextual circumstances, the successive individual transitions greatly diverged from the initial Great Transformation and hence were bound to present more or less pronounced differences among themselves. If we conceive of each individual transition as a complex of analytically separate (but interdependent) component subprocesses, we may highlight another source of differences. Such subprocesses are interrelated, but may well take place at different rates and in different sequences, under the varying historical conditions characterizing each transition: diverse "starting points," a changing international system, evolving technology, changing economic structures, changing ideological climates.

Cities and urbanization were (and are) involved and closely connected both with the unique Great Transformation and with the many individual transitions, but the city's role, meaning, and relation with regard to modernization had to be different in keeping with the variety of the paths of transition. Such diversity, however, does not necessarily prevent the formulation and testing of propositions, at different levels of generality, concerning the relationship between urbanization and modernization under specified historical and sociocultural conditions. In this sense some limited generalizations could be advanced and tested with regard to given historical epochs and/or given sociocultural areas encompassing many nations. Hopefully, a more advanced theory of modernization than the partial conceptualizations available until now could suggest some more generally valid propositions describing and explaining the relationships between types, forms, and rates of urbanization and varieties of transitional paths and modernization models.[16]

The Historical Components of the Great Transformation

The notion of secularization may be used, from one point of view, as a conceptual construct providing a common meaning to the Great Transformation, the varieties of transitional paths, and the several possible types of modern industrial societies. From another point of view, secularization can be seen as a historical-comparative construct useful for the description of concrete historical processes occurring at different times and places, with varying intensity and magnitude, particularly within the Western world, since the classical era. Both in terms of logical consistency and in terms of empirical convergence, these concrete historical processes of secularization have been associated to different extents with other trends and innovations, whose confluence finally led to the emergence of the modern-industrial complex.

I will not attempt to give an enumeration of all the components of the Great Transformation (we don't even know which are the necessary and sufficient ones), but I believe that the following roster of essential processes, trends, and innovations may prove useful:

- Growing social differentiation. Particularly in terms of division of labor, diversified forms of property, and the emergence of hierarchical strata, this development transforms the "primitive community." After the urban revolution, "higher" forms of division of labor and different and more complex kinds of social classes and stratification structures continue to evolve.
- Emergence of the individual. Both "individuation," a psychosocial phenomenon taking place as a historical process, and "individualism," the affirmation of a set of values and ideologies, become pronounced.
- Growth of the "market." With differentiation, the economy becomes a separate, relatively autonomous subsystem within the social structure.
- Scientific outlook. Once science is established as an independent realm subject to its own normative framework and its own values, the abstract, logico-empirical-quantitative approach is extended to many other aspects of human activity.
- Continuous expansion of a scientific technology applied to the production of goods and services; a technology, that is, based on modern science and not on the slow and spontaneous innovations of the artisan (pre-industrial or "organic" technology).[17]
- An autonomization — similar to the differentiation occurring in economy and in science — of ethical, aesthetic, educational, political, and other subsystems and values. Particularly important in this respect is the formation of the centralized nation-state endowed with a rational-bureaucratic organization, able to extend its intervention to larger geographical areas and to most aspects of social life.
- Social and organizational innovations necessary to activate the economy. Among these are accounting, money and credit, joint stock companies, and the like.
- The formation and consolidation of the social groups who provide the leadership and social basis for the confluence of all these trends: the urban bourgeosie. This new class is endowed with certain values, attitudes, and ideologies concerning work, science, economics, politics, and society and is able through "property" to monopolize the means of production. The emergence of "free labor" in time to generates new classes, particularly the industrial proletariat.

All this and much more led to the emergence of the first industrial society, under the particular form of industrial capitalism. Trends and innovations do not correspond to successive stages: they must be conceived as long-term historical processes, taking place to some extent along parallel lines but discontinuously and asynchronously. In fact, although endowed with certain evolutionary directionality, various historical innovations appeared in different forms and intensity, developed, and sometimes decayed, decreased, and even faded away to re-emerge later in another historical context. They certainly evidenced a tendency to be associated among themselves, to form clusters so to speak; however, in several instances during the history of Western culture these clusters were incomplete (some component was lacking), or their development was insufficient, or the form they assumed was not suitable to generate, in conjunction with other components, the definitive crystallization of the modern-industrial complex. Phases of limited secularization, particularly in Greece, Rome, and Renaissance Europe, the rise and the arrested development of a "modern" science in classical Greece, the rather controversial case of "ancient capitalism" or the less ambiguous and more advanced instances of commercial capitalism since the fourteenth century in Italy and elsewhere in Western Europe may be considered illustrations of earlier, partial, incomplete, or immature confluences of modernization components.[18] How to explain these "failures" (if such a term can be used at all) is an open question. In any case, a general theory of modernization would be able not only to account for the rise of industrial capitalism and its earlier partial manifestations but also to explain why this social, economic, and cultural development, as a unified whole, did occur only within the Western world and not in other, comparably complex and equally advanced civilizations, particularly in Asia. We do have several relatively valid explanations regarding some of the components of the Great Transformation. Furthermore, some general theoretical orientations like Marxism or neo-evolutionist theory provide a starting point for an interdisciplinary attempt to systematize the contributions of prehistory, anthropology, history, sociology, and the other social sciences. But this immense task, which in fact is the legacy of eighteenth- and nineteenth-century social thought, remains to be accomplished.

For present purposes, it is sufficient to understand that a long period of primodial modernization (in the West) is being followed by definitive modernization (throughout the world) and that the outcome is still uncertain. In the new type of society, change tends to accelerate. The first comers of the modern industrial epoch are undergoing a continuous process of transformation, while successive waves of later comers are generating new varieties of industrial societies. One of the challenges of our time is to discover how much convergence or divergence will or ought to characterize the "modernization" of the planet. The widening gap between the "advanced" societies and the "developing" or Third World societies is a related trait of the present phase of definitive modernization, and its consequences are very difficult to predict.

Secularization and the City in the Sociological Tradition

Let us now return to secularization and the associated innovations, trends, and processes whose convergence inaugurated the epoch of definitive modernization. All of them, except their incipient manifestations prior to the phase of "primordial urbanization," occurred within an urban environment, although some of the components of the Great Transformation were associated with special kinds of urban structure. This does not mean that all social change necessarily requires an urban setting. In the first place, the urban revolution itself, the long process of "primordial urbanization," consisted of innovations and transformations taking place within the matrix of the existent predominant social organization. That original organization, the primitive community and its predecessors, whatever they may have been was nonurban by definition. As Hauser indicates in his criticism of the folk-urban conception of social change, "Preurban and preindustrial societies have been capable of developing class stratification, elaborate priesthoods, status rivalry, and many other phenomena that are implicitly and unilaterally attributed to the growth of cities."[19] Secondly, even during the Great Transformation, changes on occasion originated in the rural sector. A good illustration of this is the period following the breakdown of the classic civilization and the decline of the urban Roman society. "Antiquity," Marx and Engels shrewdly noted, "started from the town and its little territory; the Middle Ages started out from the country."[20] But it would be unreasonable to deny that those specific changes subsumed under the notion of secularization as defined here, and the innovations and trends leading toward the emergence of the modern-industrial complex, could reach their full expression only in the urban setting. It was the peculiar structure of urban society that was capable of inducing such development, even if impulses originated beyond the city walls. This proposition does not mean that all urban centers necessarily give rise to secularization, let alone the particular Western type of it. Nonsecular cities have existed, as emphasized by Redfield and Singer as well as by classical sociologists like Tönnies, but all secularizing processes took place in urban structures.

The classical sociological tradition and the comprehensive theories of universal history — or philosophies of history, if one prefers — have always linked the city to secularization, even if the actual term has not been used. This close connection is, by the way, the underlying cause for the persisting confusion between the sociological concept of urbanization and the notion of modernization, as in the case of Wirth's definition. The sociological (as well as the philosophical) meaning of secularization rose in the nineteenth century. Originally it was a juridical term referring to the exclusion of an institution or a territory or other material domain from the control or jurisdiction of the church and religion. Groethuysen in discussing secularism indicates that in the realm of knowledge, science, and philosophy the term may be defined as "the attempt to establish an autonomous sphere of knowledge, purged of supernatural, fideistic presuppositions."[21] This attempt, initiated in the Western Middle Ages, flourished with the rise of modern science from the Renaissance onward and consolidated with the rationalism of the Enlightenment. The same trend occurred with regard to attitudes concerning social and political institutions. Again, the beginnings may be found in medieval thought, followed by a decisive step in the Renaissance and then progressive consolidation in the eighteenth and nineteenth centuries.

The ideologies and the philosophies of history oriented toward the idea of progress (and later its expression in evolutionistic theories) all were concerned in one way or another with the process of secularization, although the term itself was not employed. Perhaps the first sociologist to use it was Howard Becker, who defined it sociologically in terms of the transition from a "sacred, closed society" to a "secular, open" one.[22] Becker derived this conception directly from Tönnies' famous dichotomy — *Gemeinschaft* versus *Gesellschaft*.[23] Tönnies himself does not use the term secularization, but his description of the dichotomy and the historical sequence he attributes to it correspond closely to such a process. Tönnies' conceptions are firmly based on wide historical and intellectual antecedents, from Hobbes, Hegel, Gierke, Maine, Marx, and others, and represent a genuine expression of the nineteenth-century sociological tradition, including the founding fathers, Comte and Spencer. Independently from Tönnies, Durkheim's dichotomy of forms of solidarity ("mechanic" versus "organic") expressed the same basic insight and referred to the same historical process of secularization.[24] Again the Great Transformation appears at the focus of most of Simmel's sociological thinking. Like in the case of Tönnies, for Simmel (who is also usually regarded as a founder of "pure" or formalistic sociology) the assumedly timeless social "forms" are generated by historical experience and permeated with historical meaning. He regarded the capitalist order as the result of a process of market economics, individuation, growing social differentiation, and rationalism, intellectualism, growing social differentiation, and rationalism, intellectualism, abstract thinking, and universal quantification.[25] He also stressed the far-reaching correlates of a differentiated market and money economy — that is, of the emerging capitalist order. Finally, let us remember that the two greatest theories of the rise of industrial society — those of Marx and Weber—also focus upon most aspects of secularization. In Marxism, the word "secularization" is not used. However, Marxism itself has often been interpreted as the culmination of a secularizing process by which Judeo-Christian doctrines about the transcendent meaning of history are transformed into immanent human terms. As Karl Löwith has written, "Historical materialism is the history of salvation expressed in the language of political economy."[26] More closely relevant to the notion of secularization as defined here are Marx's and Engels's own sociological and historical analyses, which directly influenced Tönnies's theories. Finally, Weber (whose receptivity to Marx's and Tönnies's ideas on this topic is well known) formulated what is perhaps the most important contribution to modern sociological thinking about secularization and its relation to the city.

What explains secularization, and the reasons the urban setting, or certain types of cities, are able to generate it? The answer is a familiar one. On the structural-social side we find size, or volume of population, density, heterogeneity, both internal and external, through higher forms of division of labor, of social differentiation, of contacts and/or communications — through migration, exchange, cooperation, association or war — with different cultural patterns, values, norms. The structural economic correlates (or factors according to the kind of priority one wants to give) consist mainly of the transition from an "embedded" economy (what Heimann calls an "integrated social system")[27] to a differentiated increasingly autonomous economic subsystem. This subsystem stems first of all from the separation between agriculture on one side and trade and industry on the other (the separation of city and country), from more differentiated forms of property culminating in full private property, from the rise of the "market," with the replacement of trade — as an archaic form of exchange, rooted in traditional "reciprocity" and "equivalencies" — by the impersonal and purely economic mechanism of supply and demand, from the transformation of all products into "merchandise," from the increasing monetarization, and from the ensuing universal quantification.

This structural description of secularization is only a composite synthesis of the classic sociological contribution. Tönnies starts—as Simmel, Becker, and others have — from a psychosocial conception: the opposition between forms of human will. *Gemeinschaft* is based on organic will (*Wesenwille*), oriented toward a nonrational, nondeliberate acceptance of values and norms, legitimized by tradition and religion; whereas *Gesellschaft* is the expression of arbitrary will (*Kürville*), characterized by free choice, instrumental rationality, intellectualism, whose source is scientific knowledge and whose guiding values are given by the pursuits of individualistic interests.[28] But Tönnies does not ignore the structural social and economic factors; size, heterogeneity, and economic changes. In fact, he seems to give priority to the latter, although in association with other components. There are, in fact, three principles, which, according to him, underlie not only the contrasting poles of his dichotomy, but also the transition from one ot the other: the economic, the political and the spiritual principles.[29] This is particularly clear with regard to the transformation of the sacred city (the "felt community") into the secular city. Tönnies's *Gemeinschaft* category is not limited to the rural setting or the rural village; it can also fit a city. The city, although the "higher and most complex form of social life in general," in its "communal" expression retains a basic similarity with the village and the family, being based on the same "organic" will, equally rooted in the spontaneous natural common feeling of oneness, the same blood, soil, custom, religion. "It is only when the city develops into a 'great' city that it loses most of these characteristics." Even if some community relations may persist within it, the great city is no longer a *Gemeinschaft;* it has turned into a *Gesellschaft.*[30] The city of the community, the sacred city (or the city of orthogenetic change), does not totally lack internal differentiation: not only because of the natural "physiological" division of labor (age and sex) but beyond that, because of other forms of division of labor, particularly the artisanal division of labor. On the other hand, the existence of surplus will permit the creation of an elite of aristocrats, soldiers, priests, and men of learning. But such inequality is limited by the nature of community relations: it is a hierarchy of the same kind as exists in the family, between parents and children, since the elite and the common people continue to be united in community bonds.[31] When the bonds are broken, class struggle follows: "society" has now replaced "community." But this change is not brought about by an increase in size alone: an economic transformation, Tönnies insists, is the basis: agriculture has been separated from trade and industry, and economic inequality has increased, giving the elite, and above all a new social group of merchants, more power over the common people. Tönnies closely follows Marx in this analysis. His ideas on "society" coincide with Marxist descriptions of capitalism (and the transition follows what he calls "Karl Marx's masterful analysis of industrial development").[32] His notion of community finds its counterpart in Marx's and Engels's "primitive community" and "primitive mode of production." This is the first stage in the evolutionary Marxian scheme of human society.[33] In Marx's words, "the spontaneously evolved tribal community, or the herd — the common ties of blood, custom, language," based on the primary relationship of family and kinship, "expanded to a tribe," is "the unity of living and active human beings, with the natural, inorganic conditions of their metabolism, with nature, and therefore their appropriation of nature; nor is this only a result of a historical process." Here, too, Tönnies's assumption that "society" develops from "community" follows Marx's idea that the "historical process of separation of hitherto combined elements" starts from the primitive community.[34] Such "separation," which according to Marx is fully accomplished with industrial (capitalist) society, coincides with the sociological process of secularization. It means in the first place successive stages of increasing and changing differentiations of the "division of labor." Marx distinguishes two main forms of it: the most primitive, and also the foundation of further differentiation, he calls the "division of labor within society." It includes two subforms, also appearing successively but continuing to coexist, along with other forms throughout all history previous to the final outcome of communism. The first is the "physiological," taking place first within the family and then within the community, on the basis of age and sex; the second is local, and is possible through the contact between various communities, and the advantage of the conditions offered by the natural environment, facilitating given production. This, incidentally, originates exchange and initiates the transformation of products into merchandise. The second, more advanced form, is the division of labor within manufacturing, once more classified into two subforms of increasing specialization and productivity (from the heterogeneous division of labor, in which different parts of the same object are produced by different workers, to the organic, in which the whole operation is subdivided in a multiplicity of partial simple operations). It is important here that, according to Marx, the two main forms "presuppose certain size and density of population" and the degree of density depends not upon population alone, but also upon "means of communication."[35] Marx here means the possibility of more intense contacts, which in Durkheim's terms would correspond to "dynamic density."

One recognizes here some of the essential aspects of secularization as developed later by the classic sociological tradition. The rise of individuation (the self as an autonomous psychological entity, independent from the group, and standing as a subject vis-à-vis the object) is only possible through increasing division of labor, increasing size of population, increasing social differentiation — social strata and individualized property, heterogeneity, contacts with alien societies and foreigners: all these processes combined and multiplied by the rise of the city. "Man," Marx argued, "is only individualized through the process of history. He originally appears as a generic being, a tribal being, a herd animal, though by no means as a political animal."[36] "This sheep-like or tribal consciousness receives its further development and extension through increased productivity, the increase of needs, and what is fundamental to both of these, the increase of population. With these, there developed the division of labor, which was originally nothing but the division of labor in the sexual act, then that division of labor which develops spontaneously or 'naturally' by virtue of natural predisposition. . . ." "The division of labor only becomes truly such from the moment when a division of material and mental labor appears."[37] And when does this moment come? It occurs with the rise of the city.[38] From here the process of secularization continues toward its culmination in industrial society with increasing social differentiation, inequality, the emergence of the state and of deliberate intervention and planning, increasing domination of nature through the continuous growth of science and its conscious application to technology, dissolution of tradition, and permanent change.[39] The city played an essential role in the whole transition from barbarism to civilization. According to Marx and Engels: "The greatest division of material and mental labor is the separation of town and country. The antagonism between town and country begins the transition from barbarism to civilization, from tribe to state, from locality to nation, and runs through the whole history of civilization to the present day."[40]

The city, Marx asserts, but not any city, not the great capitals of military, theocratic, or bureaucratic empires, became the basis of the modern-industrial complex. Those societies based on what Marx and Engels called the "Asiatic mode of production" failed to develop, since they maintained the primitive communities, with their low level of division of labor, common property, and low individuation. Consequently, their cities depended entirely on the agricultural surplus, and the functions of those cities — military, bureaucratic, or religious — lacked the dynamic drive of a commercial economy. Perhaps the stagnation of Asiatic despotism was a historical accident, but in any case the only line which in fact did evolve toward the modern-industrial complex was initiated and achieved in the Western world and not elsewhere.[41] Only the classical city of the West was able to dissolve the bonds of the primitive community, to release the individual, to achieve for the first time the full privatization of property, to build a commercial quasi-capitalistic economy, a class structure, and a rational state. The "Greek miracle" failed to achieve a technological society at the time but initiated the line of evolution which crystalized in modern Europe.[42]

It was the achievement of Weber to isolate the specific traits of the Western city which were at the root of this unique process, but Marxist theories of social development did not fail to recognize the role of city and secularization. The theoreticians' historical materialism emphasizes technoeconomic infrastructural changes and class struggle. From their perspective the notion of secularization with its "principles" set forth in the definition used here might be considered a mere "abstraction," at best "an effort to sum up the most general results which arise from observation of the historical development of men."[43] Nonetheless, these "general results" are documented in the Marxist theoretical and historical analyses; and what is important for the present purposes, the role of the Western city, is unequivocally stressed.

Volume and density of population and the increasing division of labor could be found only in cities — at least until the technological revolution in communication eliminated the obstacles of space and distance. This was the structural basis which made the city the focus of secularization, and it was recognized as such not only by Marx but also by James Mill, Comte, and others.[44] But it was Durkheim with his "morphological theory" who formulated a systematic approach.

Durkheim set forth the category of organic solidarity — a social bond based on the interdependence of differentiated groups and individualized persons and corresponding approximately to the "secularized" type of social structure. The contrasting category he called mechanical solidarity. Involving low differentiation and individuation, it applies to the prescriptive, homogenous, traditional structure. As in Marx and Tönnies, organic solidarity can develop only out of mechanical solidarity. Durkheim concludes, however, that the latter never disappears entirely; it continues to coexist, although in a different form and degree, in a social setting based predominantly on organic solidarity. In a society founded on "contract," it provides the "noncontractual" element, that is, a common core of shared values and norms, which makes possible the fulfillment of the contract itself. The increase in the division of labor is generated by size and density of population. Density, however, means much more than physical proximity; its essential trait is communication. Intensity of communication, "dynamic" or "moral," density, is required to generate differentiation.[45] Material volume and ecological density alone are not sufficient: the "segmental" type of society, the juxtaposition of identical social units based on mechanical solidarity, would not produce differentiation. For Durkheim the notion of "dynamic density" is crucial in understanding the role of the Western type of city in secularization. In this sense his theory connects with elements of Marxism mentioned above and with Weber. In fact, the "segmental" type of society reminds us both of the "Asiatic mode of production" and of one of the essential characteristics which Weber attributes to the Eastern city: the coexistence of a variety of cultural groups, and a kind of heterogeneity whose "segmental" nature, coupled with caste barriers, impedes communication — that is, prevents physical size and proximity from becoming "moral" density. This would explain then why neither the spatial and demographic expansion of society — even the rise of great empires — nor urban heterogeneity, when remaining segmental, necessarily produces higher differentiation and societal complexity. In Durkheim's terms, dynamic density is impeded by the "neutralizing influence of the collective consciousness on the division of labor." Indivisibility of property in the rural commune, segregation of certain occupations in the city, religious or intellectual dogmatism are symptoms of the persistence of an "intense" form of a "collective consciousness" that prizes tradition. This persistence, even in a setting of large populations and high density, is mainly based on segmentation, which isolates "so many little societies, more or less reciprocally closed."[46]

Where segmentation dissolves, in Durkheim's view, the city, in particular the great city, not only provides the right conditions of size and dynamic density but also includes complementary factors contributing to the modification of the collective consciousness and facilitating individuation. Among these factors Durkheim emphasizes immigration because it introduces two categories of potential innovators. The "stranger" and the young become prominent. Both are agents of heterogeneity and powerful dissolvers of tradition.[47] The role of dynamic density as a key factor is also expressed in the final "urbanization" (in the sociological sense) of the entire society, since social development involves much more than the continuous increase in the proportion of population living in urban centers. It cancels the specificity of the city with regard to the "urban way of life": "The more the moral density of a society increases, the more the whole society comes to resemble a great city, including in its walls an entire nation. In fact as moral and material distance between the different regions tend to vanish away, their reciprocal relations turn out to be more and more similar to the different districts of the same city."[48] We find here an intimation that the city may fade as a distinct locus when the "urban way of life" spreads to every corner of the land, a possibility foreseen by contemporary social scientists such as Boulding and Greer.[49]

The relation between the expansion of social groups, the division of labor, and individuation had been analyzed by Georg Simmel in a book published three years earlier than Durkheim's *The Division of Labor in Society*.[50] In fact three main contributions on this subject appeared independently almost at the same time (Tönnies in 1887, Simmel in 1890, and Durkheim in 1893). The unprecedented transformations in the Western world and the culmination of the nineteenth-century intellectual tradition necessarily focused the attention of scholars on the same questions and suggested similar answers. In his essay on the expansion of social groups and the formation of individuality, Simmel uses almost the same components as Durkheim, although with a different emphasis. Growth in the size of a social group, he reasons, on the average puts more competence at the disposal of members. (For example, there may be ten exceedingly gifted people in a city of 10,000, and none in a village of 500. Furthermore, the economies of scale and the surplus production of the larger group will free additional individuals to cultivate their talent.) This leads to specialization, which in turn increases competence still more.[51] But in another essay, Simmel stresses a different powerful factor of individualization, which remains only implicit in Durkheim's and Tönnies' writings: the maltiplication and the growing intersection of social circles, which induces growing differentiation and growing individuation. While in one natural circle, family and kinship, the individual remains absorbed and his self submerged in the group; personality and freedom are acquired through his belonging to a large variety of social circles.[52] Specialized competence and a stronger sense of self operating in a money economy generate the typical mental climate of the metropolis as described by Simmel in still another seminal essay.[53]

When we absorb Simmel's theory and pass on to the writings of Max Weber, we find the notion of secularization to be important in Weber's typology of social action, forms of authority, and kinds of social relations (closely based on Tönnies' dichotomy). Secularization also occupies Weber's attention with respect to economics, science, the law, the state, and the transformation of religion into a driving force in the emergence of the "capitalist spirit."[54]

More directly related to the line of discussion I have conducted so far is Weber's theory on the particular relevance of the Western city to the rise of the modern-industrial complex. Why was it that the crucial "civic development did not start in Asia, but in the Mediterranean basin and later in Europe"? Weber's answer to this question may be summarized in three main points.

1. The concept and loyalties and concerted action of a "citizenry" based on equality of rights could not exist among the "segmental" groups composing an Eastern city. "In China the magic closure of the clans, in India the closure of the castes, eliminated the possibility of civic confederations. In China the clans as bearer of the ancestors were indestructible. In India the castes were carriers of particular styles of life upon the observance of which salvation and reincarnation depended. Ritualistically thus, the castes were mutually exclusive."

2. Only the Western city — both in antiquity until the late Roman Empire and in the Middle Ages — counted on a "self-equipped army . . . whether it was a peasant militia, an army of knights, or a burgher militia." The urban army was composed of individuals who enjoyed military independence. The "military associations" of self-equipped soldiers "were also a fundamental component in the origin of the corporate, autonomous urban community." In the East the army depended on the centralized authority of the bureaucratic-military empire and was far removed from the control of the commoners (Weber's point here resembling Marxist beliefs about "oriental despotism").

3. The Western city generated a new order, the "quasi-capitalist" order of antiquity and the "rational" capitalism of modern times, and nurtured the social group at the forefront of this transformation: the urban bourgeoisie.[55] Along this same line, a question arises about types of cities in the West. How did the classical city, not fully capitalistic, differ from the medieval city, which created the preconditions for an uninterrupted movement toward capitalism and industrialism? Weber discusses several of these differences, beginning with the "guild character of the Middle Ages city, which helped to create a specific town economy" and "made the surrounding country subservient to the town interests." None of this can be found in the ancient city, where the guilds had a different character. As Weber says, "the typical citizen of the medieval guild city is a merchant or craftsman . . . ; in antiquity on the contrary the full citizen is the land holder." This fact also affected the exercise of a citizen's rights, which were more equalitarian — at the legal level — in the medieval city. As a

consequence of the different routes to citizenship, social cleavages within the two types of cities differed. In the ancient city the major friction was between the landowner and the landless; whereas in the medieval city social conflict approached the class type of modern capitalism. Land was the basis of the wealth in the ancient city, and war was the "respectable" way of acquiring it. Although the ancient city had a considerable development of trade and industry, both were subordinated to politico-military interests. Thus, said Weber, "the city democracy of antiquity is a political guild." This trait, together with the great military strength of the city (the greatest in its time), explains "the form and direction of industry in antiquity, with relation to profit through war and other advantages to be attained by purely political means. Over against the citizen stands the 'low-bred': anyone is low-bred who follows the peaceful quest of profit in the sense of today." By contrast, trade and craft industry were deemed more honorable and more profitable in the medieval city.[56]

Each of the social sciences has something to contribute to our knowledge of secularization, modernization, and urbanization.[57] Yet such men as Weber, Simmel, and Marx were not only sociologists, but also in effect economists, historians, political scientists, and philosophers. Given their breadth, a whole section has been devoted here to "the sociological tradition," and I will continue to draw upon it in subsequent sections.

Urbanization and Modernization: First Comers and Late Comers

Thus far while considering theories of the role of the city in secularization and the other changes that compose modernization, we have been referring mostly to the "Great Transformation," to the period of primordial modernization preceding the crystallization of the modern industrial complex. But in the period of definitive modernization, in which the contemporary world is living, the city is again closely related to modernization. In fact, demographic urbanization is one of the central component processes of the whole transition.

In the present epoch of definitive modernization the character of the city tends to change continuously. One reason for change is that the whole world context is modified through the total influence generated by the individual transitions of the various nations which successively initiate and develop toward some form of modern-industrial structure. Another reason is that the economic and technological "imperatives" of the industrial system frequently shift. A third reason is that new "models" and different transition paths are appearing. We must remember that most of these modifications are expressed in terms of differences in rates and sequences of the various component processes. Demographic urbanization in particular is occurring at a different rate and in a different sequence (with regard to the other components) among the late comers (the present developing countries) in comparison with the first comers (those countries which initiated their transition in the nineteenth century and have now achieved a more advanced stage). It should be noted that the distinction between first comers and late comers is a flexible one. Among the early industrializing countries themselves one may differentiate between early and late comers (as Alexander Gerschenkron and others have done), since industrialization in Great Britain was different from the case of Germany, Russia, or the United States. For purposes of this discussion I will follow a simple distinction between the present already advanced societies (the first comers) and the present developing countries (the late comers).

In this section I will consider first the general correlation between demographic urbanization and processes of modernization, second the process as it occurred among the first comers, and finally its characteristics with regard to the present developing countries, in comparison with the former ones.[58]

General Correlations between Demographic Urbanization and Component Processes of Modernization

One way of gauging the relationship of urbanization to modernization is to construct indicators from aggregate data and then compute correlation indexes among these indicators.

The construction, selection, and use of indicators obviously present a series of very complex problems — theoretical and conceptual problems no less than problems of obtaining accurate information. Nevertheless, the use of numerical indicators is now widespread and, in spite of great limitations, offers at least a point of departure. The examples I give in this section of the indicators which one may use to measure the level of correlation between demographic urbanization and other subprocesses should be viewed as provisional.[59]

The construction of urbanization indicators in the strictly demographic sense of the term is relatively easy in comparison with the difficulties presented by the measurement of other processes. The most common way is to take as an indicator of urbanization the proportion of a society's total population residing in places each containing enough people to satisfy the researcher's definition of urban. Thus information would be sought along the lines of: "X percent of people in country Y live in settlements containing Z thousand residents." From this basis it will be possible to construct different measures of urbanization, both dynamic and static.

Much more complex is the problem presented by the indicators of social, economic, and political modernization. Conceptual and practical difficulties abound. Terminology and concepts vary considerably.[60] Psychosocial and personality traits may not be measurable at all through aggregate data. More valid and specific indicators should be constructed ad hoc, and this procedure requires surveys or similar techniques. In this sense the most comprehensive research conducted so far is the study by Alex Inkeles on social and cultural aspects of development.[61] As a first approach, however, the use of aggregate data provides some useful insights into the connections between urbanization and modernization.

In one study I have assembled thirty-six indicators of economic, social, and political modernization.[62] All were correlated with urbanization. However, as could be expected, although in most cases the coefficient may be considered rather high (e.g., .71 with GNP per capita; .87 with degree of industrial diversification; .82 with energy consumption per capita; .82 with a combined index of mass communications), the correlations were always far from being perfect. This clearly points to the existence of lags in the rate of change of urbanization in relation to the other indicators. Strictly speaking, the correlations imply no more than the existence of a generic tendency for urbanization to be associated with the component processes of modernization. In reality all these are interrelated to a variable degree, and the application of statistical techniques — factor analysis, for example — shows that the indicators behave as if, underlying the many component subprocesses, a structure or a configuration of a few independent factors or "dimensions," or even only one factor, were operating. For example, in one of the first research attempts of this type, Cattell and others isolated twelve common factors underlying the intercorrelations among some seventy indicators belonging to forty modern-industrial countries.[63] Berry utilized forty-three indicators of economic development and modernization (for ninety-three countries), finding "four basic factors underlying the forty-three indicators." Among them, one stands out — termed by Berry the "technological factor" — with much greater weight than the other three.[64] Conclusions more favorable still to the one dimensionality of the process were reached by Schnore, in his study aimed precisely at analyzing the relation between urbanization and economic development (included in his definition of social modernization). In his analysis (in which twelve indicators were utilized) urbanization appeared as one of many aspects of a single process. Although many processes can be discerned at the conceptual level, all of them seem to be closely joined empirically.[65] Correlations at the international level, such as those done by Dillon Soares for Venezuela, Brazil, Chile, and Japan revealed similar results.[66]

These and other findings are certainly useful insofar as they represent a point of departure for analysis. They confirm the hypothesis that modernization can be seen as a global process and that all the various component subprocesses are related. At the same time, considerable variations in the pattern are revealed country by country. They confirm what has been suggested concerning the considerable variations in the rhythms or rates of change, and the sequences of the subprocesses under the peculiar conditions (external and internal) that characterize the various societies in transition. The next step will be to devise a theory or a set of hypotheses encompassing the possible patterns of change and specifying the conditions and factors that in each case determine them. The relationship of urbanization to the other component processes of modernization needs to be explained under this general theory. As I have already indicated, the theory does not presently exist, and the preliminary attempts to arrive at it may take varying roads, albeit complementary ones. The construction of models could be one of the roads; empirical and historical generalization could be another. An empirical procedure would be to compare the "profiles" of development and modernization reached at a given moment by a great number of countries and try to draw from them a typology. This procedure is sketched out in a United Nations study, in which indicators of economic development are compared with indicators of "social development." In that study all nations were classified with respect to each indicator, on a scale of six categories, in order of increasing economic and social development. In this way one might be able to define as "balanced" the development of those countries which came to be situated in the same category by all the indicators — that is, those which have reached the same relative level of development in each one of the aspects considered. According to the United Nations findings, in the more advanced countries the indicators of social development and those of economic development tended to form a more "equilibrated" configuration than that of the transitional and less advanced countries.[67]

One very serious limitation in this procedure, which also applies to the correlations and factor analyses already mentioned, is that it offers no good way of comparing countries whose transition was initiated in different epochs — that is to say, under a set of very different historical circumstances at the international and the internal level. As pointed out, these circumstances vary continually and in this way alter significantly the form which change will assume in the countries having started their transition in different epochs. This effect can be clearly seen in the case of the urbanization process.

Urbanization and Modernization among the First Comers

I will consider here the relations between demographic urbanization and the growth of a modern industrial sector (manufacture), the growth of the tertiary sector (communications, transportation, trade, and services), and other technological and social transformations, particularly those related to a societal change of scale. In the case of the first comers, urban concentration appears as a necessary functional requirement, given a certain level of technical and scientific development, and certain features of the social structure (that is, certain preconditions for the emergence of the industrial society). But once the principle of instrumental rationality has spread, it can be shown how the necessities of economic rationalization, including the level of "spontaneous" behavior of enterprises in a liberal system, tend to promote ecological concentration of the population. Lampard has worked out in a very clear outline the mechanisms which, in the emergences of the first industrial society and its diffusion in the West, produced urban concentration.[68]

The specialization of functions and the concomitant interdependency create a need for a techno-economic integration, and under certain conditions, ecological concentration results. The location and size of the city will result from a balance of different elements: cost of transportation, availability of raw materials and of labor force, location with respect to the market. Costs will be reduced through concentration and the influence of these factors. Concentration also reduces the cost of investments in the economic infrastructure (such as the provision of water and energy, administrative services, and worker transport) and of "social" investments (housing, sanitary services, education, police protection). Among the external economies achieved in this way, Lampard (quoting Marshall) also classified the "psychological climate" created by the concentration of industrial activity — a climate particularly favorable to innovation, where the intellectual stimulation for change will find optimal conditions. Likewise concentration brings certain material and organizational advantages in the intellectual and scientific field: for example, libraries and laboratories. To the external economies one can obviously add the internal ones: the cost reductions derived from the enlargement of scale of economic operations.

Given these and other purely technico-economic requirements of industrial development that lead to urban concentration, the same effect is transformed into a self-reinforcing cause, not only because the force of attraction of the existing concentration has increased, but also because new needs derived from the change of scale of the urban unit have emerged: for example, the increase of the need for coordination and for organization. To this process can be added another factor which also contributes powerfully in increasing the "urban concentration": the growth of the tertiary sector, not only in response to the needs mentioned above, but also because of growth in all the other services and the rise of new forms of them. Greater industrial productivity reduces the number of workers required for the output of material goods. Meanwhile innovation continues, and the expansion of consumption for increasingly wider sectors of the population entails more jobs in that area.

One essential condition speeding or retarding urban concentration is the level of technology. Technological changes tend to produce (other conditions holding constant) changes in the type and level of concentration. This has occurred with the emergence of new forms of energy since the steam engine. The internal combustion engine and the diffusion of electric power have produced new conditions which, by comparison with the age of steam, favor what we may call "urban dispersion." Huge metropolitan areas containing numerous urban agglomerations now cover entire regions holding tens of millions of inhabitants. This new process — involving not only technological innovations but also substantial modifications in the social structure of developed countries — is transforming the city and lending new meaning to the term urbanization. The technological changes (particularly changes in the transportation system and in the mass communication media), combined with the process of "self-sustaining mobility" which characterizes the more advanced phases of the industrial society, tend to obliterate the differences between town and country.[69] Thus the urban life style, cultural patterns, and type of social structure, which (to follow Redfield's terminology) at the stage of "secondary" urbanization once distinguished the city sharply from the countryside, come to be extended to the whole society.

The absorption of "rural society" by "urban society" proceeds in the following way. First, a spectacular reduction of distance in terms of costs and of time expands enormously the geographical range over which functions can be carried on and coordinated by a centralized organization. Such expansion may find limits in the obstacles created by the political or social order, but there are practically no barriers in terms of technological, physical, and spatial possibilities. The sphere of "functional" organization, open to the redistribution and maximum differentiation of activities, persons, and "material culture," tends now to be extended to the entire nation (and even to transcend it, to the extent that social obstacles are removed so that supranational planning may take place, as in the case of the "common market" or the "multi-national corporation"). This process implies a strong intensification of the contacts and the ecological interdependency among the various regions of a country or of a multi-national region. The result is a change of scale of society.[70] Both the large metropolitan areas and the smaller cities tend to be closely integrated in a national system, and the linkage permits an extraordinary ecological mobility for some of the residents, potentially covering the national territory in its entirety.[71]

Second, in the urbanization of an entire society, large organizations come to be as important as any particular site of activity. Various private enterprises, public enterprises, unions, and other forms of association cover the national territory and influence individuals irrespective of their residence in one or another city or in urban or rural zones. Naturally the accompanying roles orient individuals toward organization on a national scale, industries on a national scale, occupational groups on a national scale. Wherever their place of residence happens to be, some members of such societies consider as one's natural site the organizational network itself, encompassing the whole country or even transcending it. They are "citizens of the nation" more than members of the urban community where — so to speak — they "accidentally" live.

The third aspect of total urbanization is linked with the mentioned revolution in the mass communication media (cinema, press, TV, radio), the profound changes in the stratification system and the effects of the increasing participation of people in consumption, education, politics, recreation, with all that is implied with regard to norms, ways of thinking and behaving, and attitudes.

Although in these ways the city absorbs the country as an industrial society matures, the city itself tends to be superseded by the nation-state.[72] When the conditions that once prevailed in only a few urban areas spread through a country, the city proper loses its identity. Paradoxically, when urbanism has been transformed into the universal life style, it no longer needs an urban location. With these final considerations we arrive at another understanding of "urbanization," a meaning which certainly conforms to the classic definitation of Wirth; limited, however, to a specific form adopted only where two other characteristics also dominate: a high level of economic development and, for the moment, its historical location within a given cultural setting, although a very wide and diffused one, in the Western culture.

Urbanization and Modernization among Late Comers

It is known that the level of demographic urbanization of the less developed countries is considerably higher than was the level of urbanization in today's advanced countries when they had reached a degree of economic development similar to the presently developing nations. According to this criterion, the idea of "over-urbanization" has been applied to the majority of the under-developed or developing countries, and this is especially relevant for Latin America, whose urbanization is higher than in all the other regions of the Third World. Already at the beginning of the 1950s, Davis and Golen observed that, with few exceptions, the less developed countries are characterized by an accelerated process of urbanization.[73] Historical data confirm this impression. About 1890, for example, a group of countries, 33.8 percent of whose population lived in urban centers (20,000 or more inhabitants), reached in terms of real product per-capita a mean index of 869 (in Colin Clark's "international units"). In 1950 a group of Latin American countries with a similar urbanization average (32.5 percent) achieved a mean index of only 624 with respect to real product per capita (lower by more than a quarter than the performance of their historical predecessors).[74]

In the experience of the first industrial country — England — the process of urban concentration advanced almost *pari passu* with that of industrial growth. A profound transformation of the rural sector resulting in the expulsion (or "release") of peasants occurred at approximately the same time a new demand for labor was created by modern industry, although, it is true, even then such demand was often lower than the released rural working. [75] If the process of industrialization is taken as the key aspect of economic development, a more adequate method to analyze urban growth in relation to industrial growth is to utilize an index which relates these two processes. In the study already quoted an index of this type was used.[76]

Among other things, the index showed that whereas in the more developed countries urbanization and industrialization are both high, in the less-developed ones urbanization is higher than the degree of industrialization. Thus the correlation between the urbanization-industrialization index and the GNP per capita, is negative (-.74). It is also interesting to observe that this inverse correlation tends to be higher at the lower levels of urbanization (and of economic development). This means that in the more advanced stages of the transition the urbanization industrialization ratio becomes relatively more independent of the level of economic development. On the other hand, it can also be noted that when countries are separated into two groups, those of earlier transition and those of more recent transition, the former group registers an urbanization-industrialization index lower by fifty percent than the second; in other words, higher urbanization in relation to the level of industrialization occurs in countries whose transition started later and more recently.[77] In the particular circumstances (social, cultural, political, economic, etc.) of the previous century and the beginning of the present one, the process of urban growth tended to be slower and occur later, when compared with economic development.

The observation of this contrast between the countries of early transition and those of recent transition has suggested the notion of "over-urbanization." The countries which are presently less developed would be affected according to this thesis by a process of abnormal or pathological urbanization, since this process failed to be restricted within the limits proper or functionally required for the level of industrialization. Some authors have rejected this position insofar as it adopts as a universal model what occurred historically in the countries which today are the most advanced in the transition.[78] In fact, even when taking into account the lessons of that historical experience, the causes as well as the effects of the urbanization process in developing countries should be analyzed as a func-

tion of the circumstances in which it is being realized, which certainly differ from those which pertained during the previous century.

In all the presently developing countries the growth of the urban population has occurred in much greater measure than the growth of the labor
force working in industry. A glance at Table 2 shows that the urbanization-industrialization ratio in general has been in continual growth. That is
to say, the urban population has grown much more than the proportion of
persons employed in industry and in other activies of the secondary sector
(Colin Clark's classification).

TABLE 2
Index over Time of the Ratio between Percentage of People Living in Cities and Percentage of Workers in Secondary Sector of the Economy[a]

Countries	Circa 1840	Circa 1870	Circa 1890	Circa 1910	Circa 1950
Great Britain	67	—	112	145	150
France	—	36	50	80	93
United States	59	—	92	107	119
Australia	—	—	126	127	150
Sweden	—	—	59	60	130
USSR	—	—	—	100	113
Argentina	—	45	96	106	141
Chile	—	—	—	93	133
Cuba	—	—	—	115	172
Eighteen Latin American countries (average)	—	—	—	—	137

Sources: United Nations, Report on the World Situation (1957); Adna F. Weber, The
Growth of the Cities in the Nineteenth Century (Ithaca, N.Y.: Cornell University Press,
1963); Colin Cla k, The Conditions of Economic Progress (London: Macmillan, 1957).

[a]The index was computed by dividing the percentage of people residing in cities of 20,000
or more by the percentage of people economically active and working in manufacturing, and
building. All figures are in hundreds.

The urban explosion in the countries of early transition was produced by
means of various successive phases which occurred in different epochs in
the various countries. Although in relative terms the great urban expansion took place in the more advanced areas of Europe during the nineteenth century, we have witnessed since World War II a new
intensification of this growth, especially in nations which, like Italy and
Spain, were until quite recently still characterized by a rather large rural

sector.[79] In the nineteenth-century wave of urban expansion, natural growth accounted for less of the increase than did rural-urban migrations, both internal and international.

At the objective (structural, mainly techno-economic) level, the causes of "expulsion from the countryside" originated in the modernization of agriculture, which allowed the "release" of a very large number of persons and the drastic reduction of employment in the primary sector. A second cause of expulsion from the countryside was demographic growth. On the other hand, this same technological and economic transformation simultaneously affected the urban side. The growth of the population employed in industry stimulated solely a first stage of the urban expansion. Thereafter, technological change and the resultant increase in productivity put a brake on the increase of the population absorbed by industry. In reality the entire secondary sector was stabilized or even tended to diminish in percentage terms. Nevertheless, at the same time the emergence of new expectations in health, education, social services, recreation, consumption, and administration, enormously stimulated the service activities. Thus it was the intensive increase in productivity in agriculture and industry that permitted the growth of the tertiary sector. All these changes created "objective" conditions of "attraction to the city." In economic terms, while the demand for rural labor was diminishing, the urban demand was growing, a demand which in the more advanced stages was not any longer based on the needs of industry but arose with the appearance of new needs for services.

At the level of norms and values, and their psychosocial (internalized) counterpart, the traditional order tended to change rather slowly for large sectors of the population in comparison with the analogous processes in many presently developing countries. The fact that in the nineteenth century there did not yet exist effective means of mass communication was perhaps one of the factors which maintained the isolation of the "peripheral" sectors within society at a time when the national bourgeoisie were vigorously promoting capitalist development. In Russia basically the same process occurred still later, since the great majority of the population, still rural, tended to maintain traditional life styles, and it was only in the course of "socialist construction" that its mobilization toward modern forms was promoted. And it must be remembered that this process was in considerable measure controlled and subjected to central planning, at the economic, the social, and the psychological order. Of course the displacement from rural to urban areas and from preindustrial to industrial cultural patterns produced profound and lasting conflicts in all countries. It is noteworthy that in several European countries migration from the countryside had very distinctive characteristics in the previous century and until World War I, in comparison with the migrations of the second postwar period. In the earlier period migration most often did not mean a definitive rupture with the traditional order. The intention of the migrant was to emigrate for a limited time with the purpose of returning after having obtained, through saving, the means to acquire land in his birthplace and thus to be able to re-establish his "normal" way of life in terms of traditional expectations and aspirations. In the migrations of the second postwar period the central motivation was the definite abandonment of the rural life style, and the decision to adapt permanently to the urban industrial culture.[80]

Summing up, it may be said that the process in presently developing countries differs from the older pattern in three main aspects: (1) the internal and external situation characterizing the starting point of urbanization; (2) the sequence in which different subprocesses have followed; and (3) the intensity and velocity of these. Let us look at each in turn.

1. With the exception of those new countries in which no preindustrial urban structure has existed, the "modern" urbanization process usually occurs in the pre-existing urban structures, that is to say, in a structure determined by the preindustrial order. In present developing nations, however, that structure was in large part formed in a situation of economic and political "dependence" with respect to the metropolis, or the industrialized nations. Both the politico-administrative needs during the colonial period (when there was one) and the economic needs derived from the export of raw materials and the import of finished products (the most common form of incorporation of a "new" country into the world market and the modern economy) profoundly affected the urban structure. Thus, already at the point of departure there is a difference in comparison with the countries in which the step from preindustrial to industrial urbanization occurred more as a function of indigenous than because of exogenous factors.

2. The sequence by which the subprocesses proceeded was modified by different factors. In the first place industrialization (that is modern factory industry) was delayed and often prevented by a conjunction of internal and external causes. Among the former we must count the type of culture and dominant attitudes, the lack of capital, of internal markets, of organizational infrastructure and of basic investments; among the latter, the external factors, it is sufficient to remember in addition to the constraints of direct colonial domination (where it existed), the particular situation of an economy entirely based on the export of raw materials and the complex of local and foreign interests favored by and allied for the maintenance of such a situation. Backwardness or lack of industrialization did not prevent, however, the release of other processes of social modernization, especially those which emerged from the diffusion of scientific and technological innovations not directly dependent on the degree of indus-

trialization. Such is the case with the drastic reduction in mortality rates which together with the maintenance (or the growth) of "traditional" birth rates led to the demographic explosion, or with the spread of mass communications media which involved the introduction of powerful instruments of subjective mobilization. The persistence of a dysfunctional agrarian structure in the majority of the less-developed countries, the enormous increase in demographic pressure, and the acceleration of processes of subjective mobilization constitute important factors for partially explaining a rural-urban migration that continues without a commensurate increase in urban employment. Incidentally, the higher level of internal immigration has also introduced, in many cases, particular "deviations" in rural-urban differentials. Although to an extent much lower than the available labor force, there was a certain transformation of the traditional structure which required some increase of urban employment. The processes indicated above, along with others, must be regarded as part of the "modernizing effects" of the primary export economy.[81] For example, the organization of the state, the establishment of social services of all kinds, commercial and financial activities, growth of the domestic market, and the beginnings of industrialization (even though limited to the production of nondurable consumer goods or to provide low-income consumer sectors) undoubtedly stirred up some new demand for labor in the cities.

It is important to notice here that the expansion of public and private bureaucracy and of services has been much greater for late comers than in corresponding stages of development in the countries of early transition. An important reason for this fact was that the models of the state and of the society, and the type or level of needs that the new institutions of the developing countries were trying to satisfy, are not the same ones that during the previous century characterized the countries of early industrialization. The contemporary needs of the present advanced nations influence expectations throughout the world. The functions of the state have tended to grow continually whatever the dominant type of socioeconomic system. And the same thing has happened with the services. It was not possible, certainly, to ignore the requirements of the higher and complex organization and services at a more modern level, once these were created elsewhere and awareness of their necessity had become widespread. Of course, this possibility of expansion of services and of public and private organizations was limited by the resources available in each country. But in many of them, the "economic expansion" based on primary exports provided relatively abundant means at least in the "primate" cities. In many cases, moreover, the expansion occurred at the expense of directly productive investment.

For all these reasons, although in very unequal measure, in the majority of countries of more recent transition, the urban occupational structure and its size were influenced by conditions not directly linked to the existence of self-sustained mechanisms of economic growth (proper) and industrialization per se (as distinct from the non-dynamic "expansion" based on primary exports). In consequence, a considerable proportion of the working-age population residing in the cities were not absorbed in services of "modern" type and remained marginal or relatively marginal to the modern forms of economy. It is this "pseudo-tertiary" sector which greatly inflates the occupational statistics of underdeveloped countries. At the same time we must note that a real tertiary sector expanded beyond the level corresponding to the degree of economic development which could have been expected on the basis of the experience of the past. This can be explained on the basis of the "modernizing effects" of the primary export economy and the "demonstration effect" of the contemporary organizational models in advanced countries, as well as the new needs noted above. Finally, the introduction of modern means of transportation, largely shaped by the needs of the primary export economy, contributed strongly to break the isolation of many areas of the national territory, thus favoring contact with urban centers and prompting migration to "primate" cities which had expanded because of their economic and political role in the export economy.

In many developing countries, after the Great Depression (1930) and particularly after World War II, industrialization was initiated or acquired a higher rate of expansion. However, the technology was often (and increasingly so in more recent times) of the capital-intensive and labor-saving type. As a consequence, even if industrial production increased considerably, the proportion of new jobs created by industry was much lower. Why was technology of exactly this type imported from the advanced countries? Engineering considerations aside, it was imported because in many cases the new industries were established and controlled by multinational corporations located in the "central" countries, and these enterprises preferred to use the same technology as in the metropolis. Their preference was partly based upon the economic advantages that can be derived from labor-saving techniques in spite of the "unlimited supply" of cheap labor available in many underdeveloped nations. In many cases the same policy is being followed both by foreign and domestic enterprises, as a means to avoid or to diminish the "social problems" confronted by the management because of labor unrest, given the relatively high level of workers' political mobilization.

3. The velocity and magnitude of some of the processes causing urban growth are much greater in countries developing today than in those which industrialized earlier. For example, never in a European country did population growth reach the level of three percent annually which nowadays characterizes certain regions. With a growth which frequently did not sur-

pass one-third of current rates, Europe was forced to send more than sixty million people overseas. To a considerable degree the present rural exodus to the cities is the substitute, in developing countries, for the great European migration of the previous century. To this must be added, as another factor of acceleration, the introduction of mass media which has eliminated or drastically reduced the psychological and physical isolation of large sections of the population and consequently facilitated their psychological and physical mobilization toward the only available focus of escape and attraction under present conditions: the cities. On the other hand, in many developing countries — particularly in Latin America — urban natural demographic increase caused by high fertility is a component of urban total growth sometimes more important than internal migration.

Urbanization without industrialization, or with delayed industrialization, is thus the outcome of a complex of interrelated internal and external conditions characterizing the transition among the late comers, at least in absence of compulsory central planning. It must be added that even the effects of such planning are not yet clear. We have seen that urbanization in Russia tended to follow the "capitalist" pattern, but this was the consequence of many different factors including the antirural bias, forced collectivization of agriculture, and emphasis on industrial development. Fascist Italy and Nazi Germany were decidedly antiurban. In Italy urban growth remained limited during the two decades of the regime, but how much this was determined by political restrictions is impossible to say, since low urban growth continued until the acceleration of economic development, in the 1950s. In China and Cuba antiurbanization policies may have been more successful, but in both cases we lack enough information to assess these (still conjectural) effects. What the consequences will be of this fact on the other component processes and in particular on economic development is a very complex problem which cannot be resolved by considering it simply as "over-urbanization" or abnormal urbanization. For now, one must recognize as real the commonly observed fact that in these countries, a part (sometimes considerable) of the urban population is marginal from the point of view of its economic activity as well as in relation to the patterns of consumption and other aspects of modern culture. As already noted, many observers emphasize the fact that the occupational structure induced by urban expansion and unaccompanied by structural changes in the economy produces a distribution of the active population which, although superficially similar to that of the developed countries, presents substantial differences. Here the service sector relates not to modern occupations but to traditional ones — for example, domestic services (which in more advanced economies tend to disappear) and other non-modern or low-productivity activities. In this sense such occupations are only a form of disguised unemployment, transferred from the country to the city.[82] It is this segment of the population that we have termed above "pseudo-tertiary." People in this situation not only do not perform activities appropriate to a modern tertiary sector, but their consumption and life styles (although not necessarily their aspirations) continue to be largely marginal with regard to modern society. Analogous arguments could be applied to a certain proportion of the population classified in the census as working in the secondary sector. Not only does this include artisan or preindustrial activities, but such a classification also takes in very low income activities and forms of disguised unemployment. In any case this is a sector of the urban population socially and psychologically distinct from the modern industrial proletariat. To these "marginals" or "semi-marginals" we must add the completely unemployed who, in some cities, represent a substantial group. The presence of the pseudo-tertiary and of the remaining marginal categories must not be confused with the overexpansion of the real tertiary to which we have made reference. This expansion, although going beyond the "historical" level expected at a given level of economic development, nonetheless generates a sector of the population which, from a social and psychological point of view, belongs to modern urban life.

To what extent does the "excess" urban population become a negative factor for economic development? According to some, over-urbanization "acts directly upon economic development, diminishing propensity for savings, discouraging agricultural production, diverting scarce resources from high yield investments to those of low return."[83] It is also asserted that excessive urban concentration, particularly concentration in primate cities, is an unfavorable condition for balanced development at the geographical level and therefore an obstacle to national integration. The phenomenon of the primacy of certain cities is found to be associated, in the peripheral countries, with an economic structure dependent on international trade. Such cities often function as points of contact between land transport (from the interior) and marine transport (to foreign lands) of primary products. Location and growth respond to the constraints of international trade (this is "outer-directed" development) and not to development balanced or integrated at the national level. The transportation system serves the same purposes and tends to multiply the "distortions" of the "syndrome of the primary export economy." The primate city and its immediate hinterland, with a disproportionate concentration of wealth, modern culture, and economic expansion, has been, according to these opinions, a negative factor for the development of other regions and of the nation considered as a whole. The material and human resources have been disproportionately concentrated in those areas to the detriment of other regions of the same country. The beginnings of industrialization do not modify this distortion, since the pre-existing urban structure tends to determine the location of the new activities, adding new factors of disequilibrium and an ecological distribution of industry frequently very unfavorable for its further development.[84]

Although very few dare to deny the existence of these negative consequences, other authors point out that the urban concentration may also have favorable effects. For example, the very concept of over-urbanization has been questioned: the concentration of scarce resources in a few urban centers may be more efficient than if they were to be spread over a wide area; the positive function of the city as a dynamic center for education and technical and social innovation may well compensate for the costs — economic and social — of over-urbanization. Even the urban marginals may turn out to perform a productive role, required by the peculiar socio-economic setting of underdevelopment. For instance, they may provide at a very small cost, goods and services for the urban workers whose access to the more expensive modern market is prevented by their low wages. In any case, the role of the city in societies which are presently developing is different from the historical role performed in the first industrialized countries. Finally, the desirability of an integrated development and modernization has been the subject of discussion. It may well be that the conditions under which both processes take place make it impossible to achieve such an integration. Or, perhaps the internal geographical discontinuities may represent a factor which accelerates the process as a whole, at least during certain stages of transition.[85] As pointed out by Hoselitz, the "generative" function or, on the contrary, the "parasitic" dysfunction of the cities, in particular the primate cities, depends upon a very complex series of economic and noneconomic causes which may intervene in each case. Unfortunately we must concur with the words of Hoselitz written long ago in the sense that the determination of these causes and of their interrelationships continues to be one of the main tasks in the study of the connection between urbanization and the other processes which affect the transition.[86]

The Effect of Modernization and Urbanization: Selected Aspects

The effect of modernization and urbanization on individuals, groups, and social institutions is universal and affects the whole social structure and the personal life of men. In this section mention will be made of some aspects of this generalized effect.

Family Changes [87]

Some degree of secularization in family relations constitutes a necessary condition of development. It is also one of the consequences or correlates of modern urbanization. It is well known that the scope of primary relations (such as those that characterize the family) should be kept to a minimum to allow for the secondary type of relations required by the institutions peculiar to a modern society. Primary relations (that is, "community") are diffuse, affectively charged, particularistic, and governed by ascription, while secondary relations ("society") are characterized as specific, affectively neutral, universalistic, and based on achievement. Accentuating this second type of relation seems necessary to reach a sufficient specialization of function and institutions and at the same time the optimum allocation of workers on the basis of efficiency. From this point of view, the sphere for the application of kinship relations should be reduced to a minimum along with all types of extended family relations. It has been pointed out, however, that this requirement is a source of tension implicit in the very nature of industrial society and perhaps a possible intrinsic limit to secularization. Indeed, the permanence of primary groups (and especially of an institution like the family) is often considered a functional and universal requirement, at least in historically observed societies, in the sense that it discharges functions that can be accomplished only in structures of this type (such functions as the socialization of the child and the creation of an intimate group for the sustenance of the adult personality).[88] The whole of the social structure, especially the stratification system, is affected by this limitation. The impersonal milieu created by the predominance of secondary relations emphasizes the necessity of the continuous reformation of primary groups; thus, for example, small groups defined by secondary relations (e.g., work groups) tend to become transformed into primary ones if the interaction is prolonged. The kinship group itself, extended beyond the bounds of the nuclear family, never disappears. On the contrary it tends to remain at least as a preferred field of recruitment for spontaneous primary groups.[89]

Another consequence is that substantial modifications occur in many aspects of the primary relations themselves. Without losing their primary character, they acquire characteristics differing from those they held or were given in traditional society. In particular, interpersonal relations within the nuclear family tend to become more egalitarian, for there is greater participation by all members in the group's different activities, as well as greater access to the decisions of the group; and the stability of the group itself comes to depend more on volition than on mechanically applied normative prescriptions. One of the most important phenomena of this whole process — one that can be taken as a general measurement of levels of secularization — is spontaneous (not politically induced) birth control, insofar as it means the introduction of deliberate instrumental rationality into one of the most intimate spheres of human life. It appears fairly clear that all these results are nothing but an extension of the principle of elective action to larger areas of behavior. The process is characterized by its emphasis on new values, particularly in the affirmation of the individual and his full development. This is a field dominated by ideological controversies; it is here that the most resistance arises. It is also a question open to scientific debate as to whether primary relations are rigidly molded by the changes in social organization required by development or whether certain structural alternatives exist that, on the one hand, assure the minimal conditions of development and, on the other, maintain traditional forms in primary areas of behavior.

Various authors have criticized the generally accepted hypothesis of a close correlation between the type of industrial structure and the predominance of the nuclear family. On the one hand, a functional equivalent of this type of family may exist in developing societies; on the other hand, there are examples of nonindustrial societies with nuclear families of the Western type. Instead of assuming that the nuclear family is inevitably associated with industrialism, it has been suggested that a great degree of indeterminacy characterizes the relationship between family structure and other parts of the social structure. Perhaps a wider range of family types is compatible with the industrial structure. If so, the diffusion of the nuclear family in Western developed societies must be seen as a historical coincidence: those countries were characterized before the transition by such a family type, rather than developing it as a consequence of the transition itself. This historical coincidence, moreover, can be interpreted the other way around. Inverting the causal relation between the industrial-urban structure and the nuclear family, we could consider the existence of this type of family as one of the preconditions facilitating the rise of industrial society (emphasizing the value of the individual, diminishing the scope of ascriptive relations and so forth).[90]

These and other criticisms of the hypothesis of a close functional relation between the isolated nuclear family and the industrial structure are, of course, of great importance and should be kept in mind; however, they do not seem to support the contrary hypothesis of an almost complete indeterminacy or absence of correlation between the two. Rather, in many cases, the facts can be interpreted in accordance with the hypothesis. Japan is a good illustration, often cited as the classic case of the permanence of the traditional family despite its advanced level of techno-economic development. In that country, the divorce rate appears to diminish instead of increase with the advance of industrialization; at the same time, the divorce rate in rural areas is higher than that in urban areas. Thus in Japan we find correlations exactly the opposite of those established in Western countries. Yet rather than negating the hypothesis of the interdependence between the nuclear family and the industrial structure — as might seem superficially to be the case — Japan's experience could be interpreted, on the basis of a more detailed examination of the data, as a confirmation of the hypothesis. Such is the conclusion of some of those conducting research on this topic.[91] The "starting point" in the case of Japan "was a society in which lineage and not matrimony was sacred." Divorce was permitted, and the divorce rate was high. But it was a different type of divorce from that of the West: it was a "traditional" type of divorce, adjudicated by the family group and exercised essentially in favor of this group and its continuity (for example, the repudiation of a sterile woman). Industrialization and urbanization weakened this type of family and the ideas that sustained it. The individual began to emerge from the kinship group, and marriage began to be seen as an individual affair. Consequently the decline of the divorce rate should be seen as a symptom of the weakening of the traditional structure. On the other hand, the authors could distinguish another type of divorce, of a Western variety, based on the individual decisions of the partners. This type of divorce — an expression of the nuclear family that was emerging in the transition toward a more advanced industrial structure — was, on the contrary, increasing. In other words, the total divorce rate represented a balance between two opposing tendencies: a decrease in "traditional" divorce and an increase in "modern" divorce, the former taking place in rural areas, the latter in urban areas.

The Japanese example is sufficiently illustrative of the type of modifications (or better, specifications) that should be introduced in the generic hypothesis of correlation between modern family type and industrial structure. The basic characteristic is the introduction of a normative system of the elective type in relations previously prescriptive. But the form of the transition depends on the pre-existent traditional structure, and the family type that emerges is probably considerably influenced by such a structure. In particular, the speed of the transition, as much as the degree of electiveness in the field of familial relations, can vary widely.

On the other hand, it must be recognized that the ideological trends and the demonstration effects generated by the pattern of family life in advanced urbanized and modernized areas exercise a powerful influence on developing countries and that the structural effects of urbanization and industrialization on the family, if any, are likely to be reinforced or even created by changes in attitudes promoted by such effects and ideologies.[92]

Adjustment, Integration, and Marginality

The phenomena of adjustment, integration, and marginality are analytically (and often empirically) different but closely related. Adjustment as used here refers to the individual (or group) ability to perform the roles in the various activities in which he (or the group) participates without suffering excessive or unbearable psychological stresses. It is a concept related mainly to the individual or the primary group (although the phenomenon itself may be determined by social structural factors). The second phenomenon, integration, is conceived in collective terms — participation in the larger society or a significant subsector of the larger society forming an inclusive sociocultural group (such as a local community, a neighborhood, etc.). Marginality is defined with reference to integration — that is, attenuated, incomplete, fractious participation in one or more spheres of activities, and exercise of roles in a given society, subsystem, or area of activities. The notion of marginality also embraces the idea of the extension of social rights — that is, it involves awareness of exclusion from the exercise or the benefits of social (political, cultural and economic) rights. The marginal thus is also the excluded, the segregated individual or group. Because of these double aspects which usually coexist in concrete phenomena, the meaning of marginality, participation, and related concepts is highly ambiguous. It is convenient to distinguish several "moments" which may be successive or contemporaneous but are analytically different: (1) "release" and "availability," (2) mobilization, (3) integration. In the first stage, individuals and groups are "released" from traditional (or at least from pre-existing) structures. They lose their previous integration and become "available" for new roles, new behavioral patterns, new forms of participation. Such release may occur through "objective" factors (such as external circumstances which impede the actual functioning of the previous structure or adverse material or environmental conditions) and/or through "subjective" factors (cultural difusion, impact of mass media, and the like). In any case it is produced by a loss of correspondence between attitudes and aspirations on one side and possibilities of action and satisfaction on the other. "Availability" may originate different processes. Anomie, maladjustment, and social and personal disorganization are some possibilities. Persistence of those archaic traits which can be adapted to the new requirements of the new "objective" circumstances and the emergence of different types of "fusion" between traditional and modern are other possible results. Psychosocial mobilization occurs when the released individuals and groups acquire new attitudes and values, aspire to new roles or to new patterns of participation, including new forms of consumption (of material and emotional goods). Mobilization, in other words, is readiness to be incorporated into new patterns of behavior and institutions. How psychosocial mobilization is expressed in actual behavior depends on the situation, particularly with regard to the concrete possibility of participating in the new areas and/or the legitimacy of such participation in terms of the dominant values of the society and its hegemonic sectors. We may speak of assimilation when there exists both the concrete possibility and the legitimacy of the given form of participation. When one or the other or both are lacking, psychological mobilization may be translated into conflictive mobilization, that is, in some sort of social movement (in a very large sense: political, religious, or forms of nonideological rebellion, peaceful or violent). Integration thus may occur through assimilation (changing the individual or groups) and/or through social change, whereby the society or the relevant subsystems are transformed so as to make possible and/or legitimate the participation of the mobilized sectors. Mobilization through conflict and integration through social change are particularly relevant in the case of class, ethnic, religious, ideological, or political cleavages, between the mobilized marginal sectors and the established sectors of the society.[93]

The notions of "release," "availability," and "mobilization" must be remembered when considering marginality. In a general way, marginal people are the nonintegrated or nonparticipants in the modern structure, but there are many states of "nonintegration": persisting integration into archaic structures, unused release or availability, mobilization through psychosocial conflict. On the other hand, these processes do not usually occur at the same time in all the aspects of life for the same group or even the same individual. Finally, areas of marginality must be distinguished, that is, the activities, roles and institutions in which the individual or the group is prevented from participating (because the social system, or subsystem, lacks the capability of absorption and/or through direct or indirect rejection, discrimination, or segregation) or cannot participate (for lack of motivation, attitudes, or skill). Let us mention some of the major areas of marginality: (1) nonparticipation in the productive system, or economic marginality (unemployment, disguised or not, and other forms of "redundant" jobs, discussed in the previous subsection); (2) marginality in consumption (deprivation of the use of modern goods and services); (3) ethnic marginality (not participating in the dominant culture in a society which discriminates against "minorities" — here participation is likely to consist of protest and struggle); (4) marginality of the traditionals (lack of modern attitudes and skills); (5) political marginality; (6) educational marginality; and (7) marginality with regard to real opportunity of social mobility. A crucial problem is the determination of the correlation between the forms of marginality. The concept of marginality is distinct from the category of exclusion — that is, individuals and groups socially, culturally, and ecologically located outside the society (usually the national society, urban or rural). Therefore the marginal man is by definition an incongruent participant with regard to the set of areas in which he is expected to participate, such expectation being determined on the basis of an image of his rights and obligations. Here incongruence means participation in some areas of the expected set but nonparticipation in others. Thus a person may be a legitimate participant (i.e., may be integrated) in the modern productive structure (say as a worker in a modern industrial plant), objectively mobilized in the sphere of politics (as a militant in a radical nonlegitimate political movement), psychosocially mobilized with regard to modern consumption (because of his unfulfilled aspirations), and still "unreleased" and traditional in the area of family life and kinship relations. Most important of all, the modern and the traditional sometimes are not clearly separated even within the same area of behavior or in the same institution. They may be fused in various ways. Release is usually partial release; it does not necessarily involve disintegration and successive reintegration into completely new patterns. It may occur through the persistence of integration within traditional norms, values, and attitudes which become somewhat adapted to modern conditions. Consequently there are many degrees and forms of marginality: from the extreme marginality of those living in peripheral and backward regions or in isolated traditional communities within the nation to the relatively reduced marginality of the urban migrant who, though segregated in his shantytown or slum neighborhood, paticipates in some activities more exposed to modern communication media than the isolated inhabitant of the peripheral areas.[94] Marginality is not necessarily related to individual maladjustment and social disorganization. The rural migrant to the city may maintain his or her psychological adjustment by remaining integrated into some sort of encapsulated rural setting recreated within the urban center and moving gradually toward participation in the modern sector. This process of "urbanization without breakdown," found in both advanced and developing countries, is based on the persistence of primary ties: kinship groups, extended family relationships, a *compadrazgo* (Godfathership) system, combined in certain cases with voluntary associations or with particular conditions offered by the neighborhood.[95] On the other hand, the transference or the creation of these highly integrated but segregated environments in the city may perpetuate marginality in different forms, particularly under conditions of discrimination of any sort. In other cases when the "sheltered" environment is not created or maintained, then the classical urban problems may be expected (family breakdown, delinquency, suicide and mental illness). Here we usually find marginality and maladjustment, a situation which tends to become self-reinforcing, especially when extended over more than a generation, since it affects early socialization and education, diminishing or seriously impairing the intellectual and emotional development of the young child.

The phenomenon of marginality in economic, political, social, and cultural development was prominent among the first comers and affected a considerable proportion of the population. But concepts and habits of perception likely to make anyone conscious of the phenomenon hardly existed. The fact of "nonparticipation" remained to a large extent unseen except for progressive politicians, social thinkers, revolutionaries, and intellectual traditionalists wishing to criticize the emerging new world. This partial blindness or distortion was caused by the fact that the notion of participation in the national society was still ignored or rejected by the dominant elite, as is clearly shown by the struggles over extension of civil, political, and social citizenship.[96] On the other hand, many aspects of social mobilization proceeded at a much slower rate among the first comers than in the Third World today. Not only was the movement of the masses into the modern sector slow, but the shock was often confined to the area of work and production, while in other spheres, like consumption and social rights, traditional attitudes and expectations could be maintained if an individual found them still comfortable. Furthermore, the process of mobilization in both its objective and subjective aspects was, by and large, rather discontinuous — that is, it occurred in great successive waves, often separated one from the following by lapses of more than a generation. In fact, the entire urban working class remained relatively segregated from the national society and from the various spheres of modern culture until very recently. Its incorporation and integration into the national system only began to be evident with all its effects in the last few decades, as the economies of the industrial countries reached the stage of greater maturity. It may be important for today's developing countries to notice that this integration occurred only after economic growth had advanced considerably.

This is not to say, of course, that mitigating conditions and lack of a concept of marginality removed all difficulties. Discontinuities and the occasional phases of accelerated mobilization did provoke very acute conflicts and tensions which in some cases put the system in a revolutionary crisis. Economic marginality, in the form of permanent or temporary unemployment, was always painful, particularly during the cyclical crises. The persisting traditionalism of the masses, the still valid "deference pattern," and the effective "safety valve" of mass overseas emigration damped but did not eliminate the explosiveness of the "social question." Furthermore, marginality — or its "developed" equivalent, "poverty" — has by no means disappeared. Relatively large sectors of the population in the more advanced nations are still deprived of the benefits of the affluent society. This problem is particularly frustrating in the United States, for this country is by far the richest in the world, while its share of poverty (variously estimated to affect from twenty to forty percent of the population) is probably larger than in several developed but less affluent countries.[97]

Certainly marginality is not the same everywhere. For instance, its composition, size, ecological location, and forms of recruitment vary in advanced and in developing countries. In the former the marginal group is mainly composed of older workers, retired persons, and young adults prior to the first job, while in the latter the category contains a relatively large portion of the population. Marginality in developed regions is becoming more and more a typical urban problem (although, even there, pockets of depressed rural areas can be found), while in the Third World, most of the marginals — sometimes up to one-half of the population — are rural (but urban marginality is more visible). Nonetheless there are disturbing coincidences between the two cases. In the first place it seems that, whatever the other contributing factors, the relation between the total capacity of absorption into the modern productive system and the rate of growth of the working-age population sets the proportion of marginal population at anz given moment. Delayed development (and its external and internal causes) in conjunction with population explosion is the main determinant in developing countries; but in advanced ones, technological changes (particularly automation) and other structural conditions, considered by a number of economists as responsible for the surplus population, also indicate a similar incapacity, an incapacity which threatens to "marginalize" new categories of working persons in all strata. In both regions, it is from the less favored segments of the population that the marginals are selected. In fact, everywhere what are often regarded as causes of marginality or different types of it (ethnic, educational, etc.) should be really considered as determinants of the selection, through which is "filled" the structurally given "quota" of marginals. Blacks and other disadvantaged minorities in the United States, Indians and other ethnic groups in Latin America, recent migrants, particularly from backward areas everywhere, contribute disproportionally with their size to the total marginal population. Persistent marginality in a context of high development clashes with the promises and the potentialities of a technological society even more than the marginality associated with delayed industrialization and development in peripheral and dependent areas does.

Modernization and the Urban Crisis

The "urban crisis" is, in a sense, coetaneous with the city itself, or at least the secularized city. Since ancient times the city has been regarded as unnatural or sinful, contrary to divine design and human nature. Modern theories of history regard secularism and the "world cities" as the culmination of the life cycle of a civilization and the beginnings of its end. At the same time the city has been exalted as man's greatest achievement. Since the first crystallization of modern society, the city, its role, its contrasts, and its problems have been prominent in the attention of the intellectuals and the public. Nineteenth-century social science, as well as literary essays and fiction, produced an impressive picture of the glaring contradictions at the dawn of the urban-industrial civilization. Reflecting an anti-urban bias but also dire reality, a considerable portion of the intellectual tradition in urban sociology is pessimistic. The Chicago school and its European background were more concerned with personal and family disorganization than with adjustment, more with disintegration than with integration; both emphasized the anomic aspects of urban life. Most of the intellectual trend around the theme of mass society is equally pessimistic. Idealization of the mythical "community" of the past and a negative image of the emerging industrial society contributed to maintain the same bias in many theoretical and empirical studies up to the present.

It is also true that a vigorous reaction took place in America and, at an earlier time, in Europe. As noted, hasty generalizations concerning the breakdown of family life and primary relationships, disappearance of the extended family, isolation and alienation of individuals, and other "evils" attributed to urban mass society, were revised, and a more balanced view of the city began to emerge. The new approach to the "urban way of life" came from a more optimistic perspective of modernization. Instead of perceiving the modern city as endemically affected by disorganization and anomie, or in any case by a low degree of integration, certain observers conceived it as based on a different kind of integration, that is, what we have called here the secularized type of social structure. As Halbwachs put it long ago, "Complexities of urban societies should not be confounded with anomie."[98] Many of the "evils" of urban societies could be interpreted as "transitional" problems, likely to be obviated in the "normal" course of economic development and social and political modernization. The great vitality shown by the neocapitalistic model after World War II in the United States, in Europe, in Japan, and elsewhere, a more balanced view of socialist societies (and their viability in creating a modern expanding economy), the prospect of "peaceful coexistence" and the increasing "integration" of all sectors of the population into the national society in many parts of the world, and the growing institutionalization of industrial or class conflicts all contributed to this renewal of optimism.

But with the acceleration of change, typical of modern civilization, a new awareness of the "dark" side of urban life is prevailing again. Both the whole industrial civilization and its particular forms (East and West) are in question. Not by chance this trend appeared most clearly in the more advanced societies, particularly the United States. Loss of identity, maladjustment, family crisis, and disorganization were still there. Poverty was suddenly rediscovered, while other old and new urban problems became more and more visible: the decay of the central city, the growth of the "ghettos," the "fall of megalopolis," the breakdown of urban transportation, the rapid obsolescence of public services, the spread of crime and drugs, the vulnerability of the city to the urban guerrillas, the alteration of the ecological balance, the crisis of city government, and all the rest.

Although some of the pessimism and some of the actual difficulties of the city may be simply transitional or can be imputed to an arbitrary component of a particular socioeconomic system, the contradictions of the modern city must be confronted within a larger context. The birth of the modern-industrial complex, its spread over the planet, and the universal urbanization which accompanies it are the most crucial events in the history of mankind. They involve an extraordinary extension of human control over the use of natural forces, through an ever-expanding natural science and power technology. This development led to the emergence for the first time of a real world history, the actual creation of a planetary system based on the close interdependence of all its regions, in terms of the requirements of the new technology and the new economy. Through the continuous expansion of human productivity it created the real possibility of abolishing scarcity and poverty for all mankind and of liberating the spiritual energies formerly absorbed in the struggle for subsistence. Industrialism also implies the possibility of the ultimate disappearance of the city and its replacement by a sort of universal urbanization — in the sociological and to a certain extent in the demographic sense.

This tremendous explosion of the power of man has its threatening side also. In the first place, the immense material productivity already attained is not for the most part devoted to worthy human needs and values even in the wealthy countries. Nor have the political, social, and cultural obstacles to extending productivity to the Third World, as well as the marginals in the advanced areas, been overcome. Secondly, the "control" and the productive use of natural forces entails a "cost" in terms of the detrimental consequences of altering the equilibrium of nature itself. Though more science and more technology could help to solve this problem, the task would require the coordinated effort of all mankind through a cooperative, deliberated, and rational action. But this coordination must confront formidable social and cultural obstacles generated by the peculiar course of the historical process leading to the rise of the modern-industrial complex in its diverse versions. Although the scientific, technological, and economic orders have obliterated all frontiers, making the planet one unified system, the old sociocultural partitions will persist in terms of sovereign nation-states — separate organized and conflicting units, characterized by a sort of international stratification based on the domination of a few "super powers" — struggling among themselves for world hegemony. This anomic situation at the international level not only precludes the urgently needed rational planning in technological, scientific, economic, and social realms, but it also is perpetuating and expanding to an unprecedented level the production of the "instruments of death," diverting productivity from the creation of the "instruments of life" still so much needed by the majority of men. Above all, the persistence of the economically and technologically obsolete nation-state maintains an endemic situation of "local" or "limited" wars and the ever-present menace of a general armed conflict among the super powers, with the inevitable "final solution" of the "humanity problem" through nuclear Armageddon. Most if not all the contradictions, threats, and promises of industrial society are to be found at the roots of the "urban problems" of the metropolis and the megalopolis of our time, and it seems rather futile to analyze urbanization without reflecting also on modernization in the broadest sense. The outcome of present difficulties will depend on man's capacity to create through social and cultural innovations the institutions necessary and sufficient to control and direct the material power he has achieved toward the betterment of his life — and not direct this power toward his own extinction. After all, industrial society was generated by the confluence of a series of such innovations — the Western city being one of them, and perhaps one of the most crucial. Only a similar or a higher level of social creativity may provide a solution to the tragic problems confronting contemporary man and his cities.

Notes

* Reprinted from *Modernization, Urbanization and the Urban Crisis*, Gino Germani (ed.) (Boston, Mass.: Little, Brown and Co., 1973).

1. Hope Tisdale Eldridge, "The Process of Urbanization," *Social Forces* 20 (1942), 311-16; reprinted in J. J. Spengler et al. (eds.), *Demographic Analysis* (Glencoe: Free Press, 1956).

2. United Nations, "Étude sur les données relatives à la population urbaine et à la population rurale dans les récensements récents," *Études Démographiques*, no. 8 (1950), Chapter 1.

3. Louis Wirth, "Urbanism as a Way of Life," in A. J. Reiss, Jr., *Cities and Social Life*, (Chicago: University of Chicago Press, 1964), pp. 64-83.

4. For a critical review of the literature on this subject, see Leon Bramson, *The Political Context of Sociology* (Princeton: Princeton University Press, 1961), Chapters 2-3.

5. Wirth himself makes this distinction quite clear. See "Urbanism as a Way of Life," p. 66.

6. See Max Weber, *The City* (Glencoe: Free Press, 1958), pp. 91-120.

7. See Robert Redfield and Milton B. Singer, "The Cultural Role of the Cities," *Economic Development and Cultural Change*, 8 (October 1954).

8. See Alessandro Pizzorno. "Développement Economique et Urbanization," in *The Sociology of Development*, Transactions of the V World Congress of Sociology, Vol. 2 (ISA, 1962).

9. Eric E. Lampard, "Historical Aspects of Urbanization," in Philip M. Hauser and Leo F. Schnore (eds.), *The Study of Urbanization* (New York: Wiley, 1965), pp. 519-54.

10. G. Germani, "Secularization, Modernization, and Economic Development," in S. M. Eisenstadt (ed.), *The Protestant Ethic and Modernization* (New York: Basic Books, 1968), 343-66.

11. Cf. K. Polanyi, *The Great Transformation* (New York: Farrar and Rinehart, 1944), Chapter 4; K. Polanyi et al. (eds.), *Trade and Market in the Early Empires* (Glencoe: Free Press, 1957), p. 71 and *passim*.

12. In the past, modernization was totally identified with Westernization because of Europe's head start. The "new states" of the early modern period were Western colonies such as the United States and the countries of Latin America, and they adopted the Western model (capitalism accompanied by limited representative government) without hesitation, openly equating "progress" with European civilization. This of course served Western imperialistic ambitions very well.

At present, decolonization, increased nationalism, and the availability of several models of industrialization and forms of fusion of pre-existing cultural patterns with the new industrial institutions have helped to show up the ethnocentric aspects of Westernization. But of course this reaction itself can be carried too far if the fact of European initiative is utterly denied. On premodern foundations of modern society, see T. Parsons, *The System of Modern Society,* (Englewood Cliffs, N.J.: Prentice Hall, 1971).

13. The source of this table is Lampard, "Historical Aspects," p. 524.

14. Pitirim Sorokin, *Social Philosophies of an Age of Crisis* (Boston: Beacon Press, 1951), Chapter 13.

15. Polanyi's book entitled *The Great Transformation* has already been cited in note 11 above.

16. General schemes hypothesizing stages of modernization or social and economic evolution have been formulated by social philosophers, historians, economists, and sociologists, particularly the nineteenth-century evolutionists. The usual traditional vs. modern dichotomies are essentially an oversimplified two-stage scheme. An example of a schematic stage-like process with limited application to nineteenth-century economic development can be seen in Alexander Gerschenkron, *Economic Backwardness in Historical Perspective* (Cambridge: Harvard University Press, 1962), pp. 353-66. For a more circumscribed study, see G. Germani, "Stages of Modernization in Latin America," *Studies in Comparative International Development,* 5, no. 8 (1969-70). In many theories the appearance of the city or the role of given types of cities is stressed as a particularly important evolutionary step. See for instance, the critical review of economic theories by Bert F. Hoselitz, "Theories of Stages of Economic Growth," in Hoselitz et al. (eds.), *Theories of Economic Growth* (Glencoe: Free Press, 1960).

17. Precapitalistic (or preindustrial) technology is, according to Sombart, empiric and organic; that is, empiric in the sense of not deliberately founded on applied or basic scientific research and organic insofar as it continues to be rooted "within the sphere of living nature," See Werner Sombart, *Il Capitalismo Moderno* (Torino: UTET, 1967), Chapter 9 (29 of the German edition).

18. Edward Meyer, Michael Rostovzeff, Alfons Dopsch, et al. maintained that the difference between the Graeco-Roman economy and the economy of a modern society was only quantitative and not qualitative, an interpretation in turn rejected by Bücher, Rodbertus, et al. Instead of comparing the ancient economy with modern capitalism, Max Weber emphasized the differences between the occidental and the oriental city, finding in the former the type of social organization which, with the innovations of European medieval cities, would generate in time the new industrial order. See Harry W. Pearson, "The Secular Debate on Economic Primitivism," in Polanyi et al. (eds.), *Trade and Market.*

Why did ancient capitalism fail? Why were more machines not invented? Why the return to the "economic primitivism" of the early Middle Ages? None of the answers proposed by Rostovzeff seem complete and sufficient, but we may retain as interesting his suggestion that, among other factors, the decadence of the cities and of the urban bourgeoisie, through their incapacity to integrate into a more civilized life the internal rural and urban masses, was an important component in that failure. See Rostovzeff, *Storia Economica e Sociale dell' Impero Romano* (Florence: La Nuova Italia, 1953), Chapter 12.

The failure to develop modern science and scientific technology, given the level achieved by the Greek thinkers, is another puzzle. Was it Christianity, or barbarian invasions, or the inability of the Romans to absorb this part of the Greek heritage that smothered science? Or was it the slave basis of ancient society, as Farrington, among others, maintains? A similar puzzle is presented by Chinese science. Again, here the "socioeconomic" hypothesis of the evolution of Western science, as against the "arrested" process in China has been maintained by Needham, in his monumental history of science and civilization in China, with his imputation to the "agrarian bureaucratic" structure of Chinese society, the "failure" to develop an indigenous tradition of scientific knowledge that might have surpassed the West. See Benjamin Farrington, *Science and Politics in the Ancient World* (London: Allen and Unwin, 1939), and Joseph Needham, *Science and Civilization in China* (Cambridge: Cambridge University Press, 1959), Vol. 3, Chapter 19, sec. k.

19. Philip Hauser, "Observations on the Urban-Folk Dichotomies as Forms of Western Ethnocentrisms," in Hauser and Schnore (eds.), *Study of Urbanization*.

20. Karl Marx and Friedrich Engels, *The German Ideology* (New York: International Publishers, 1969), p. 11.

21. B. Groethuysen, "Secularism," in the *Encyclopedia of the Social Sciences* (London: Macmillan, 1934), vol. 13.

22. Howard Becker, "Ionia and Athens: Studies in Secularization," in Leopold von Wiese and H. Becker, *Systematic Sociology* (New York: Wiley, 1952), Chapter 25, and H. Becker, *Through Values to Social Interpretation* (Durham: Duke University Press, 1950), Chapter 5.

23. F. Tönnies, *Gemeinschaft and Gesellschaft* (London: Routledge and Kegan Paul, 1955).

24. Emile Durkheim, *The Division of Labor in Society* (New York: Macmillan, 1933).

25. N. J. Spykman (ed.), *The Social Theory of Georg Simmel* (New York: Atherton Press, 1966), Book 2, Chapters 6-7, and Book 3, Chapters 1-2.

26. Karl Löwith, *Meaning in History* (Glencoe: Free Press, 1964).

27. Eduardo Heimann, *Teoría de los sistemas económicos* (Madrid: Editorial Tecnos, 1968), Introduction.

28. Tönnies, *Gemeinschaft and Gesellschaft*, Book 2, first part.

29. F. Tönnies, *Principios de Sociología* (Mexico, D.F.: Fondo de Cultura Económica, 1942). Book 5, Chapter 1.

30. Tönnies, *Gemeinschaft and Gesellschaft*, Appendix, sec. 4.

31. Tönnies, *Principios de Sociología*, Book 1, Chapter 2, sec. 6; *Gemeinschaft and Gesellschaft*, Appendix, secs. 2-3.

32. Tönnies, *Gemeinschaft and Gesellschaft*, p. 64. On the influence of Marx on

Tönnies, see J. Leif, *La Sociologie de Tönnies* (Paris: Presses Universitaires de France. 1946). pp. 106 ff.

33. Marx's thought on social evolution, which is receiving considerable attention from Marxist social scientists at present, is most completely formulated in Karl Marx, *Pre-Capitalist Economic Formations*, ed. E. J. Hobsbawm (New York: International Publishers, 1964), although it passed through many modifications both before and after the original edition of that work. In any case, the Marxian scheme should not be taken as a rigid theory of fixed deterministic successive stages but as a set of hypotheses to "facilitate the arrangement of historical material." The supposed stages "by no means afford a recipe or schema as does philosophy, for neatly trimming the epochs of history" (*German Ideology*, p. 15). See Maurice Godelier for a nondeterministic interpretation of Marxist evolutionary theory: *Antropologia, Storia, Marxismo* (Parma: Guanda, 1970), pp. 31-3.

34. Marx, *Pre-Capitalist Economic Formations*, pp. 66, 86, 106. This position is similar to Polanyi's "embeddement."

35. Marx, *El Capital* (Mexico, D.F.: Fondo De Cultura Económica, 1946). Vol. 1, Chapter 12, sec. 4.

36. Marx, *Pre-Capitalist Economic Formations*, p. 96.

37. Marx and Engels, *German Ideology*, p. 20; Marx, *Pre-Capitalist Economic Formations*, pp. 94-6.

38. Marx and Engels, *German Ideology*, p. 143.

39. On the differentiation of property, through the sequence of precapitalist to capitalist social formations, see Godelier, *Antropologia*, pp. 33-48. On the emergence of the state, and incidentally the crucial importance of its Greek form, see Friedrich Engels, *The Origins of the Family, Private Property, and the State* (New York: International Publishers, 1967), Chapters 4-5. On the role of science, technological evolution, permanent change, and dissolution of tradition, see part 1 of any edition of the *Communist Manifesto* and the third part of Engels' *Antiduhring*.

40. Omitted

41. Nondeterministic interpretations of Marxism stress among other things a diversity in the possible lines of evolution.

42. Engels, *Origins of the Family*, Chapters 4-6.

43. Marx and Engels, *German Ideology*.

44. Marx in *Das Kapital* refers to J. Mill and others. Durkheim in the *Division of Labor* quotes Comte in this sense. See also Celestin Bouglé, "Revue Générale des théories récentes sur la division du Travail," in *L'Année Sociologique* (Paris: Alcan, 1901-02).

45. Durkheim, *Division of Labor*, Book 2, Chapter 2, sec. 1.

46. Ibid., secs. 1-2.

47. Ibid.

48. Ibid.

49. See also the commentary by Don Martindale and Gertrude Neuwirth in Weber, *The City*, p. 62.

50. Georg Simmel, "Uber Soziale Differenzierung," in *Staats-und Sozialwissenschaftliche Foschungen*, ed. Gustav Schmoller (Leipzig,1890), Vol. 10.

51. In writing this section I consulted *Sociología* (Buenos Aires: Espasa Calpe, 1939), a Spanish translation of Simmel's *Soziologie* of 1908. In *Sociología*, competence is discussed in Vol. 2, Chapter 10.

52. Simmel, *Sociología*, Vol. 2, Chapter 6.

53. Simmel, "Grosstade und Geistesleben," in von Zahn (ed.), *Die Grosstadt* (Dresden, 1903).

54. Most of Weber's analysis of secularization is to be found in his *Wirtschaft und Gesellschaft*, 2 vols. (Tübingen, 1925). On the economic evolution from primitive German agrarian communities to capitalism see Weber's volume translated as *General Economic History* (New York: Macmillan, 1961). Also available is *The Protestant Ethic and the Spirit of Capitalism* (New York: Scribner, 1958).

55. See part 3 of Weber's *General Economic History.*

56. Weber, *General Economic History*, Chapter 28.

57. See esp. chaps. 2, 3 and 6 of my book *Modernization, Urbanization and the Urban Crisis.* Of course the literature on the subject is immense, and even a summary review of it would be far beyond the scope of this book. I would like nonetheless to add a note regarding two subjects: the rise of the market and individuation.

As for the former, in the book edited by Karl Polanyi and others, *Trade and Market*, Polanyi ventures an interesting hypothesis about the rise of the market and about the replacement of trade based on traditional rules of reciprocity by trade based impersonally on supply and demand. The scene is ancient Athens, and the hypothesis is based on an ingenious interpretation of Aristotle's writings. "Aristotle living as he did on the borderline of economic ages (pre-market and market economies) was in a favored position," Polanyi concludes, to perceive the essential difference between the two types of trade, and to witness the incipient process of differentiation of the economy away from the undifferentiated social system. See Polanyi, "Aristotle Discovers the Economy," in *Trade and Market.*

Some of the aspects of individuation as seen by anthropologists, historians, and psychologists are considered by Clyde Kluckhohn in Chapter 3 of my aforementioned book. Other very important contributions from the perspective of "psychohistory" can be found in writings by Meyerson, Barbu, and Fromm, among others. Meyerson has analyzed the notion of person, relating its evolution, the psychological changes in the awareness of the self, within the context of sociostructural change and the evolution of ideas (philosophy and religion). Taking into account primitive societies and oriental cultures, he devotes most of the analysis to the transformation of the Western man in classical Greece and Rome. See Ignace Meyerson, *Les Fonctions Psychologiques et les Oeuvres* (Paris: Vrin, 1948), Chapter 2, sec. 2. Barbu relates the political and economic changes in the Greek city to the rise of awareness of self and individuality and conducts a parallel analysis on the structural changes and the emergence of a modern highly individuated personality in sixteenth-century England. See Zevedei Barbu, *Problems of Historical Psychology* (New York: Grove Press,1960). Finally I must mention the well known book by Erich Fromm, *Escape From Freedom* (London: Routledge and Kegan Paul, 1945), in which a detailed psychological examination of the process of individuation during the Renaissance and the Reformation can be found.

58. This section is partly based upon Gino Germani *Sociología de la modernización* (Buenos Aires: Paidós, 1969), Chapter 5.

59. Alfredo Niceforo wrote what was probably the first text about indicators of modernization: *Les Indicateurs Numériques de la Civilisation et du Progrès* (Paris: Flammarion, 1921). That the kind of data required for construction of indicators has become more and more readily available is in itself an indicator of modernization. Among the more interesting compilations in the field may be mentioned B. Russet, K. Deutsch, et al., *World Handbook of Political and Social Indicators*

(New Haven: Yale University Press, 1964). An earlier example of the same type, though limited to economic development, is the *Atlas of Economic Development* prepared by Norton Ginsburg (Chicago: University of Chicago Press, 1961). Other projects using a number of indicators are described and analyzed in Richard J. Merrit and Stein Rokkan (eds.), *Comparing Nations* (New Haven: Yale University Press, 1966). The above references use only numerical data, but there are attempts to use nonstatistical information as well. An example of this is the work by A. S. Banks and Robert B. Textor, *A Cross Polity Survey* (Cambridge: MIT Press, 1963), in which all the variables are "nominal" or "ordinal" and are used dichotomously. A recent overview of indicator construction and use may be found in C. L. Taylor (ed.), *Aggregate Data Analysis* (Paris: Mouton, 1968).

60. Cf. United Nations, *Report on the World Social Situation* (1961), part II. Notice also that J. Drewcowski and W. Scott have constructed an index designed particularly to measure the "quality of life" in countries of different cultures: *The Level of Living Index* (Geneva: United Nations Research Institute, 1966).

61. See Alex Inkeles and David H. Smith, "The Fate of Personal Adjustment in the Process of Modernization," *International Journal of Comparative Sociology*, 11, 2 (June 1970), 81-114. Inkeles has isolated a syndrome of attitudes, values, and ways of acting which define modern man from a psychological perspective, and this definition is independent of cultural and national traits, since it turned out to be the same or very similar in six widely different countries: Argentina, Chile, India, Israel, Nigeria, and Pakistan. "Making Men Modern: On the Cause and Consequences of Indiviual Change in Six Developing Countries" is the title of a paper presented by Inkeles at a meeting of the American Association for the Advancement of Science, Dallas, 1968. An interesting attitude study on modernization in two Latin American countries is Joseph Kahl's *The Measurement of Modernism* (Austin: University of Texas Press, 1968).

62. See *Sociología de la modernización*, pp. 161-62.

63. Raymond B. Cattell et al., "An Attempt at More Refined Definition of the Cultural Dimensions of Syntality in Modern Nations," *American Sociological Review*, 17 (1951), 408-21.

64. Ginsburg, *Atlas*.

65. Hauser and Schnore, *Urbanization*.

66. Gláucio Ary Dillon Soares, "Congruency and Incongruency among Indicators of Economic Development: An Exploratory Study" (paper presented at the Conferencia Internacional sobre Investigación Social Comparativa, Buenos Aires, 1964).

67. UN, *Report on the World Social Situation* (1961).

68. E. E. Lampard, "The History of Cities in Economically Advanced Areas," *Economic Development and Cultural Change*, 3 (1954): 81-136.

69. "Self-sustaining mobility" refers to the process of continuous upgrading of most of the population through the circulation (from the top to the bottom of the stratification system), of status symbols attached to consumer objects and activities, the spread of the automobile being a good example. Some occupational upgrading occurs also (the lower occupations are transferred to machines or perhaps to migrant foreigners). See G. Germani, "Social and Political Consequences of Mobility," in S. M. Lipset and N. Smelser (eds.), *Social Structure and Mobility in Economic Development* (Chicago: Aldine Press, 1966).

70. See *Modernization, Urbanization, and the Urban Crisis,* Gino Germani (ed.) (Boston, Mass.: Little, Brown and Co., 1973), Chapter 12.

71. Ibid.

72. Cf. Martindale's commentary in Weber, *The City.*

73. Kingsley Davis and Hilda Hertz Goldsen, "Urbanization and the Development of Pre-Industrial Areas," *Economic Development and Cultural Change,* 3 (1954).

74. The data for this computation were taken from Adna F. Weber, *The Growth of the Cities in the Nineteenth Century* (Ithaca, N.Y.: Cornell University Press, 1963), pp. 144-145, and Colin Clark, *The Conditions of Economic Progress* (London: Macmillan, 1957), Chapter 3. See also G. Germani, "La Ciudad como Mecanismo Integrador, *Revista Mexicana de Sociología,* 29 (1967), 387-406.

75. Lampard, "The History of Cities in the Economically Advanced Areas."

76. *Sociología de la Modernización,* p. 166.

77. The urbanization-industrialization index is computed by dividing the indicator of urbanization (percentage of total population living in cities of 20,000 or more inhabitants) by the indicator of industrialization (percentage of labor force working in manufacturing). The smaller the index, the lower the urbanization in relation to industrial employment. Less developed and less urbanized countries (with an urbanization of twenty-four percent or less and an average per capita GNP of 247 dollars) had an index rating of 300 on the average; the rating was 237 for countries with an average of 900 dollars GNP per capita and twenty-six to forty percent inhabitants living in cities of 20,000 or more. For the more developed nations (1219 dollars GNP per capita on the average, forty-one percent or more urbanization), the index figure was 200. The correlation between the urbanization-industrialization index and GNP was — 0.91 for less developed nations; — .87 for the somewhat more developed ones and — .68 for the advanced nations. The countries more developed in 1913 had for the period 1950-55 an index of 177; for those less developed in 1913, the index was 336 for 1950-55.

78. See V. N. Sovani, "The Analysis of Over-urbanization," *Economic Development and Cultural Change,* 12 (1964): 113-22.

79. After 1945, especially in the Common Market, the movement of the population from the country to the cities attained the proportions of a veritable exodus. As of 1960, it was estimated that in the six Common Market countries, the rural-urban movement would continue, involving many more millions of people, in the immediate future. See G. Beijer, *Rural Migrants in Urban Settings* (The Hague: Nijoff, 1963). On migrations in the nineteenth century, see A. F. Weber. *The Growth of Cities.*

80. Ibid.

81. Both the primary export economy and the first stages of industrialization (for instance, import substitution and the start of a consumer goods industry) generate a certain "economic expansion" thus providing a surplus which may have "modernizing effects." This was the experience of Latin America and of other underdeveloped areas. See Germani, "Stages of Modernization in Latin America."

82. Peter T. Bauer and Basil S. Yamey, *The Economics of Underdeveloped Countries* (Chicago: Chicago University Press, 1957), Chapter 3.

83. What J. Friedmann and T. Lackington have to say with reference to Chile reflects a widespread opinion that is applicable to analogous situations. See "Hy-

perurbanization and National Development in Chile," *Urban Affairs Quarterly*, 2 (June 1967).

84. Gunnar Myrdal, *Economic Theory and Underdeveloped Regions* (London: Duckworth, 1957), Chapter 3; Bert H. Hoselitz, "Generative and Parasitic Cities," *Economic Development and Cultural Change*, 3 (1955), 287-94; Wilbur R. Thomson, "Urban Economic Growth and Development in a National System of Cities," in Hauser and Schnore (eds.), *Urbanization*, Philip M. Hauser, "The Social, Economic, and Technological Problems of Rapid Urbanization," in Bert F. Hoselitz and Wilbert Moore (eds.), *Industrialization and Society* (Paris: Mouton,1962); Bhilip M. Hauser (ed.), *Urbanization in Latin America* (Paris: UNESCO, 1961); Philip M. Hauser (ed.) *Urbanization in Asia and the Far East* (Calcutta: UNESCO, 1957); International African Institute (London), *Social Implications of Industrialization and Urbanization in Africa, South of the Sahara* (Paris: UNESCO, 1956); United Nations Office of Social Affairs, *Report of the World Social Situation* (1957), Chapters 8-10.

85. Albert O. Hirschman, *The Strategy of Economic Growth* (New Haven: Yale University Press, 1958); Benjamin Higgins, "An Economist's View," in José Medina Echavarria and Egbert De Vries (eds.), *Social Aspects of Economic Development in Latin America* (Paris: UNESCO, 1963), Vol. 2, part 2; Sovani, *op. cit.*; V. E. Faría, "Marginalidade urbana" (unpublished manuscript.).

86. Hoselitz, "Generative and Parasitic Cities."

87. This section is partially based on Gino Germani, *Politica y Sociedad* (Buenos Aires: Paidos, 1962). Chapter 3, sec. 2.

88. Talcott Parsons and Robert F. Bales, *Family Socialization and Interaction Process* (London: Routledge, 1956), Chapters 1-3.

89. See for instance Michael Young and Peter Willmott, *Family and Kinship in East London* (Glencoe: Free Press, 1957); G. Germani, "Inquiry into the Social Effects of Urbanization in Working-Class Sector of Greater Buenos Aires," in Hauser (ed.), *Urbanization in Latin America.*

90. William J. Goode, *World Revolution in Family Patterns* (Glencoe: Free Press, 1963), Conclusion.

91. T. Kawashima and K. Steiner, "Modernization and Divorce Rates in Japan," in *Economic Development and Cultural Change*, 9 (1960), 213-39.

92. Goode, *World Revolution*. Chapter 1 and Conclusion.

93. This theoretical framework of mobilization is formulated extensively in Germani, *Sociología de la Modernización*, Chapter 2.

94. Good illustrations of the variety of incongruent situations may be seen in Chapter 11 of Germani, *Modernization, Urbanization, and the Urban Crisis, op. cit.*

95. See, among others, William Mangin, "Latin American Squatter Settlements," *Latin American Research Review*, 2 (1967): 65-98.

96. T. H. Marshall, *Citizenship and Social Class* (Cambridge: Cambridge University Press, 1950), Chapter 1. See also Reinhard Bendix, rcf50 Nation Building and Citizenship (New York: Wiley, 1964), Chapter 3.

97. Herman P. Miller, "The Dimensions of Poverty," in B. B. Seligman (ed.), *Poverty as a Public Issue* (New York: Free Press, 1965).

98. Maurice Halbwachs, *Les Causes du Suicide* (Paris: Alcan, 1930). Chapter 15.

3.

Self, Society and History

Ego-consciousness, the clear perception of oneself as a separate individual, completely different from all other selves in the world, and the sense of personal identity and uniqueness are the result of complex socio-cultural processes. They are not "given" to the human individual as such: they are conditioned by the type of social structure and culture in which the individual has been socialized. They were not necessarily the same in primitive societies, or in Homeric Greece, or in the fifth century B.C. Athens, or in the Middle Ages, or in the Renaissance, or in modern times. They may vary within the same society, in the different social classes, or in different social and cultural contexts. Different degrees of ego-consciousness and different degrees of "individuation" correspond to different types of social structure: in certain types, and under given conditions, the growth of ego-consciousness is facilitated and a higher degree of individuation may be reached.

There is a tendency to conceptualize the growth of individuality as an evolutionary process. While it is true that under the conditions of a typical primitive social structure, the degree of individuation is usually very low, it must also be recognized that modern society is typically oriented toward the rise of a higher degree of ego-consciousness. But the process cannot be said to be unilinear, nor can it be conceived of as one of uniform orientation towards higher individuation. Not only may different cultural contexts produce different types of processes, in this respect, but even within the context of Western culture, there have been various stages of relapse into lower degrees of individuation. It must also be remembered that considerable differences may coexist within the same society among different sectors of the population. For instance, the elites may be thought to always have been more individuated than the common people and the urban setting to be more favorable to individuation than the rural or folk community.

But even if we cannot think in terms of strict, deterministic evolutionism, it is true that the great transformation, the transition from pre-industrial to industrial society is characterized by growth in the degree of individuation. The contributions of social science in the nineteenth century, and even more so in the present one, have emphasized the role of individualism in the basic changes which took place in society. Modern society itself includes as one of its essential characteristics a high degree of individuation.

Some of the more typical developments in modern culture may be considered precisely as an effort towards greater ego-consciousness. Not only psychoanalysis but most of modern psychology is oriented towards an increasing self-awareness of the individual as a separate self, and increasing the individual's level of objectivity in dealing with his own self (or to use Herbert Mead's expression, in perceiving oneself as others perceive oneself).

In modern society there are also counter-currents which tend to reduce the degree of self-awareness and individuation. In fact the more important aspect of "massification," is precisely the danger of de-individuation and loss of identity. The structural traits of modern society do not facilitate the rise of ego-consciousness; there are aspects which in fact tend to reduce it, and as a result we have the apparent paradox of a society which has reached the highest degree of individuation, and which at the same time includes powerful factors which tend to reduce it.

The growth of individuation can be examined in a historical-cultural perspective. I will give some examples of important contributions of both cultural history and anthropology.

Some of the earlier theoretical contributions to this problem can be found in the dichotomic typologies such as Durkheim's "mechanical versus organic solidarity" or in Tönnies' "Gemeinschaft versus Gesellschaft." Direct reference to the problem of individuation has been formulated, in connection with a similar typology, by H. Becker in his well known concept of "sacred vs. secular" society. In these typologies we find a common trait: in one type of society individual consciousness is still merged within collective consciousness. The individual is not separated from the group, his own ego is undifferentiated from the group. In a sense "he" is "the group." In the opposite type the individual has "emerged" from the group, he is now a real self-conscious ego and clearly separated from environment and from other selves.

M. Mauss, an anthropologist and sociologist of the Durkheimian school, formulated one of the first contributions, based on ethnographic data on the problem of rise of the individual, as a separate person. He pointed out the historical and social nature of the notion of "person" and "ego." He emphasized the fact that in present primitive societies, as well as in ancient Western societies, the idea of the "person" as an individual stems from the notion of "personage." The individual in these societies tends to be a set of roles. He has a set of positions (statuses) within the social structure and his identity is no more than the sum of such set of positions. He has a precise location within this social relation network which makes up the society and all his personal identity is no more than this personal location. The same location puts him also within a series of successive generations: he is less an individual than simply an element of the social structure. J. Murphy, a British anthropologist, writing some ten or fifteen years later, formulated a more complete theory of the development of individuality, analyzing the process in ancient societies, and relating it to changes in the social structure. According to Murphy, "in the small group in which the earliest true men lived, such as the food-gatherers and hunters of the Paleolithic Age, and those of the same economy today, there was for each member a limited individuality." Ego-consciousness at this stage "has still the atomistic divided impulsive character of the animal mind which moves swiftly from one instinctive reflex to another every moment. . . ." The precondition for the rise of an individuated consciousness is the appearance of a unified consciousness. Following Durkheim and Levy-Bruhl, Murphy attributes this important step, not to the individual, but to the group. That is, the individual starts becoming conscious of himself as a member of the group, as an element of a whole and not as a separate individual. Ego consciousness will emerge from this stage, once other changes take place in the social structure. It may be noted that at an individual level, some psychologists have adopted rather similar conceptions. In contrast to what we may call the Rousseauian notion of the priority of the individual over society, such psychologists as H. Wallon, or G. H. Mead, have described the emergence of the individuated self out of the matrix of the group. Mead especially has given a "naturalistic" account of the rise of the self, on the basis of social interaction.

The first stage, in which the individual still lacks a unified consciousness, Murphy calls "the primitive horizon." The transition to the next step, the stage of group-consciousness called "the tribal horizon," is the result of drastic changes in the social structure which are originated by the introduction of agriculture and the domestication of animals. Such changes involve a sharp increase in the number of individuals (what Durkheim called an increase in the "volume" and "density" of society), and a higher level of differentiation. This is a more complex type of society, with an increased number of statuses and roles. But real ego-consciousness is not fully possible at this stage. It takes a further step in the complexity of social organization to create the conditions favorable for the emergence of the individual as such. This step is the appearance of the city. This stage, the "civilized horizon," will in time cause a further degree of individuation and the emergence of a real ego-consciousness. This change is also expressed in many aspects of the culture, such as religion or art. Thus, while within the "tribal horizon" "the objects of man's worship are the impersonal Spirit of Animism, or the vague, ill-defined and nameless powers of his Polydaimonism," in the urban societies, in the "civilized horizon," "the spirits become personal gods, and the nameless powers are deities with a certain humanlike individuality." As Murphy observes, in the ancient civilization the personality of the gods are an index of the degree of development reached by the individual personality in these societies.

This third stage in the emergence of the self, the "civilized horizon," has been further analyzed by a French psychologist — I. Meyerson. To him, the evolution of selfhood is just one example of the historicity of psychological functions, an illustration of the changing human nature. Meyerson used the evidence provided by different disciplines to describe the various stages in the emergence of the person as a full-fledged ego and a clear awareness of oneself as a separate individual. Such evolution, within the Western tradition, is shown through the changes in the meaning of the Greek and Latin words *persona* (Latin) and *prosopon* (Greek). The evolution in both languages is similar: from "mask," "role," to "being" and "individual." In this transition, according to Meyerson, the role of religion and philosophy, was especially important. The contribution of the Greek and oriental as well as such philosophical schools as religious beliefs and ideas, stoicism and Neoplatonism are important expressions and landmarks in the emergence of the individual as a separate self, a person conscious of himself as such. According to the French philosopher Brunschvig, it was from the Stoics that men learned to say "me," and that they became aware both of the moral and psychological aspects of selfhood. Christianity received this heritage and further reinforced it with religious meanings and particularly with the metaphysical notion of the person as an individual soul.

The emergence of the self must not be considered as a kind of unilinear, irreversible evolution. The various approaches to this problem tend to emphasize the connection between the characteristics of the social structure and the degree of individuality and awareness of selfhood. Within the same society different groups may be differently affected by such characteristics, so that their respective degree of "individuation" may vary a great deal. For instance members of the elite are likely, in any society, to be more "individuated" than the rest of the population. Certainly the urban context tends to emphasize individuality and clear awareness of selfhood. On the other hand the "great transition" from nonindustrial to modern society has certainly been marked by greater diffusion among the general population of a higher degree of individuation. That is, while in traditional societies, even in higher and complex historical cultures, high individuation was usually found among the elite, in the modern industrial society such a degree of individuation is required in much larger sectors of the population.

The dramatic emergence of the individual with the dawn of the modern world has been vividly described in the well known statement of Burckhardt. "In the Middle Ages both sides of human consciousness, that of which was turned within as that which was turned without, lay dreaming or half awake beneath a common veil. The veil was woven of faith, illusion, and childish prepossession, through which the world and history were seen clad in strange hues. Man was conscious of himself only as a member of a race, people, party, family, or corporation — only through some general category." The development of individuality in the Renaissance has been analyzed by many authors. Among others, E. Fromm has provided a psychological analysis of the historical process of growing individuation in modern times and has also suggested some parallelism between this process and psychological growth of the individual.

An important contribution may be found also in recent work of anthropologists. M. Leenhardt, for instance, has shown how contact with the Western world has brought real individuality, the living experience of selfhood to some Melanesian tribes, whose culture had remained in extreme isolation, and who, even from the point of view of physical anthropology, have been considered as a kind of "living fossiles.".

But there is no reason to believe that the evolution towards higher individuation is an irreversible trend. Within the limited scope of the present paper I can only mention the existence of some powerful traits which in the present mass society, seem to threaten individuality and tend to generate deindividuating forces.

4.

From Traditional to Modern Society

A World in Transition

Ours basically is an age of transition. If change is a normal feature of society, then the modern world is witnessing the emergence of a type of society radically different from all previous historical forms, with a rhythm of transformation the rapidity of which is no longer measured in centuries, but in years. Change in the modern world has other characteristics which are unusual: it embraces all regions of the planet, all social groups and all individuals. In the past, vast regions remained relatively isolated as others changed, and there always persisted a great layer of the population which dwelt on the margin of change. In 1800 scarcely 2.4 percent of the world population lived in cities of 20,000 or more inhabitants; the remainder spent their lives in the country in agricultural pursuits. Practically isolated from the dynamic centers, generation succeeded generation without appreciable modification occurring in any of the essentials of life. But now there is no longer a corner of the globe which can remain isolated. Real "universal" history has emerged, replacing the "parallel histories" of the past. If more than twenty percent of the inhabitants live in cities of this size, and more than forty percent work at nonagricultural occupations, then means of communication and the facility and frequency of contact have quite completely destroyed all barriers, and the rural areas are equally affected. In some countries and continents this transformation is very advanced; they are the countries that today we generally call "developed." In others, the transformation is taking place or has recently begun, but the rhythm of change is becoming faster and faster. While England took 140 years to get beyond the phase that Rostow calls take-off, the timespan was reduced to sixty years for the United States, to forty or fifty years for Japan, and to much less for Australia and Russia. This acceleration of the rhythm not only affects the economic process, but also embraces all aspects of change.

The characteristic of transition, which is the coexistence of social forms which belong to different epochs, has stamped an especially antagonistic quality on a process which is inevitably lived as crisis. This occurs since it implies a continuing rupture with the past, a laceration which not only divides persons and groups, but affects the individual consciousness, in which attitudes, ideas, and values pertaining to different stages of the transition coexist.

This profound transformation is reflected in many sociological theories, classic formulations and also in recent contributions. It is a question of a change which embraces all aspects of human life: economic organization, social stratification, family, morality, conventions and political organization. Moreover, its impact implies substantial changes in the forms of thought, feeling and the bearing of people. It implies profound transformation in the structure of the personality. It is no accident that a considerable part of sociological theory is devoted precisely to studying this great process and that the other human sciences are concerned with the same topic, although frequently they work under a distinct problematic structure and conceptualization. What we generally refer to as "economic development" is none other than change itself as seen from the perspective of the economist. The problem of technological change and its repercussions is another aspect of the same process. The abundant literature on crisis, with the theme of moral progress versus material progress, shows other facets of the current anxiety over change.

The Dichotomy: Traditional Versus Modern

What is the initial and what is the "final" state (or at least the direction) of the process? Notoriously there is no agreement on the definition of "economic development" or "modernization." Nevertheless there is a certain consensus on its main traits. Among these traits are generally counted not only economic indices, but also "social conditions" of development. Global production per capita level of investment and standard of living are some of the most frequent indices. But there are usually many others: birth rate, general and infant mortality, distribution of the active population by branch of activity, general and technical education, scientific development, technology, type of stratification, family organization, forms of state organization, types of international relations, degree of individuation, level of rationality, suicides, and divorces. The problem of the definition of economic development and modernization (or that of measurement related to it) naturally has an interdisciplinary character and implies a series of value decisions. And the solutions usually adopted are, implicity or explicitly, based on a dichotomous model (initial state versus final state) very familiar to sociologists. Economic development is conceived of the passage from a "traditional" society to a "developed" society. The former is characterized above all by a subsistence economy, the latter by an expansive economy based on a growing application of "modern" technology. Whatever the divergencies of points of view may be on this or that aspect of this dichotomy, it clearly reflects the classic formulation of

Tönnies, Durkheim, Becker, Redfield and others. On the other hand, when a specific "ideal type" is used, it often happens that the empirical type of the most "developed" countries (socialist or Western, according to ideological preference) assumes the role of final goal, or final orientation, of the trend toward development. For these reasons the "social factors" of the process are perceived as the necessary and sufficient conditions for producing a type of society similar to the constructed model, or the empirical one adopted as a final goal.

This dichotomous typology is the immediate result of an extreme simplification. At the same time the limitations and the utility of all typologies reside within it. Two points might be made from this general observation: first, the two opposite types should be considered the extremes of a multidimensional continuum as present and historical experience demonstrate. Second, although maintaining the simplicity of the dichotomy, it would always be necessary to qualify the extreme onesidedness of the polar types. It would be appropriate to distinguish the multiplicity of forms of both ends of the continuum. For example, the usual type of "traditional" society corresponds better to the extreme case, frequently called "folk" society. Nonetheless, the much more complex historical societies, the "preindustrial urban" societies are also subsumed under this extreme type, despite their profound and substantial differences. The same oversimplifications often occur at the other end. "Modern-industrial" society is a generic category, including a whole range of different types. Only in assuming a variety of social structures at the point of departure, as well as at the point of arrival, can the idea of the multidimensionality of the tradition be maintained.

Another significant limitation of the dichotomous model is that is obscures, or possibly negates, the functional role of the persistence of traditional patterns in the process of modernization or the wide range of compatibility of both elements in modern institutions. Certainly the actual, or empirical, existence of "mixed" societies would not invalidate the model (since the two poles are conceived as "ideal" types not to be found historically in any "pure" form). Nonetheless by implication the model could suggest the persistence of traditional or archaic patterns as an obstacle to modernization, and never as a support or an aspect of it. The dichotomy would acquire an ideological bias in favor of "modernity." The ideological use of the model may lead in other directions. For instance, in many cases it involves an idealization of tradition, as illustrated by the classical example of Tönnies, or it may give exclusive emphasis to the internal structural change in the process of transition, leading to the neglect of the meaning and the impact of such international factors as the economic and political hegemony of the "central" countries over the "periphery."

All these limitations impose severe restriction on the analytic use of the dichotomic model. On the other hand it is very difficult to escape it. In any case it seems legitimate and necessary to identify the universal and necessary characteristics of the transition, as well as the constant elements in industrial society. The usual dichotomous typology, "traditional" vs. "industrial" society, is a convenient and perhaps a necessary point of departure. But any further analysis would require a typology of the various and divergent forms of transition and of industrial societies as well. Unfortunately, while it seems possible to delineate the general characteristics of industrial society, the construction of a valid typology of industrial societies and types of transition should be sought not only in the differences among the various possible "starting points" (types of traditional societies), and historical circumstances characterizing the transition, but also in the variation in the possible types of sequences among the many partial primary and secondary processes.

Secularization as the Central Component of the "Modern-Industrial Cultural Complex"

"Modern-industrial" society is defined in terms of three main structural traits (called here for the sake of convenience "secularization"), required by, and associated with, scientific knowledge, technology, and economy in such a way as to lead to the use of "high energy" and to the maximization of efficiency in the production of goods and services. These traits may be regarded as a basic (although generic) core to be found in any industrial society, and as universal requirements for its existence and maintenance. However, beyond the institutional setting required for the attainment of the increasing high energy use, and an increasing efficiency in productive technology, allowance must be made for a wide range of structural and cultural variations (including many mixed "traditional-modern" institutions and structures) that is, many types of industrial societies. Whether future evolution will bring increasing homogeneity or increasing diversity is a question which remains to be answered.

Although a certain degree of secularization (one which may vary under different historical and sociocultural conditions) is a necessary condition for "high energy" use and high efficiency in productive technology, it is not a sufficient one. In fact there are various instances of secularization not followed, or not accompanied by, high energy use or increasing efficiency in technology. In these cases, this association was instead a historical fact, to be explained in terms of a unique and very long historical process, which once it occurred, originated a new cultural complex called the "modern-industrial society." The "great transition" leading to the emergence of the first historical case of this new type of society must be distinguished from the great variety of forms of transition which occurred later in the process of its diffusion, adaptation and transformation, first in Europe and other Western societies, then in the rest of the world.

Secularization is conceived here as a complex process including three basic modifications of the social structure:

1. Type of social action: from prescriptive to elective action
2. Acceptance of change: from institutionalization of tradition to institutionalization of change
3. Institutional specialization: from a relatively undifferentiated complex of instutions to a higher degree of institutional differentiation and specialization.

These changes occur at different levels. At the psychosocial level they affect attitudes and behavior, while at the normative level they affect institutions, values, statuses, roles, and other norms. But they don't necessarily involve all the members of a society, all types or areas of behavior and attitudes or all institutions and values. Secularization usually begins in relatively small groups (involving either the transformation of preexisting minority sectors or the emergence of new groups), leaving the great majority of the population relatively unchanged. Also, from the point of view of geographic diffusion, these ruptures are localized in determined territorial areas (in some cities) while the remaining areas may be relatively unaffected during the first steps of the transition. The emergence of groups bearing new attitudes and values, or the transformation of preexisting groups, is an expression of modifications produced in the society. They constitute a reaction to the fact that certain institutions of the preexistent social system no longer function as normatively expected. I am referring here to the active response (the "mobilization") of groups made available by such disintegration who generate innovations in both attitudes and behavior. We are speaking of minority or elite groups (in a broad sense to distinguish them from the masses), for even when the process of dislocation has affected large parts of the population, the active response begins to arise from small sectors, either because the impact is particularly great on preexistent elites, or because new elites emerge from the interior of those sectors made "available." The active response, the "mobilization" of large segments of the population, also constitutes an essential aspect of modernization — but this is usually a "later" process, that is, a process that does not necessarily precede the first stage of the transition.

Among the three basic modifications mentioned above, the change in the type of social action is the more general requirement for the existence of modern industrial society. Institutionalization of change and institutional differentiation and specilization may be considered to a large extent consequences of the predominance of "elective action." For this reason, in describing the three modifications, a more detailed analysis will be devoted to this topic.

"Prescriptive" to "Elective" Action

Increase in rationality (especially instrumental rationality) is usually considered one of the main traits of secularization. In this sense it is maintained that "rational action" (or at least some type of rational action) tends to replace "traditional" action, in many areas of behavior. While the validity of this approach is not denied, in the present discussion "rational" action will be considered as a particular type of action within the category of "elective action." Not all elective actions are rational actions, and while secularization certainly involves a strong tendency towards increased rationality, its more general trait is the exercise of individual choices — even if such choices are not always "rational."

"Elective" and "prescriptive" actions occur within different types of normative frameworks which may be considered as "pure" types, or as opposite poles of a continuum along which it should be possible to classify "mixed" (empirical) types. "Prescriptive" action takes place within a basically rigid normative system that limits the margin of possible variation by the actor. In the case of "elective" action, the normative framework not only is less rigid but actually operates differently. In the first case, a specific course of action is normatively imposed (and subjectively internalized) for each specific situation. In "elective" action, the normative system still regulates ends, means, and the relation between them, but it is characterized by the imposition of a certain degree of choice on the actor, rather than by the prescription of a fixed course of action. We may take as an example situations arising from a comparative analysis of industrial and nonindustrial societies. In the latter, status is more frequently ascribed than acquired. The son inherits the position of the father; the choice of profession does not imply a real decision, as there is a prescribed response to the problem of occupation. Furthermore, the actor has internalized a series of patterns that motivate him to occupy the position of his father, and he is socialized to develop the proper attitudes. The problem of the economic activity of the subject is thus resolved by society. On the other hand, what is the norm in industrial society? Here the prescription is that of choosing a profession. But does there exist absolute liberty to do so? Here also we find a series of conditions that the actor must (in the normative sense) take into consideration: his vocation, his aptitudes, his money, his social connections. Furthermore, the required choice must be made in accordance with certain criteria: the choice of an occupation is criticized if made in an "unrealistic" manner — for example, if one decides to be a pianist without considering the relevant aptitudes. The demand that one must choose an occupation is a norm that must be respected. The man who allows his parents to choose his occupation for him will be considered too dependent. A person who selects his father's occupation simply because it is his father's, demonstates an "abnormal" affective dependency on his father. It is always hoped that each person will choose an occupation in accordance with his vocation and his choice is judged on such criteria. But it is essential to note that the criteria for this choice are prescribed. In this type of action, then, a normative system exists, but it is different from that system typical of "prescriptive" action. In one case, simply the assignment of a determined occupation is prescribed. In the other, the choice is prescribed, as is also certain criteria for making it. In the type we have called "prescriptive," one does not lack a certain latitude in his interpretation of the norm. It is possible that concrete situations may vary from the "typical" situations envisaged by the norm; here arises the necessity of "interpretation" to determine whether it is suitable to apply the norm. Thus there arises a series of possible vacillations and deviations from that which is socially prescribed. But this whole margin of variation does not change the nature of the prescriptive action which is characterized by its assignment of a determined response before a given situation (also "culturally defined"). Although it admits a certain margin of variation that can become fairly broad, it is not based, as is "elective" action, on a prescription to choose, an affirmation of individual liberty (and the responsibility for the exercise of this liberty), as a value sustained by the culture ("individualism"). It is rather tolerance rooted, in the absence of sanctions against deviations that arise, in the concrete application of a norm, either as the result of chance in this application, or as the product of a certain imprecision in the circumstances which accompany each concrete situation and which make the socially established norm more or less applicable to each.

The individual character of decisions taken within the system of "elective" action contrasts as well with another characteristic that can be assigned to the "prescriptive" ideal type. In the latter, any decision that is taken within its fairly rigid and narrow limits tends to be a decision of the collective order, that is, taken by the group as such, considering its own interests, which may be above, and at times in conflict with, those of its present members. Not only is the choice of a spouse (and also divorce in some cases) based on an interpreation of relevant traditional rules, but also this very interpretation is charged to the familial group and not to the individuals directly affected. It is obvious that all action is action by single individuals, but in "prescriptive" action the individual acts as the carrier of group norms, values and interests, rather than his own or individual ones.

Collective choice in a system of "elective" action is based on very different norms and assumptions. This can be illustrated by the ideology of public opinion as expressed in liberal rationalist thought: here the decision of the group is assumed to be reached through the accommodation of individual wills, each individual supposedly deliberating and deciding as an individual.

It is important to distinguish the "elective" normative framework from the situation of anomie. Structural anomie has often been confused with the situation that arises in a type of society in which "elective" action predominates. Historically, the development of the concept of anomie is linked to the formulation of the concept of "elective" action; for example, both are found in Durkheim (cf. his two types of "egoistic" suicide). Durkheim also indicates that this phenomenon originated as a result of rapid change from one type of society (rural, traditional, with a mechanical solidarity) to another (urban, industrial, with an organic solidarity). But it is clear that this "origin" is only one of a number of possibilities and that anomie can develop as much in predominantly "prescriptive" structures as in those characterized by "elective" action, although historically it has been in the latter that it has been observed most frequently.

Rational action may now be defined as a type of "elective" action in which the criteria of choice are based on some type of rationality (usually instrumental rationality), and this is the case for actions carried on in many areas of behavior in industrial society. But there are also "elective" actions which are based on nonrational criteria or which combine rationality with other criteria. This occurs, for instance, when the individual is required in his choice to express his own personality genuinely, such as the "vocational" component in the choice of an occupation, or the emotional component in the choice of a mate. The more general and essential trait which distinguishes this type of action from traditional behavior is the existence of genuine individual choice, even if such choice is normatively expected to be based on nonrational criteria.

Most social actions in every society, traditional or modern, are based on habit. If a type of action is defined by its normative system, the fact that certain actions are empirically performed without reflection or deliberation is not relevant when one judges the "elective" or "prescriptive" normative nature of the action. Although it would seem obvious that all traditional action is at the same time habitual, it is possible to show that these are two analytically distinct categories. Habitual action requires no explicit reflection over all or part of the moments that are integrated in the course of the action. The reflection and integration take place partially, or totally, below the level of consciousness or at least, if there is a consciousness of execution, there is still no explicit reflection as to the opportunity for undertaking the action, the means employed, the ends chosen, and the conditions considered. All of this is kept at an implicit level, when not totally below the threshold of consciousness, and action responds more or less automatically to a given situation. Now a prescriptive action is not necessarily automatic or based on habit. It may require reflection and even deliberation. Thus a nonhabitual prescriptive action supposedly elevates to the conscious level the internalized norms, so as to identify the situation, to determine if it corresponds to that foreseen by the norms, and eventually to resolve the problems of interpretations and adaptations of the norms themselves to concrete situations. As mentioned earlier, the prescriptive character of a normative system does not eliminate a margin of variation, indeterminacy, and indecision. Certainly many prescriptive actions are performed by habit: phenomenologically they seem to be automatic or almost automatic reactions to given situations. But this does not mean that all habitual actions correspond to a prescriptive framework. The important point to be stressed here is that "habit" may correspond to an "elective" framework. The case of an "elective" action that is taken in whole or in part below the conscious level, without a reflective or deliberative phase, may seem a contradiction (an "elective action," or an action "by choice," without "choice"); but the paradox is resolved by the fact that the habitual aspect of the action is set in the context of an "elective" normative system.

An "elective" action which has been repeated many times becomes almost habitual and the whole elective and deliberative process becomes permanently implicit. This pattern can be seen in many economic actions taken in industrial society. In this type of structure, the normative system is of the "elective" type and demands instrumental rationality. However, many economic actions take place in a routine and habitual manner without a deliberative process of rational choice of means. This is certainly the case in much action by consumers who become used to spending their income in a routine or almost automatic manner, and it is true of numerous actions taken by managers or entrepreneurs. With respect to habitual action by consumers, one may object that they are following "prescriptive" norms defining the "proper" level of living of each social group. Although this cannot be denied, it must be remembered that in an industrial society, the "ascriptive" (or traditional) character of these norms is gradually diminished by the stimulus towards greater consumption. An impulse for higher levels of aspiration, an impulse at the same time institutionalized, introduces strong elements of choice into the consumption pattern. For example, according to some research on consumer behavior, its character (habitual or not) depends on the importance of the purchase and whether or not it is repetitive. The case of habitual action by a manager reveals most clearly the relation between habit and choice. Take the example of certain expenditures such as those for advertising. Often they are made entirely automatically based on decisions made once and never, or seldom, re-examined. The same is true of many other managerial decisions (pricing, calculation of costs, and restocking). Many political actions in stable democracies have this "habitual" character as well, in spite of the expressly "elective" nature of their normative systems. It is obvious that the habitual character of these actions does not mean that they are "prescriptive." They are actions of an "elective" type (corresponding to an elective normative system) but they are performed as habitual actions. The great majority of actions are habitual, corresponding to the functional process whereby behavior which was once conscious passes to an automatic, unconscious, repetitive level. A very large part of culture is not manifest, but appears in behavior patterns under the form of habitual action. Furthermore, to the degree to which we can differentiate the various normative systems, we are also able to distinguish their elective or prescriptive character (in the senses used here).

We must clarify the notion of "habit" as used here, for it refers only to behavior which is learned and which, in some way, has reference to a system of norms; that is, applies to regulated conduct. It is possible that this behavior may become completely automatic (at the conscious level), or may have been so since it was learned, if the process of internalization took place very early in the life of the individual; but even in these cases, the observer can infer the existence of a normative system that molds the apparently automatic behavior.

Finally, we must mention one last possibility. Although historically one can observe a tendency towards the successive extension of the "elective" normative system, in all societies (including the urban, industrial, "developed" ones), there are important areas organized within a "prescriptive" framework. In spite of this, it is possible that "traditions" may be redeveloped in areas characterized previously by choice. In this case, the rise of a prescriptive system is the result of a process linked to changes that include a sphere of values and norms of a wider significance than the specific area in which the changes themselves can be verified. Given the significance of this process, the mere fact of "habit" is not sufficient to accomplish such a transformation in the normative system (an action does not become a tradition solely because it is repeated); however, it is possible that the passage from an elective to a prescriptive system is accompanied often by habit.

From the Institutionalization of Tradition to the Institutionalization of Change

Traditional society is rooted in the past, rejecting all that is new while reaffirming the repetition of preestablished patterns. All change, in this type of society, is seen as profoundly abnormal and as always constituting a violation of the norms. In industrial society, on the other hand, change becomes a normal phenomenon, one anticipated and institutionalized by the norms themselves. These set the rules of change. The most illustrative example of the rules of change, other than the example of the economy, may be found in science, where assertions are always provisional. They can always be replaced by others, but always according to the established methodological canons. These canons, therefore, constitute the normative system of change itself.

The institutionalization of change and "elective" action seems somewhat of a paradox in view of the essential function that forms of integration, based on a prescriptive framework, perform for the maintenance of stability. Here one may find a structural source of tension which may induce further elements of change.

Institutional Differentiation and Specialization

Preindustrial society, especially the preliterate type, has a relatively undifferentiated structure for the performance of functions. In industrial society, each function tends to be specialized, with a tendency to spawn a series of structures, each increasingly specific and limited to determined and clearly fixed tasks. This can be seen especially in the realm of economic activities, an area where, in preindustrial societies, clearly differentiated institutions are not found. On the contrary, it is the family which, in this area as in others, assumes the central role. The family, the local community, and religion are all tightly linked and embrace the greater part of human activity. With industrial society comes an increasingly accentuated differentiation of function. The economy assumes particular importance and creates its own organization. The same process occurs in education, political activity, recreational or expressive activity. It is essential to observe here that old institutions are also transformed and specialized.

All societies involve differentiation and relative structural complexity; in this respect one should establish a clear distinction between the labels applied to "primitive" cultures, preliterate ones, and "historical" nonindustrial societies, in which the degree of differentiation and specialization is undoubtedly much greater than that of the former. But in modern societies the process continues to the extreme of modifying the type of structure. Thus it is also legitimate to distinguish this type of society from the "historical" nonindustrial ones.

It should also be pointed out that the increasing specialization and differentiation of corresponding normative spheres tends to give rise to a plurality of value systems (insofar as they are also adaptable to institutional specialization). Each institutional sphere tends to acquire autonomy of values. This in no way affects the hypothesis of the interdependence or interrelation of all the parts of the social structure, integrated to varying degrees around central and common values. It is obvious, however, that with respect to this last type of integration, secularized societies are characterized by much less "valuation congruence," although this does not eliminate the possibility of the existence of certain underlying common values.

From the point of view of economic institutions, change thus presupposes the emergence of a specific normative system, governing both economic values and attitudes, with its correlates at the levels of motivation and personality type.

Minimum Universal Requirements: The Extension of Secularization in the Spheres of Science, Productive Technology and Economic Institutions

One of the more intriguing problems of the social sciences is the definition of the minimum universal conditions for the functioning of an industrial structure. In the past century England could be taken as the paradigm answering this question. Everyone knows now that there are various models for industrial society and various types of transition. But from here two questions arise: to what point must the process of secularization proceed, and which are necessary and which are accidental consequences of this process (considering their extension to different sectors of society as well as their degree of intensity)? We can postulate the existence of a limit, as a universally functional necessity. If this is so, in all industrial society the secularization process itself will have to develop within a normative framework which assures a minimum base of integration. This opens the question as to whether, for the functioning of industrial society, a certain degree of secularization must be extended to all sectors of society, or whether this is necessary only in those spheres most closely linked to economic development (that is to "high energy" use and high efficiency technology). Finally, we should also answer the question of whether it is possible to limit secularization to a certain level and restrict it to determined sectors or if, on the contrary, we are dealing with a process endowed with an internal autonomy that, once begun, reaches a maximum of intensity and extension beyond control.

Discussions of these themes have occupied a considerable part of sociology, as much in the last century as in the present. And a good part of the ideological controversies of our day take the form of distinct and opposite positions on this very problem. The difficulty in keeping the discussion on a purely scientific plane, free from valuational and ideological connotations, is obvious here and does not require special commentary. Formulations in functional terms often mask ideological positions. Limiting the discussion to purely economic concerns (as in many discussions of the conditions of economic development) does not eliminate these connotations. It simply eliminates them from the realm of possible discussion, turning them into inexplicit premises of tacit assumptions behind positions which appear on the surface to be purely technical or economic.

It will be difficult to avoid all these valuational connotations in the following discussion. The criterion to be used in describing the scope of secularization, in both its extension and its intensity, will be that of the minimal conditions for the functioning of a type of social organization compatible with the basic requirements of economic development. We shall now attempt at least partially to answer these questions.

All society presupposes as a universal functional requirement is the existence of a minimal level of normative integration. This term indicates the existence of an underlying nucleus of norms shared by all the members of the society. Adopting a sufficiently broad definition of norms, this means that the common nucleus would have to include cognitive elements, as well as valuational and regulative ones. "Sacred" or nonsecularized societies accord this requisite considerable preponderance: the three features previously pointed out, i.e. the prescriptive character of action, perpetuation of tradition, and the undifferentiated character of institutions produce as a consequence the very high degree of homogeneity and stability that all typologies attribute to this type of society. Nevertheless, as our discussion of "elective" action and the institutionalization of change demonstrates, societies characterized by a high level of secularization also rely on a certain degree of normative integration, the very minimum necessary to assure the existence of the criteria of choice and change.

An appropriate illustration can be found in modern science. Science, as mentioned before, is an example of the incorporation of the mechanics for change into a system. To expand this example: each discipline is composed of a series of propositions of a provisional character — that is, potentially, each proposition can be substituted for the other. Permanent change, however, takes place within a fixed system, based on criteria governing the acceptance or rejection of propositions. Only in this way is it possible to speak of a "science" relatively integrated with respect to both substantive contents and the human group bearing and believing in those contents: the scientists. The society, the social group of scientists, will exist as such only as long as its members continue to participate within the common normative framework, that of the criteria for accepting and rejecting scientific propositions. The so-called crisis of science, from the end of the past century to the present, seems to be precisely a discussion of the validity and universality of this normative framework itself. But since this debate has been limited to the philosophical sphere, without disturbing the concrete labor of the scientists relying on the essentials of this normative framework, it has not dislocated or disintegrated science as an institution or human group. The latter could occur, however, with the absence of normative consensus.

Secularization in the field of science, technology and economy seems to be a minimum universal requirement for the existence of industrial society. A degree of secularization in the three areas is also a precondition (that is, a primary process, as defined earlier); but the degree of the primary pro-

cess at the beginning of the transition and the nature of secondary processes of secularization in the same area, will vary a great deal according to the
social setting and historical circumstances of the transition.

Modern science, as well as technology, is distinguished by the three
aspects of secularization: "electivity," "institutionalization of change,"
and "increasing specialization." Science should be distinguished from all
other intellectual activities or forms of knowledge (as for example theology and philosophy) — a distinction affecting not only the content of science, but also its material and social organization in teaching and
research. The principle of its functional autonomy should be dominant
without limitations. In the field of natural science secularization is certainly a primary process, but its extension to the social sciences takes the
form of a secondary process, varying again with the different cultural settings and historical conditions.

In the economy the process of secularization signifies first the differentiation of specifically economic institutions, that is, those organized on the
basis of norms and values free from connotations of religion, morality,
aesthetics, or prestige, and generally oriented towards the demand of efficiency, that is, incorporating instrumental rationality as a basic principle
of action and the institutionalization of change. Whatever the variance of
political or economic organization in industrial society, all the basic
aspects of the economy are transformed. Economic activity will probably
be concentrated in a type of specific organization that, whatever its legal
system (private, collective, "mixed," state-sponsored), should be characterized mainly by rationality and all of its consequences, such as bureaucratic organization. Forms of property, exchange, division and
organization of labor, distribution and allocation of human and material
resources to different sectors of the population should be oriented towards
the principles of efficiency and change. A phenomenon of "mobility"
should be produced in all those aspects as they acquire their own dynamism, unhampered or minimally hampered by the sociocultural structures
pertaining to the other sectors of the society.

Historically this secularization of the economy has taken place in various forms. In countries of earlier modernization this assumed the economic and political form broadly termed "liberal." But in those countries
where the process occurred later, or is taking place now, there have
appeared a great variety of other forms which can generally be called
"nonliberal." Furthermore, in these same countries, significant transformations have been experienced which have distinctly removed them from
primitive structures. Although it is difficult to arrive at a conclusion on
this point, it is obvious that the rise of industrial society can be accompanied by either "liberal" or "nonliberal" forms, as long as both result in
secularization in the three spheres of science, technology, and the econ-

omy. But this mere affirmation leaves unanswered some of the major questions related to the conditions that determine the appearance of one form or the other, the stability of each one, the comparative cost of the various forms of development, and their consequences for the other aspects of society.

In each of the sectors indicated (science, technology, economy), the process of secularization should be extended to all levels: the normative level and the motivational level (or that of personality). In other words, the attitudes corresponding to the new normative framework of the secularized society must be internalized and the new personality types suited to this sort of structure must emerge. This has often been pointed out in the emergence of managerial attitudes and, in more advanced stages, "general" motivations adapted to industrial work and to the capacity of responding to the particular incentives of this work.

This section has attempted to define the minimum requirements for the existence and maintenance of any industrial society. In the remainder of this chapter a series of other changes usually associated with secularization will be described. Their degree of universality, however, is open to discussion except when they are relevant to the three main fields of science, technology, and economy. These are the forces which make for growing homogenization of industrial society. But against these factors there are opposing trends favoring diversity, especially the differential rates and sequences in the component processes and the variations in social and cultural conditions at the beginning of and during the transition.

Impacts of Secularization on the Patterns of Social Relations and on Personality Types

Secularization usually involves an important change in behavior patterns: changes in forms of social relations and in personality types are the most relevant here.

In all typologies it is quite clear that industrial society tends to reveal a type of social relationship very distinct from that prevailing in traditional society. The well-known opposition between primary groups and secondary groups expresses this need for distinction. The first relationship is defined by Cooley by its intimate character, by its immediacy ("face to face" group), and by the "fusion of individualities" that results. To this "primary-secondary" dichotomy others can be added, all of them pointing to analogous phenomena: the opposition between the type of relation characterizing the family, the small local community or the work group, and the impersonal relations involved in the fulfillment of roles by persons who are totally interchangeable, in a way typical of bureaucratic organizations. In industrial society, primary ties do not and cannot disappear, since the human personality would not develop properly, and, once formed, would not remain integrated if it did not relate to primary groups. But these primary relationships tend to function at a level compatible with the functioning of the society. They cannot decrease below a certain minimal threshold, since, if they do, the individual and the society will suffer grave disorders. But industrial society must emphasize impersonal relations oriented toward the principle of the greatest efficiency, that what is important is the task, not the person. This instrumentalization has an insurmountable limit, since each person also needs recognition and needs an intimate circle in which he can develop and be supported. The fact is that the family may lose many functions and may decrease in number of component members, but it must persist as an intimate group and as the proper setting for the socialization of the child. This can be turned around, and in part opposes exigencies or functional requirements of the industrial society. It can easily be pointed out that it creates an important source of tensions and conflicts. The continuous formation of primary relations in a situation of interaction in small groups, although the origin of the interaction may be a relationship within a secondary group (for example a group of workers in a big factory), is well known. Remember the distinction, often exploited by a certain wing of industrial sociology, between formal relations (secondary ones) and informal relations (primary ones) in the work situation.

The dichotomies referred to have a convenient formulation in the pattern variables of Parsons. He treats concepts constructed within the theoretical context of a general theory, and for that reason are not directly transferrable to other contexts. But allowing for this reservation it seems clear that, inasmuch as they articulate and differentiate dimensions of what in the original dichotomies are undifferentiated monolithic conceptual blocs, they can be of extraordinary utility for the description of types of industrial and traditional social structure.

According to Parsons' formulation, in extremely simplified form, all social relations, categories or roles can be analyzed along five dimensions, each dimension represented by two opposing poles. These dimensions can be described in the following way.

Affectivity Versus Affective Neutrality

It can be presumed that in all social action the final aim is the attainment of a certain gratification. Nevertheless, each action can be seen as either immediately gratifying in its fulfillment or as merely instrumental for a future end. In this case the expression of "affect" is postponed and the action itself does not gratify affective attitudes. It should be noted that like all social action, it always presents multitudinous aspects. It is possible that a "neutrally affective" role (with respect to its own specific end) may offer certain gratifications in other ways. For example, one can work in order to obtain a salary which at the same time will be employed for the satisfaction of certain needs. The principle aim of work can be merely the necessity for salary (work is a means toward the salary), but one can find a certain satisfaction in the task itself. That is to say, the same action on the one hand is affectively neutral, while on the other hand it is affectively loaded — it gives expression, for example, to a "calling" or vocation.

Particularism Versus Universalism

The relative expectations of a determined role can be defined in such a way that they may refer to a particular person, in specific and untransferable form, or to any member of a category of defined persons in agreement with determined criteria. For example, the mother-son relation or the relation between friends are particularistic, since the two people included in the relation have to be two specifically determined persons, and if either of them should change, the relationship itself would disappear. It is true that all the norms that regulate the above-mentioned relations are expressed in general terms (for example, "honor thy father and thy mother"), but these terms state only the particular obligations of all who fall in that role classification. If instead the norm stated, "honor all mothers for the fact of being mothers," then it would be a question of a relation of a universal type. An example is the merchant-customer relation.

Diffusion Versus Specificity

A relationship may cover only specific aspects and be extremely specialized in its content, or it may cover a very broad, barely defined area. For example, the relationship regulated by a contract is exceedingly precise: obligations and rights are clearly delimited so that the contract regulates only the sphere covered and defined in it. But there are other types of relationships in which such limitations or specificity do not exist. Thus the limits of friendship are in general diffuse (although at times one can have limited friendships for a specific interest, for example to play chess). Familial roles are equally diffuse (formal legal definitions, for example, cover only a small area of the expectations that according to custom are assigned to these relations). In reality limits are very difficult to establish (recall, for example, the mother-son relation, and the difficulty of fixing limits in the reciprocal obligations and rights between friends).

Ascription Versus Achievement

This distinction refers to the well-known dichotomy of ascribed versus achieved status (and roles). The first is attributed to persons by virtue of what they are, by their nonelective attributes, for example by their sex (men or women), age (child, adolescent, elderly person), or their ancestry (caste, inheritance). The second expresses what they succeed in doing, their accomplishments. For example, whoever passes certain examinations will achieve the status of doctor. We must make clear that ascribed status can be classified in two categories: of the classificatory type, when status is ascribed for possession of features determined through birth; or of the relational type, when status is ascribed by virtue of entrance into a determined relation with a group or person, for example, the in-law relation in marriage.

In Parson's formulation, there appears also a fifth pair of concepts: "Orientation toward private interests versus orientation toward collective interests," which is less relevant to the present purpose.

It is possible to classify the different social structures utilizing these concepts. In the typology employed in this exposition the two types of societies, "traditional" and "industrial," are characterized by the predominance of certain types of roles according to the preceding distinction. In the traditional society, ascriptive, diffuse, particularistic, and affective roles prevail; roles of a universal type in industrial society are differentiated and acquire great importance — achieved, universalistic, specialized and affectively neutral roles. Nevertheless, there are certain sectors of the structure (i.e. the family) in which roles of a primary type (ascriptive) continue to predominate. The different parts of a social structure can require different types of organization which necessarily accentuate determined types of roles, among those possible according to the previous classification. Thus the kinship group and the family are characterized by ascription, particularism, diffusion, and the affective weight of the relationship and by the fact that among its members the interest of the group prevails over and above that of the individual. And these characteristics of the family group are bound up with functions that it itself must fulfill, in a way that will remain the same in any type of global society. On the other hand, activities directed toward the material maintenance of the society where consideration of efficacy and the fulfillment of the task are essential, always require a structure in which they have, one way or another, the principles of achievement, universalism, specificity and neuturality.

It might be convenient to reiterate an observation of central importance related to the dichotomous typology employed. Both its poles, traditional and industrial society, possess an extremely high level of abstraction and generality. It would be necessary to make successive distinctions within each one so as to arrive at an adequate taxonomy of types of societies, based on valid theoretical principles, that would allow the multiplicity of existent empirical types. In the case of industrial societies, the fact that other very distinct models were added to the historical model offered by Western Europe poses the need of a theoretical system on which to base comparisons. Parsons, utilizing his "pattern variables," has suggested a classification of this type, but it is necessary to add that, with the exception of the "ascription-particularism" and "achievement-universalism" forms, the rest do not seem convincing with regard to their applicability to other historical forms of industrial societies. Let us momentarily turn aside from this problem. Besides, the fact that the industrial structure tends to superimpose a variety of cultures, each with its own peculiarities, implies the necessity of reckoning with the principia media that assures the applicability of abstract models in changing historical situations.

The transition toward industrial society creates, and makes its prerequisite, new types of personality. Societies in which prescriptive action and particularistic and diffuse roles predominate will have a more distinct personality type than an "elective" structure, with universalistic, specific and affectively neutral roles. Here again there are numerous typologies that in one way or another relate to this problem (although frequently in very different contexts). We can therefore speak of a "traditional" type whose mental structure and orientation is dominated by the internalization of norms of a prescriptive type, and the two types formulated by Riesman, "inner-directed" and "outer-directed," which would correspond to two stages of transition toward industrial society, according to the Western model. The first is characterized by its orientation toward a certain system of internalized goals, which allows self-guidance, self-made decisions, and the absence of prescribed courses of action characteristic of the traditional type. This is "gyroscopic" personality would be succeeded, in the most recent stage of industrial society (what C. Wright Mills calls the "overdeveloped society"), by the "radar" personality, in which there also persists action of an "elective" character, but whose guide would be "the others." Here the need to be guided by others would be internalized. "Adjustment" and the tendency to conform would not spring from the fulfillment of prescriptive norms but would emerge from "a special sensitivity toward the actions of others." This is what Riesman calls the "radar personality" existing in the era of "human relations," of psychotherapy, of "adjustment." This typology has been cited as an illustration; its application is dubious, without further comparison with other social structures within the general type of the industrial society or with other cultures, as well as with the same type of structure. Nonetheless there are certain features that seem peculiar to developments in industrial society.

In treating these typologies it is undoubtedly necessary to bear in mind the fact of internal differentiation of all society, the fact that the different groups which integrate society possess different types of personality and that, because of the asynchronous character of change, types corresponding to different stages will coexist.

Secularization and the Stratification Systems

The development of an advanced economy imposes at least two requirements essential to the stratification system. In the first place, just as the division of labor is subjected to the principle of efficiency, traditional types of stratification also undergo substantial change. A great number of obsolete offices and occupations disappear, while a growing number of new activities arise. In the second place, the assignment of people to different tasks which in most underdeveloped societies tends to be based on the ascription system must now be substantially transformed to an achievement basis. In other words, the stratification system must assure greater social and ecological mobility so that the recruitment of personnel for different positions in the occupational structure is governed by the principle of efficiency, rather than by other considerations such as family, religion or ethnicity. It is for this reason that a relatively open class structure must be considered one of the requirements, or a basic condition for, the functioning of an advanced economy. It is known that the degree of social and ecological mobility in developed society is still very far from the theoretically possible maximum of strict equality of opportunity and access to all positions according to the principle of efficiency. There are certain obstacles in all known societies to the attainment of maximum social mobility, that is, the principle of maximum instrumental rationality in the assignment of people to different functions and tasks. It is a debatable question whether such obstacles represent a universal characteristic of all society or are merely features observed in all historical societies up to the present, but not necessarily linked to all types of social structures (in other words, the obstacles may disappear in some future type). In any case, the present existence of such obstacles indicates a limit to the process of secularization in the sector of social stratification. It has been noted that this limitation is bound up with other functional requirements, for example the necessity of maintaining family institutions.

In spite of these limitations, however, and regardless of the economic and political forms assumed in the modernization process, societies reaching a certain level are preoccupied with establishing normative mechanisms which, without modifying the stratification system, tend to compensate partially for the obstacles limiting the rational selection of personnel, especially for scientific and technical tasks. Thus, in the early phases of developing societies, the need for universal primary education was proclaimed, followed by its extension to the secondary level and by the establishment of other educational reforms capable of rationalizing the recruitment system. It is important to observe that if, on the one hand, this was the result of the greater cultural and political participation of the popular classes, it also was and is a response to the need for a maximum use of human resources. This tendency, however, could coexist with a contradictory phenomenon: the growing numerical limitation and inaccessibility of the highest levels of the class structure (especially in the so-called "power elite"). In this case, greater mobility and a rational distribution of personnel would take place solely in the lower and middle levels, while an opposite tendency would appear at the top of the structure.

Extensive secularization of the stratification system must be considered a later process. In fact, according to some widely known theories, what is needed to initiate the process of modernization is some kind of partially blocked upward or downward mobility, some type of status deprivation. This may be considered a form of mobility not fully accepted, or fully legitimized in terms of the still predominant values and norms of the society, that is noninstitutionalized or de facto mobility. Such a situation is likely to cause the displacement of a group, to mobilize it against the status quo and eventually to transform it into a modernizing elite. In contrast with this process of noninstitutionalized mobility, the mobility required for the smooth functioning of a mature industrial society must be fully institutionalized. A certain degree of complete mobility (mobility in all dimensions of the stratification system) should be normatively expected (within the structural limits indicated in the previous discussion). Such institutionalized mobility is then a requirement for the stability of any industrial social system, even if the various types of industral society offer different solutions for this general requirement. A related secondary process is the rising aspirations of the lower strata who everywhere tend to achieve in practice the equalitarian principles somewhat implicit in industrial society. Along with other aspects, this process gives rise on the one hand to the protest movements characteristic of industrialization, while on the other hand it becomes a powerful factor for further change in the social structure. In one way or another it leads to actual increase in the participation of the traditionally excluded sectors.

The great variations in rates and sequences of the various processes composing the transition may generate widely divergent patterns in the stratification system of industrial society. Taking as a reference the Western experience, it may be said that in these presently advanced countries both structural and psychosocial changes tended to follow the more mature stages of economic development. The spread of rising aspirations among the great majority of the individuals belonging to the lower strata was more gradual, and tended to keep pace with the actual structural transformation of the stratification system, especially with changes in its profile (as with the expansion of the middle strata) and the institutionalization of mobility. In presently developing countries, other types of sequences may occur. In the more common case, attitudinal changes, the so-called "revolution of rising expectations", are taking place at a much less advanced stage of economic development, and the rate of the mobilization process is much higher than in the Western case. This means that new attitudes are created without existing counterparts in the occupational structure, the stratification system, the actual rate of mobility (and most often its legitimation), the level of consumption and other forms of participation in the modern type of life. As is well known, this situation turns the "rising expectations" into "rising frustrations." In the Western experience, widespread social unrest and deep social conflict accompanied the extension of participation (in its various forms), but the integration of the emerging sectors of the population was able to take place through gradual reform because the structural changes produced by economic development permitted a relatively easier absorption of the conflicts. It must be noted that not all differences can be imputed to the higher rate of mobilization of the larger strata and the ensuing social pressure "from below." Other significant factors intervene to turn such potential pressure into a powerful means for drastic social change: the type of available elites and their attitudes, the types of predominant ideologies, the existence of various and contrasting models for development, and the peripheral and often subordinated position of the developing countries.

A different type of sequence, less common than the one just described, involves structural changes in the stratification system very similar to those in advanced societies, but which is based on a less developed economic structure or, more precisely, an "economic expansion" as distinguished from economic development proper. This "modernizing effect" is possible in relatively rich countries with a medium level of per capita income, where the rate of urbanization, the degree of bureaucratization, and the growth of a modern service sector, especially education, have been higher than the rate of industrial growth proper and have taken place at less advanced stages of economic development (compared to the Western model). The considerable expansion of the urban middle strata is likely to cause sociological and psychosocial consequences very similar to those observed in fully advanced societies. However, when the society lacks the corresponding economic structure, this type of "premature" modernization of the stratification system has given rise to serious obstacles to further development. This is the case of some of the relatively developed but stagnant Latin American countries such as Argentina and Uruguay.

Secularization and Political Organization

Only two aspects of this complex question have been selected for the present discussion. The first concerns the rational organization of the state as one of the necessary conditions of development, the well known formulation of Max Weber and others. The experience of recent decades suggests the possibility of certain significant variations in the forms in which rationalization takes place. In the countries most advanced in the process, the type of administrative and political organization tended to be rationalized to the maximum. At the same time, the type of authority assumed this same form, with traditional and charismatic components diminishing considerably. In countries where change began much later, however, the organization of the state acquired a rationalized form while the type of authority, particularly on the highest levels, assumed nonrational forms.

It is possible that this phenomenon is related to the particular necessities of normative integration found in countries undergoing a very rapid process of secularization: in these cases, the loyalty to the national state and its symbolic personification reach the necessary intensity only if accompanied by forms of charismatic authority. It is probable, moreover, that this phenomenon is related to the general tendency towards centralization. Thus those countries would pass almost without transition from what we can call traditional centralization to the newest forms of concentration of power which are linked to advanced forms of technical and economic development.

The second aspect concerns the degree of participation of the popular strata in political institutions. Although there are also striking differences between advanced and developing countries, in both, the degree of participation indicated above is much higher than that usually observed in traditional society. It is difficult to distinguish whether this experience in participation constitutes a necessary condition of development, or whether it is an implication (an inevitable consequence) of this. At any rate, whatever the political form assumed the position of the popular strata in developed societies varies substantially with secularization, as it has been defined here. This increase in participation is undoubtedly a result of changes in social stratification, but it is also part of the rupture of the limits of the local community and the transfer of loyalties to the national community. The extension of political participation is a secondary process and here again one may observe that it is taking place at a different rate and in a different sequence with regard to the stages of economic development in presently developing countries, as compared to the past experience of more advanced ones. The pattern is the same as was noted with regard to the stratification system: an acceleration of the growth of political participation involving an inversion of the sequence between economic development and this partial process of social modernization.

Secularization and the Family

Some degree of secularization in familial relations constitutes a necessary condition of development. It is well known that the scope of primary relations (like those that characterize the family) should be kept to a minimum to allow for the secondary type of relations required by the institutions peculiar to a developed society. Primary relations, as opposed to secondary relations, are diffuse, affectively charged, particularistic, and governed by ascription; secondary relations, however, are characterized as specific, affectively neutral, universalistic, and based on achievement. Solely by accentuating this second type of relation will it be possible to achieve an extreme specialization of functions and institutions and, at the same time, the optimum allocation of personnel on the basis of efficiency. Consequently, the sphere for the application of kinship relations is reduced to the minimum, as are all types of extended family relations. It has been pointed out that this is a source of tension implicit in the very nature of industrial society and perhaps a possible intrinsic limit to secularization. Indeed, the permanence of primary type groups (and especially of an institution like the family) is often considered a functional and universal requirement in the sense that it discharges functions that can only be accomplished in structures of this type (as the socialization of the child and the creation of an intimate group for the sustenance of the adult personality). The whole of the social structure, especially the stratification system, is affected by this limitation. The impersonal milieu created by the predominance of secondary relations emphasizes the necessity of the continuous formation of primary groups; thus, for example, small groups defined by secondary relations (as work groups) tend to become transformed into primary ones if the interaction is prolonged. The kinship group itself, extended beyond the bounds of the nuclear family, never disappears. On the contrary it tends to remain at least as a preferred field of recruitment for spontaneous primary groups.

Up to now, we have dealt with the necessary reduction in the operative limits of primary relations to the isolated nuclear family and spontaneous primary groups. Another consequence is that substantial modifications occur in many aspects of the primary relations themselves. Without losing their primary character, they acquire characteristics differing from those they held or were given in traditional society. In particular, interpersonal relations within the nuclear family tend to be more egalitarian, as there is greater participation by all members in the group's different activities, as well as greater access to the decisions of the group, and as the stability of the group itself becomes based more on volition than on mechanically applied normative prescriptions. One of the most important phemomena of this whole process, one that can be taken as a general measurement of levels of secularization, is birth control, that is, the introduction of deliberate instrumental rationality into one of the most intimate spheres of human life. It appears fairly clear that all these results are nothing but an extension of the principle of elective action to larger areas of behavior.

This process is characterized by its emphasis on new values, particularly in the affirmation of the indivdual and his full development. This is a field dominated by ideological controversies and it is here that the most resistance arises. It is also a question open to scientific debate as to whether these results are rigidly determined by changes in social organization required by development, or whether there exist certain structural alternatives that, on the one hand, assure the minimal conditions of development, and, on the other, maintain traditional forms in these areas of behavior.

Various authors have criticized the hypothesis of a close correlation between the type of industrial structure and the predominance of the nuclear family. While a functional alternative of this type of family may exist in developing societies, there are examples of nonindustrial societies with nuclear families of the Western type. The hypothesis has been advanced that suggests that a great degree of indeterminancy between the family structure and other parts of the social structure exists, and especially that a wider range of compatibility between the industrial structure and family type is possible. Therefore, the diffusion of the nuclear family in Western developed societies would be rather a historical coincidence: those countries were characterized before the transition to such a family type, rather than developing it as a consequence of the transition itself. This historical coincidence, moreover, can also be interpreted in another sense. Inverting the causal relation between the industrial structure and the nuclear family, we could consider the existence of this type of family as one of the preconditions facilitating the rise of industrial society (emphasizing the value of the individual and diminishing the scope of ascriptive relations.

These and other criticisms of the hypothesis of a close functional relation between the isolated nuclear family and the industrial structure are, of course, of great importance and should be kept in mind: however, they do not seem to support the contrary hypothesis of an almost complete indeterminancy or absence of correlation between the two. Rather, in many cases, the facts can be interpreted in accordance with the hypothesis. Japan is a good illustration, often cited as the classic case of the permanence of the traditional family despite its advanced level of technical economic development. In that country, the divorce rate appears to diminish instead of increase with the advance of industrialization; at the same time, the divorce rate in rural areas is higher than that in urban areas. Thus, in Japan we find correlations that are exactly the opposite of those established in Western countries. But rather than negating the hypothesis of the interdependence between the nuclear family and the industrial structure this could be interpreted, on the basis of a more detailed examination of the data, as a confirmation of the hypothesis. Such is the conclusion of some of those conducting research on this topic. The "starting point" in the case of Japan "was a society in which lineage and not matrimony was sacred." Divorce was permitted and the divorce rate was high. But it was a different type of divorce from that of the West. It was rather a "traditional" type of divorce, determined by the family group, and exercised essentially in favor of this group and its continuity (for example, the repudiation of a sterile woman). Industrialization and urbanization weakened this type of family and the ideas that sustained it. The individual began to emerge from the kinship group and marriage began to be seen as an individual affair. Consequently, the decline of the divorce rate should be seen as a symptom of the weakening of the traditional structure. On the other hand, the authors could distinguish another type of divorce, of a Western variety, based on the individual decisions of the partners. This type of divorce, an expression of the nuclear family that was emerging in the transition toward a more advanced industrial structure, was increasing. In other words, the total divorce rate represented a balance between two opposing tendencies: a decrease in "traditional" divorce and an increase in "modern" divorce. Concomitant with this process, an inversion was observed, i.e. a higher rate of divorce in urban areas.

The Japanese example is sufficiently illustrative of the type of modifications (or better, specifications) that should be introduced in the generic hypothesis of correlation between "modern" family type and industrial structure. The basic characteristic is the introduction of a normative system of the "elective" type in relations previously of a prescriptive nature. But the particular forms of the transition depend on the preexistent traditional structure, and it is probable that the family type that emerges is considerably influenced by such a structure. In particular, it is possible that the rapidity of the transition, as much as the degree of the extension of "election" in the field of familial relations, can vary widely.

Secularization, Growing Participation and National Identity

If the local community constitutes the territorial base for the traditional society (and for the great majority of the people, including preindustrial historical societies, this is the case, as the rural population is physically and psychologically anchored to a piece of land), in the industrial society this typical base is the nation. The process of the formation of nationalities in the West is too well known to require more than a mere allusion. What is being noted here are two circumstances: in the first place, the replacement of the local community and the corresponding transference of loyalties is part of the process of growing participation characteristic of the industrial society; in the second place, the rupture of the local community and the emergence of the nation takes place violently throughout the world, so that now, with the rapid disappearance of the last colonial territories, the "sovereign" state organization is practically universal. However, this process is not only disturbed by the great unevenness in the development of the various countries (and the persistence of their dependence on the advanced countries) but also, more importantly, by the fact that it becomes mature through the national state (with its normative aspects, values, ideologies, and corresponding attitudes) precisely at the moment in which this organization is ceasing to correspond to the requirements of a world in which distance has disappeared, and interdependence is total. The rise and universalization of the nation-state occur in conflict with the rising of a universal system of highly stratified power. All this happens, moreover, amid conflicts between hegemonic countries contending for domination of the world.

One of the traits of development is its expansive character: it implies permanent change, technological progress, and the continued advance of the "frontier" from the geographic point of view as well as the social. Because the process is ongoing, every region and marginal group will be included in the new form of civilization. Perhaps as a repercussion of other changes in the social structure, for example, demographic or other changes, or through mass communication, the equilibrium of the old society breaks down and disappears. People are set in psychological and physical motion. Great international and internal migrations occur. The peopling of the Americas reflects this phenomenon. And the great rural-urban migrations which have acquired so much importance have the same meaning. The incorporation of marginal groups comes about in two ways: by the geographic diffusion of the new way of life, the new technology and new economic forms; and by the concentration of people in those areas which have reached a high level of modernization: emigration to the most developed countries, migration from the country to the city and internal migrations to the most advanced areas. These migrations also imply upward social mobility. They are accompanied by changes in the system of social stratification, especially expansion of the middle strata and the extraordinary growth of new occupational roles. Educational benefits are extended to more and more people, and finally, in keeping with improvements in the new living standard, the patterns of consumption previously reserved by the middle class are diffused to continuously increasing sectors of the population.

The small local community, which for a thousand years was the major concrete reality for an enormous majority of the planet's inhabitants, disappears. It is absorbed in global society, in the multitude of secondary relations that each individual is called upon to accept by virtue of the multiplicity of roles assigned to him. These relations, including those with "primary" groups, supposedly based on "face to face" relations, no longer need physical proximity to persist. Sound, light and people can move with sufficient rapidity and facility; as a consequence, the nation of "physical proximity" changes completely in sociological significance. The psychological preeminence of the small community was once fundamental since groups essential for the life of the individual coincided with it: family, kinship group, friendships, in the first place, and occupation and other activity groups. But now these are not confined to a single geographical location: the minimal unit is the nation. And the "location" of an individual is in an "occupational network" covering the country, and perhaps several countries. Of course it is still not so easy to emigrate from one's own country or city; but the mobility of the population is extraordinarily greater than it was in the past. And except in the lagging marginal areas, where traditional ties prevail, there is almost no bond that can resist the strain of an individual's need to find work or advancement.

In the Western countries this rupture with the local community, and the emergence in its place of a new psychologically significant territorial unity, first occurred among the strata that were the carriers of the new forms of life in the nascent bourgeoisie. Frequently this took place by the transference of the old persona loyalty (for example, to the monarch) to an impersonal loyalty (the nation). What is interesting here is that this transference produced not only the need for mobility typical of industrial civilization, but also the claim of the new strata to full participation in political power. The sentiment of nationality is bound up here with citizenship. One belongs to the nation, has rights and obligations toward it: one is a citizen of a nation. This leads to an important conclusion: the feeling of belonging to the nation and the transference of loyalties are produced simultaneously with complete forms of participation and with the claim and then the effective practice of political participation.

In the marginal groups, which at the beginning of the process are the great numerical majority of the population, a similar process occurs. The popular strata acquire national loyalty, a feeling of identification with the nation, insofar as they participate, and the process involves them not only as mere instruments but as citizens.

The political evolution of the European popular classes clearly demonstrates this. It shows that the internationalism of the leftist movements which could be a coherent ideological expression for the elite was, for the mass, an expression of protest against that national society which rejected them while recognizing as its only and real citizens its most privileged members: the nascent middle classes and the bourgeoisie. Insofar as the movement of participation proceeds, the popular strata acquire sentiments of national identification, and the internationalism of the left tends to become transformed.

In undeveloped countries and others where the transition was initiated much later, the feeling of nationality becomes the most powerful of the "ideologies of development," replacing the Protestant ethic and other attitudes that historically accompany and promote the beginnings of the transition in the Western countries.

If we now recall the particular structure of the industrial society, and the fact that the institutionalization of change, elective action, and the growing specialization of institutions introduce certain internal tensions and make it necessary to maintain common values as a minimum base for integration, we may understand the other basic components involved in the emergence of the nation.

This nucleus of common values is gained through national identification. Nevertheless, it is proper to distinguish the difference between countries that are advanced in the process and those that are presently undergoing it. In the West, the transition was both preceded and accompanied by a value system especially suited to an industrial society: the affirmation of the individual and his autonomy, the primacy of reason, the emphasis on liberty and equality. The principle of nationality grew coherently out of such values. In "progressive" political thought of the past century, for example, there was no general opposition between the sentiment and the affirmation of nationality on one side and these values on the other. This implies that the normative nexus and the community of values necessary to sustain the bases of a pluralist society ere not only identified with a given nation, but also with this complex of values. The emergence of new nationalities and the violent acquisition of national identification on the part of the people and groups moving without transition from small local community to national community have given a distinct content to contempoary nationalism.

Secularization and the Demographic Transition

One typical symptom of transition is demographic change. According to the well-known model, traditional society is characterized by "high demographic potential," and high birth and mortality rates; there is later a phase of transition in which first, mortality rates decrease, and then, after a varying lag (several decades), birth rates begin to diminish. Finally, in the most advanced stage, birth rates tend to stabilize (or in times of prosperity to grow again) while the mortality rate continues to decrease, although only to a certain limit. This final phase has been termed "low demographic potential." This scheme is so symptomatic of all other processes bound up with the transition from traditional to industrial society that some writers, like Riesman, have used it as a point of reference in describing other changes in the field of personality and attitudes. As is well known, this transition is tightly bound to the extension and improvement of sanitary methods and knowledge, and a general rise in the living standard, all of which reduce mortality, especially infant mortality, and spectacularly prolong life expectancy. Decline in birth rate is an expression of the elective action in family life, leading to planned parenthood. Given the asynchronous character of change, transformations in the demographic order occur with different rhythms and in different groups of the same society. If in the primary phase of "high demographic potential" there doesn't seem to be marked difference in birth and death rates between urban and rural areas, or between groups of different socioeconomic levels (although there can be a direct correlation between number of surviving offspring and social position, it is not very pronounced), in the transitional phase there appears a typical series of very marked differences which are symptomatic of the degree of development reached by each group and each zone or region within the country itself, or of each country in an international context.

First to reduce mortality, and then birth rates, are the countries, zones, and groups most advanced in the transition: Western European countries are thus the most advanced in the process, and within them the urban middle classes, followed by the urban workers and then the inhabitants of rural zones. The phase of transition is marked here by differential birth rates (and mortality): (1) inversely correlated with the socioeconomic level (more birth in the lower classes); (2) inversely correlated with the urban character (more birth in rural zones); (3) inversely correlated with the degree of development (more birth in less developed countries).

This transition also produces substantial changes in the age composition of the population, with all of its repercussions in other parts of the structure. The number of children and adolescents diminishes proportionately and at the same time the number of aged increases. The age pyramid which in traditional structures has a wide base tends to change form, restricting the base and increasing the central part (double inverted cone). The increase in the proportion of the aged begins a series of new problems in a context which lacks not only material facilities but also an adequate normative framework. The role of the aged is uncertain in a society of isolated nuclear families. The normative vacuum creates the need to respond imaginatively to the situation in replacing outmoded traditions.

The different rhythms and sequences of demographic transition in presently less developed countries, compared to those which entered the process in the last century or before, may place them in a very special situation. According to some, here is where we will find one of the most serious obstacles to economic development.

A phenomenon in old industralized countries which is widely known but bears mentioning, is that the lowering of the mortality rate precedes by a considerable period the lowering of the birth rate. Consequently, before the industrial revolution, births and deaths tended to be stable (with a small excess of births); after the change, the vegetative balance becomes greater, and the population begins an extraordinary increase, unprecedented in human history. The European population that reached around one hundred million is 1650 was almost two hundred million in 1800, and more than six hundred million in 1950. That is, the population which had remained stationary for centuries exploded, with the beginning of modern science, technology, and economics.

What happened in Europe between the nineteenth and twentieth centuries is now happening elsewhere. But while in England, for example, the lowering of the mortality rate was relatively slow (around 1700 the crude rate was twenty to one thousand, in 1850 it was twenty-two out of a thousand, and eleven out of a thousand in the next century), in countries which are only now entering transition, the application of preventive sanitary means, and other factors, produce a rapid and spectacularly drastic reduction of mortality rates. But while other changes in the social structure have not yet occurred — for example, there is no industralization, and a great many institutions and attitudes follow traditional patterns — the other side of the relationship, the birth rate, grows higher. We would say "highest" judging by Europe, where, including the epoch prior to the industrial revolution, it was less than thirty-five per thousand, whereas in many of today's underdeveloped countries it reaches as high as fifty per thousand. The result is that the population of these countries grows with a much greater rhythm. Consequently, the possibility of economic development probably rests on a higher rate of inversion. In effect, to the increase of inversion necessary to expand the economy there will have to be added another increment proportional to the growth of the population (what some call demographic inversion), and this is meant simply to maintain at least the same level of capitalization per inhabitant. Age composition, particularly in the primary phase, also shows negative aspects owing to a lower proportion of the population of work age.

Aside from the differences noted between countries of early and late industrialization, it should be remembered that both the peculiarities in each culture and the divergent forms presented by transition considerably influence demographic change. Generally all societies tend to regulate the demographic equilibrium in some ways. The substantial difference between preindustrial and industrial societies consists of the fact that in the former, regulation occurs through prescriptive mechanisms, while in the latter the normative pattern becomes elective and assumes the form of individual control of births. But certain features of the structure can project a very great influence on the speed as well as on the forms of transition. Here family organization assumes a central role; for example, the birth rate changes in Western countries might seem to be facilitated by the type of family prior to transition, while in other countries of late development, different forms of familial organization can retard (although it is doubtful that they can impede) individual control of births.

Recently, different criticisms of the model of demographic transition have been advanced. It has been pointed out that in certain cases in Europe the primary effects of transition produced an increase, not a decline, in the birth rates, because of the breakdown of those traditional mechanisms which contributed to keeping the birth rate at a lower level. Also, in relation to the decline in mortality, other hypotheses have been advanced about the particular form assumed in the Western countries. In Latin America itself, recent studies show the first impact of modernization has produced an increase in the birth rate. But this apparent deviation from the model of the demographic transition has been explained in terms of better sanitary conditions of the population and an increase in the duration of the life of the female, and therefore, an increase in the period of fertility. In any case it seems that the general model of demographic transition remains essentially unaltered. The criticisms cannot get beyond a simple, more detailed specification of the hypothesis itself.

Secularization in Other Aspects of the Social Structure

It has already been noted that education tends to spread to the whole population and that it becomes necessary to reduce the differences in educational opportunities caused by stratification.

Another essential condition is the change in educational content: a very great increment in scientific and technical instruction is required and, as is known, this requirement usually clashes with prestige values which are assigned in traditional societies to nontechnical forms of knowledge. This applies particularly to the humanistic form of upper-class education, but also to other attitudes and values, especially religious ones. The problem which must be resolved here is that of defining the limits of this transformation of educational content, and of determining to what degree it is possible to integrate the two types of education. This question is tightly bound up with the extension of secularization to other areas of knowledge besides those referred to as "natural." If indeed the rise of a natural science is a condition immediately linked to economic development, the extension of this type of knowledge to the sphere of human actions is probably another necessary condition, determined more by the transformation of the social organization and interpersonal relations than by economic development directly. The less direct character of this link and the fact that this sphere of knowledge is more impinged upon by the values of the traditional society can explain the greater resistances to the secularization of knowledge in the social sciences. At any rate, historically this process of secularization strictly accompanies economic development, and the advances in scientific sociology in particular in all countries in recent years has been universally recognized as an expression of this process.

According to the general principle of institutional specialization, those structures that in the past tended to encompass the whole society must now be circumscribed by well-defined specific functions. We have already seen that this is the case with respect to family organization and kinship groups; another illustration is religion. The importance of religion especially in the first stages of development (as much in a positive as in a negative sense) is well known and will not be dealt with here. We wish to point out, however, that as an essential condition of development, religion also acquires a specific sphere, i.e. it must be transformed into a specialized institution. This has a series of consequences on the other results (implications) of development, for example, on changes in the family, the position of women, education, science, individual values, etc.

The present discussion does not attempt to cover all the aspects of secularization but has been limited to a few, selected for their importance or as appropriate illustrations of the process.

5.

The Asynchronous Nature of Change

Asynchronism is a general feature of change and implies, in addition to the distinction between "parts" and "sectors," the simultaneous use of three dimensions: cultural, social, and motivational. The notion of underdevelopment emerges precisely because of geographic asynchrony, but it also extends to simultaneously implied multiple levels.

Geographic asynchrony. Development occurred at different times in various countries, and this very asynchronism may exist in different regions of the same country. The notion of underdeveloped country or region emerges from this fact (plus other assumptions not analyzed here, such as the conception of development as a necessary universal process). They will be distinguished thus: "central" and "peripheral" countries, and, within the same country, "central" and "peripheral" regions. It is precisely to this and similar types of asynchronism that the notion of the "dual society" refers.

Institutional asynchronism. Different institutions or groups of institutions experience changes associated with modernization and economic development with different velocity, so that institutions typical of different "phases" or "stages" coexist in a region or area (implicit notions include integration, adjustment, equilibrium and "correspondence" of parts).

Asynchronism of different social groups. Certain social groups are altered more rapidly than others; this produces analogous coexistence of groups corresponding to different phases. "Objective" (occupation, education, socioeconomic status) as well as "subjective" (attitudes, social character, social personality) characteristics of certain groups correspond to an "advanced" stage, while others correspond to a "backward" phase.

Motivational asynchronism. Not only is motivational asynchronism implied in the previous points (in relation to institutions and groups), but owing to the multi-sided role of an individual in different groups and institutions, asynchronism penetrates the individual mind. Attitudes, ideas, motivations and beliefs corresponding to successive "stages" of the process, coexist in his psyche. (Because of this, change is perceived and felt as "crisis," and corresponding ideologies may originate.)

The notion of asynchronism can be considered a commonly held assumption for most theories on social change. What is being pointed out here is the generalized character that should be assigned to this phenomenon, which should therefore not be conceived of as limited to geographic unevenness or to cultural lags among certain sectors of the culture ("dual" societies, material culture versus non-material culture or infrastructure versus superstructure). Rather it should be seen as embracing the total structure, and both the analytically separable dimensions of the sociocultural world (cultural, social, motivational) and its concretely isolable parts or sectors. To this general formulation we add only a few other observations.

In the first place, regarding geographic asynchronism and "backwardness," the different countries that initiate the process do not necessarily repeat the same phases or stages undergone elsewhere. This means that the present state of economic development and modernization in more advanced countries influences (or can influence), with differing scope and intensity, the process in less developed countries. From the methodological point of view, this implies the need for conceptual schemes taking into account the sociocultural features of the specific area treated and the present state of the process in more advanced countries insofar as they may exert an influence on the area in question. Obviously, all sociocultural phenomena are affected by the incidence of asynchronism on the one hand and local peculiarities on the other. Another complication is added by the fact that each "part" of the society may be affected in a distinctive way and with different intensity. The final observation refers to the degree of transferability of the diverse features of development, a problem which anthropology studies with special attention, but which is also taken up by economics, sociology and political science.

At the same time, I must also emphasize that the notion of asynchronism implies the notion of integration, in its two forms: integration by adjustment (at the normative and the psychosocial level) and value integration. The different velocity of change will produce, in effect, coexistence of partial structures "corresponding" to different global structural models (according to the current scheme, partial "modern" structures coexisting with "traditional" ones). Coexistence could be perceived in contrasting ways according to the point of view of the observer. What would be judged "disintegration" in relation to the traditional society would be judged as "modernization" from the point of view of the industrial society (for example, modernization in attitudes of women and youth, which conflict with the "patriarchal" authority of the husband and father). But it should be recognized that this simple interpretation of asynchronism is inadequate since it oversimplifies important and more complex aspects of the phenomenon.

Thus it must not be forgotten that the assignment of a partial structure to a specific model of society depends on the investigator, and his choice should be made on the basis of a theory concerning the "correspondence" of the given partial structures with other parts of the model. What should

be known are the minimal functional requisites necessary to the maintenance of the structures in question, or at least their degree of reciprocal
compatibility. But although there are some partial hypotheses, a general
theory applicable to "industrial society" does not exist.

On the other hand, the very notion of "different velocity of change"
should be further clarified. The existence of "adjustment" or "correspondence" between partial structures also supposes "interdependence," that is
to say, assumes that modification of partial structures will produce repercussions in those others in relation to which they were "adjusted" before
the occurrence of change. How can it be said, that despite a change in the
attitudes of women and youth, attitudes, expectations, and the fulfillment
of paternal and marital roles will remain unmodified? The hypothesis can
be formulated that, with an alteration of the situation (derived from
changes in the behavior of the other participants in the structure, deviating
from social roles that are normatively fixed and psychologically expected)
there will be a certain reaction (for example, intent to apply forcefully
prescriptive solutions by the existent norms). This "reaction," however,
will itself be a modification of husband and father behavior as expected in
the "ideal" roles normatively assigned to those statuses. The fulfillment of
such roles, therefore, is not invariant (faced with modernization of certain
participants), but the modification produced was not effected according to
the orientation adequate for attaining a new adjustment compatible with
the "modern" model. In other words, when one speaks of asynchronism
and more especially of "backwardness," what is indicated is not the
absence of change in the "lagging" parts, but rather that change is not
congruent with the assumed model. Only in completely isolated parts of
the structure is it possible to speak of immobility or "being static." Such
would be the case with disequilibrium between two geographic areas,
where there is no communication, or between social groups rigidly isolated
by caste and similar barriers. But these are limiting cases, which in the
present epoch, given the spread of communcations and the elimination of
geographic barriers and of ecological and social isolation, can be considered virtually nonexistent. Therefore the mere awareness of such backwardness, on the part of the backward group, implies an essential change
in the group itself, whatever form this recognition may assume (it may well
be violent rejection or servile imitation or, more likely, ambivalent attitudes).

What we have called coexistence of partial structures distinctly affected
by the process of change does not therefore imply a mere "contemporaneity of the noncontemporaneous." Instead it may involve a whole range
of situations whose variations may depend, among other things, on the
reaction of the backward sectors and on the forms of adjustment or rejection they may assume. The degree of communciation between the parts

and sectors of the social structure acquire a role of singular importance in this respect. The rise of an international system involves the extension of these phenomena of asynchronism to the entire planet.

The Demonstration Effect

There are two important phenomena that characterize asynchronism at a high level of communication and a rapid rhythm of change. There is on the one hand the "demonstration effect" and on the other the "fusion effect."

The "demonstration effect," according to the apt expression coined by J. Duesenberry, refers to the consumer in his propensity to consume and save as affected not only by the level of income, "but also by the difference between his income and the highest level of consumption of others with whom he may enter into contact." That is, knowledge of the existence of such a level produces similar aspirations, and this affects consumptton and savings. Savings tend to be reduced and almost disappear, with the modification of the relative position of the family in the income hierarchy, even in the case of an actual real income increase. The "demonstration effect" notion, inspired by the concept of "conspicuous consumption" formulated by Veblen, has been extended by Nurske from the realm of individual consumers to that of international relations: here the "demonstration effect" is generated by the knowledge that the less developed countries have of the standard of living reached in the most developed countries, and in the present epoch, to be precise, of the level reached by the United States. This includes countries that, by virtue of their social system, are at odds with that nation, but assume as a goal the standard of living in that country.

It has already been said that the mere recognition of underdevelopment, on the part of a group or a country, in itself implies the introduction of an essential factor for change. This is equivalent to extending the applicability of the notion of the "demonstration effect" from levels of consumption, from economic behavior, to many other aspects of the social structure: to forms of material and nonmaterial culture, to forms of social organization, to the degree of participation in a global society and its "most modern" expressions, to interpersonal relations, especially as the aforementioned aspects come to affect concretely the life of the common man. Therefore the "demonstration effect" is translated partially into modes, attitudes, aspirations, and partially into ideological expressions in politics, economics, labor relations, and many other areas. This does not imply neglect of the role of different and contrasting "ideologies of development" and opposite historical models of development. What should stand out clearly here is that the foundation of the goal is common, whereas what constitutes the essentials of the ideological conflict is the form for attaining it. Moreover, we cannot ignore the fact that certain structural forms of advanced industrial society tend to "look alike" despite their different historical development.

The "demonstration effect" not only affects those partial structures in the process of changing and rapidly becoming "more advanced," but also introduces modifications in those lagging behind. It doesn't seem possible to formulate more precise propositions on the nature of this influence, but it will be necessary to give some general outlines.

The most serious theoretical problem emerges from the psychological and ideological character of the "demonstration effect" and the causal role it can play in relation to nonphysical elements of the structure. In other words, we are confronting here the old problem involved in many theories on social change: hegemony of the "infrastructure" over "superstructure," of "material" over "nonmaterial" culture, of "real" over "ideal" factors, of the role of ideas in history and the like. My general assumption in this respect is that no priority whatsoever should be granted *a priori* to any "dimension," "level" or part of the social structure. At the same time it will be recognized that, depending on the concrete historical situation, different causal priorities may arise. This is equivalent to rejecting a general hypothesis about the ordering and weight of the different factors, and instead using hypotheses of the most limited applicability (to areas, types of structure, and determined periods) to be verified each time through investigation. It is not so much a question of "theories of the middle range" as with Merton, as much as of *principia media* (Mannheim) of historically limited validity. On the other hand, the use of these hypotheses or "historical laws" does not deny but rather requires the use of theories of the middle range applicable to a given sector of social facts with relative independence of their historical or geographical validity.

I must also mention the fact that the demonstration effect is conditioned by the circumstances in which contacts are verified and by the characteristics of the process of communication. Finally and decisively, an essential factor is given by what we may term conditions of receptivity on the part of groups subjected to its influence.

The Fusion Effect

The "fusion effect" is one of the phenomena produced in the confrontations between ideologies, attitudes, motivations originated in advanced societies and beliefs still operating in groups, countries or areas which are totally or partially backward. Frequently ideologies and attitudes corresponding to advanced processes of modernization, on reaching areas and groups still characterized by traditional features, do not disrupt this context but reinforce those traditional features, not in the name of the past structure, but as "very advanced" products. In other cases, although on the verbal level an ideology in no way tends to differ from the meaning assigned to it in originating zones and groups, its psychological significance in "backward" or "archaic" groups becomes strongly influenced by the traditional contents.

In the following paragraph I shall present some illustrations of the "fusion effect," between attitudes corresponding to an advanced stage of modernization and "archaic" attitudes in presently developing countries. In these illustrations I shall emphasize the fact that the "advanced" attitudes are themselves the result of a transformation of the society. In the earlier stages of the transition they were very different from the form assumed in later stages. It is, however, this more advanced expression which is diffused in the developing world (through the "demonstration effect"), and which combines with the surviving preindustrial attitudes through the operation of the "fusion effect."

In the first place I shall describe briefly some attitudes and traits characterizing the earlier stage of the transition in Western countries, and will compare them with modifications which emerged in the later stages of the process. Secondly I shall show some of the results of "fusion effects" of these more advanced traits, in their diffusion in presently modernizing countries.

Democracy with limited participation. The "rational" organization of the state and bureaucratic authority predominate (according to the Weberian formulation), accompanied by the formal rights regarding the liberty of the individual (particularly freedom of contract, work, movement and expression). However, actual participation in the life of the community is limited to certain social groups. This limitation embraces notably the political sphere (complete political rights reserved for the bourgeoisie) but also implies that the popular classes are not integrated in the new forms of the society.

The previously indicated fact also means that in these first stages only some groups are fully modernized (at the level corresponding to the period considered); other sectors, especially the popular classes, urban and rural, are still, at the cultural and motivational plane, in a "traditional" stage, whereas the economic process is transferring them to a more developed structure of production (urbanization and industrialization).

On the ideological and motivational planes, the group which is leading the process, the "bourgeoisie," possesses attitudes and ideas that not only powerfully shape its psychological impulse for the realization of its task, but also offer it the basis for legitimating its position and the conditions under which the transition occurs. These attitudes correspond to the so-called "capitalist" or "bourgeois" spirit, to the early entrepreneur type with all his charcteristics, including a specific Weltanschauung, a definition of achievement and goals, of obligations and rights (as seen in the Protestant ethic and in Riesman's inner-directed character). With regard to the legitimacy of its position and of its roles these are clearly the result not only of the political philosophy of the epoch, but of the prevailing great conceptions of the world (evolutionism, Darwinism) and in the economic field, in a very precise way, of the postulates of the classic economy.

This legitimacy not only possesses full strength for the ruling groups but it also accepted or passively supported by the popular groups. It is clearly true that while in this epoch all the great social protest movements are created, and ideologies emerge, which will seriously threaten this legitimacy, the great majority of individuals generally remain outside these movements. In reality, they are located outside the sociocultural context in which the conflict is set; they still belong, relative to this problem and in all the aspects of life (except in its economic function), to the "traditional society."

It is necessary to point out another important aspect of asynchronism in this period with regard to consumption attitudes. Though with regard to production the ruling group is fully modernized (dynamic character of industrial production), attitudes concerning consumption continue at the traditional level of a nonexpansive economy. This is clearly the situation among the popular classes, whose levels of aspiration are extremely low. As for the bourgeoisie, the limitation is produced through the mechanism of "capitalist ascesis" (the "deferred gratification pattern," the "abstinence" of the classical economists). As a result of such features (and in conjunction with other factors mentioned here, such as innovations in technology and foreign expansion), an unprecedented accumulation and extraordinary development of the economy was produced, with all its concomitants in the different spheres.

Successively, the previously explained conditions underwent a profound transformation, whose essential points we shall try to sum up.

Limited democracy is followed by progressive enlargement of participation leading to forms which we may term "total participation." This signifies not only the integration of the majority into political life and its inherent rights, but also a much greater participation of the popular classes in the urban-industrial culture (its "modernization"): its incorporation, objective and psychosocial, in the national society, its new habits of consumption, its new levels of aspiration, which also become expansive.

In addition to this, the new expansive character of consumption now requires new forms of production, and becomes predominant in the middle and upper classes. The "capitalist asceticism" is replaced by new attitudes which correspond, moreover, to the "new" organization which is assumed by the enterprise. The great corporation emerges and with it the "entrepreneur" is replaced by a human type, the "director," or the "manager."

Instead of Riesman's inner-directed man there is the outer-directed man; instead of emphasis on production there is emphasis on consumption.

State organization is transformed, and the same change of role which occurred in business affects the political parties, the unions, and other significant structures in modern life. New forms of social stratification appear; new occupations emerge which are the bearers of new attitudes. Universal bureaucratization leads to the "employee society."

The ideological climate, at the same time, experiences a substantial upset. On the one side, movements which questioned the legitimacy of the order postulated by classical economy are successful in creating new forms of state and economy in extensive regions (also creating new forms of legitimacy). On the other side, new equalitarian principles of "social justice" become commonly accepted by all social groups, and extensive legislation emerges which completely replaces the "free contract" of the previous epoch. This situation does not eliminate but has different effects on extremist ideologies which may continue battling to attain still more radical changes.

The nations most advanced in the process now exercise various forms of world hegemony. They not only provide "models" for the peoples of countries on the road to development, but also, by virtue of the international level of struggle, one way or another influence very deeply their structures, their internal groups and their transition.

Now let us describe the influences and repercussions of these phenomena in countries which have begun their economic development more recently. As was already indicated, these repercussions are inseparable from local conditions, so that here again I will use generalizations that somewhat distort reality.

In developing countries, the process of fundamental democratization is found already completed or very advanced. The significance (Mannheim) of politics for the popular classes of these countries is incomparably greater than for more advanced countries in the first stages of their economic transformation. This means that among the popular classes the level of aspirations with regard to consumption, living standard, working hours and social rights tends to approach those of presently developed countries. Though small changes in the standard of living may still produce positive effects on social consensus, such effects are likely to be exhausted more rapidly than in the past and must be replaced by new and more favorable improvements. That is, the process is speeding up.

Among the middle and upper classes, on the other hand, it will be impossible or very difficult to find attitudes similar to those prevailing in the stage of "capitalist ascesis"; here is a fact of great general significance. The new advanced attitudes of the stage of "emphasis on consumption" can become "fused" with the surviving ideals of the seigneurial life, the ideology of the upper classes in traditional society.

Due to circumstances mentioned before, in developing countries consumption attitudes corresponding to a developed economy coexist with an underdeveloped productive technology and organization.

Another field where the fusion of advanced stage attitudes and patterns of traditional society acquires great force is in the realm of political ideologies. Here the popular classes have incorporated the equalitarian thought, the aspiration to social rights, the criticism of the legitimacy of the capitalist order in developed countries, while they still strongly maintain the noneconomic attitudes of traditional society, into which the institutions of the industrial society have not penetrated. Thus the lack of legitimacy of capitalist values in a society still dominated by traditional ethical standards in economic life, is fused with modern "post-capitalist" ideologies favorable to socialist reforms of industrial society.

Among the ruling classes there is an analogous fusion between "noneconomic" traditional attitudes and recent influences of the extension of social rights and diffusion of equalitarian ideals. The "moral condemnation" which so frequently characterizes the traditional attitude about "economic" activity, becomes bound up here with connotations of the new ideological climate of the developed countries, where in more or less radical fashion there is the necessity to justify anew the economic institutions (and on grounds very different from those shaped by the ideologies of the nineteenth century).

The absence of legitimacy in underdeveloped countries can therefore affect not only the popular classes that reject the existing social order but also the ruling group with insecure legitimacy. A situation radically distinct from that of very advanced countries in the first stages of their development is thus presented. The extraordinary channeling of forces required at the beginning of the process is only possible through the coexistence of a minority absolutely sure of its legitimacy to rule and of the validity of its task with a mass that, despite protest movements, still has not questioned the validity of such a task. In this way the huge human sacrifices required by development may be implicitly justified. On the other hand, this occurred in countries currently advanced at an incomparably slower pace than is evident at present.

The dilemma synthesized in the foregoing points will become even more obvious if we recall how some countries, whose development began in this century or at the end of the last, have confronted it.

Japan and Russia are contrasting examples chosen from several possibilities. In Japan there was a traditional ruling class which took the initiative in transforming the prexistent structure with only such alteration as was strictly necessary. But once a sufficiently advanced state of development was reached, the question was open as to at what point this structure would be preserved. Actually the post-war years would seem to show that the diffusion of "modernization" cannot be contained or limited. The crisis of legitimacy will be posed, at an advanced stage, when the benefits of modernization are being effectively extended to the larger sectors of the population. But the case of Japan seems quite exceptional when the situation of presently underdeveloped countries is taken into account. In Russia the exigency of legitimacy and the motivational impulses necessary to a channelization of efforts were radically different from those of the developed nations of the West. If in the latter there was a "mystique of capitalism," in Russia a forceful "mystique of socialism" was employed; perhaps it would be more exact to say a mystique of the "socialist nation." Thus the high price of development was justified and the legitimacy of the ruling groups was maintained. Again, in this case, the new demands are increasing at a fairly advanced stage of economic development.

The ideological circumstances and politics of the majority of developing countries today could not be explained or understood without accounting for the above-stated facts. The emergence of multiple ideological currents, which put the emphasis on the "national" and the "popular," on "social justice" and the legitimacy required by the new circumstances in which development is realized, are intended to mobilize and channel the immense energies necessary to carry it out. Of course, the significance of such movements transcends the function just mentioned, since they are bound up with other changes within contemporary society, but there does not seem to be any doubt about the substitutive role they are destined to fulfill.

With the problem of legitimacy we get to one of the essential questions posed by economic development, relating to the type of political organization in which it should take place. Here we clearly have a problem of values, a choice that should be formulated explicitly, since the ensuing plans put into execution depend on it. The role of the social sciences is fundamental in this respect: the clarificatory function of "models" or "typologies" of development is sufficiently proven and needs no comment.

6.

The Total Transition

Economic Development, Social Modernization and Political Modernization

The theoretical problems posed by the asynchronous nature of change are not easily solved. It could be suggested, however, that by distinguishing, within the total process of transition, a series of component processes, the principle of asynchronism, or unevenness, could be introduced into the analysis. At the same time the distinction could prove fruitful in emphasizing some of the factors underlying the variety in the forms of transition. I will distinguish three main component processes: economic development, social modernization, and political modernization. These distinctions are currently employed, but the definitions implicitly or explicitly used are not always clear, and in any case are far from uniform among social scientists. For this reason some indication will be given of the meaning assigned to these distinctions in the present context.

Again, for the same analytic purposes each of the three main processes should be perceived of as composed of a series of partial processes. However, though mention will be made of some components, this series of distinctions will not be pursued further.

The main processes and their component subprocesses are interrelated as shown by the statistical correlations usually observed among them. But, as indicated in the discussion on asynchronism, such correlations are far from being perfect, and should be interpreted as no more than the expression of a tendency for certain indicators to be associated. What can be inferred from the historical experience is that the various subprocesses may occur at very different rates and may show different sequences among them. Differences at what may be considered the "point of departure" of the transition and in the various internal and international conditions under which the transition takes place may be responsible for such variations in rates and sequences.

Economic development and social and political modernization are defined here primarily as processes of structural change. The total transition is conceived as a cumulative process, into which at any given moment the results of its previous course become incorporated as determining factors in the future course of transition. In each process the definition is based on the application of the basic principles characterizing the "modern-industrial complex."

Economic development is tentatively defined as a structural transformation of the economy, by which the mechanisms functionally required for "self-sustained growth" are permanently incorporated into it. The ideal type of a developed economy may be characterized by the existence of a series of main traits:

a. the use of high energy and high efficiency technology in all branches of economic activities (including primary);
b. the existence of appropriate mechanisms (institutional and human resources) for the permanent creation and/or absorption of technological and organizational innovations. Such mechanisms should ensure the continuous rise of new dynamic sectors, to compensate for, or to replace those, whose dynamic role in the economy is decreasing, or which have reached their maximum possiblity;
c. the predominance of industrial over primary production;
d. a higher ratio of capital investment to national product;
e. high per capita productivity;
f. predominance of capital-intensive over labor-intensive activities;
g. higher independence (or less dependence) of the national economy on foreign trade (in terms of its proportion to GNP at given population levels), of its strategic importance to the maintenance of growth and its diversification as regards types of goods and number of countries and;
h. more equal distribution of GNP, both in terms of socio-occupational strata, sectorial activities and geographical areas.

The process of economic development is defined as the transition towards an empirical economic structure described by the traits mentioned in the above "ideal type."

One should distinguish between economic expansion and economic development. The first may be defined as a process of steady growth in per capita GNP over a relatively long period of time, which lacks some of the structural components of economic development enumerated in the preceding paragraph.

This does not mean that economic expansion does not involve structural change. In fact, it is also a process of structural change, but is not sufficient for "self-sustained" development. Economic expansion may (and such is indeed the more frequent case) take place on the basis of the modernization and expansion of some specialized primary production, its integration into the international market, and the accompanying commercial and financial expansion with all its further repercussions on the econmy and its "modernizing effects" in other sectors of the society. Economic expansion may eventually originate or be transformed into, a process of economic development. Perhaps it may constitute at least one of its preconditions. While there is no agreement in considering it a necessary precondition, it can be said with more certainty that is not a sufficient precondition. The reorientation of the economy and the introduction of the structural changes required for economic development cannot, in fact, be assumed to be automatically induced by a certain degree of economic expansion. Only under certain conditions may economic expansion become a step in the process of economic development.

The concept of political development is even more controversial than economic development. Perhaps three major traits may be singled out: first, the "rational organization of the state" (in Weberian terms), including high efficiency in performing the expanding and increasingly diversified, specialized and centralized functions of the state in an industrial society; second, the capacity of leading and absorbing structural changes in economic, political and social spheres, while maintaining a minimum of integration; and, third, some sort of political participation of all or the great majority of the adult population. Other components which are usually included may be conceived as consequences or aspects of the three traits enumerated. This is the case, for instance, of "nationhood" which could be conceived of as one aspect of total participation, or "stability," here subsumed under the capacity of absorbing and leading change, without disrupting the social system.

Finally social modernization is largely conceived of as a residual category, best illustrated (rather than defined) by a series of component processes:

a. the "social mobilization" of an increasing proportion of the population;[1]
b. urbanization, i.e. increasing demographic concentration in urban areas (often one of the most typical expressions of mobilization);
c. other demographic changes, such as decline in death and birth rate and subsequent changes in the age structure;
d. changes in the family structure and in the internal relations of the nuclear family, as well as with regard to kinship groups;
e. changes in the local community and especially its integration into the national community (as a social aspect of political participation);
f. changes in communications;
g. changes in the stratification system: modification of the stratification profile (first a reduction of the traditional intermediate strata, then an expansion of the modern middle strata), modification of the nature of the cleavages between strata with the final emergence of a "stratification continuum", increase in "exchange" mobility, increase in "structural" (transitional) mobility, emergence of a form of permanent mobility "by growing participation" (based on a mechanism of "self-sustained mobility" consisting of the continuous occupational upgrading and the continuous transference of status symbols from top to bottom);
h. changes in the scope and forms of participation, particularly extension of civil and social rights to the lower strata (similar to the extension of political participation);
i. extension of modern forms of consumption to the same groups, extension of education and the resulting extension of feelings of participation and increasing identification with the community;

j. other important changes in such institutions as church, voluntary associations and forms of leisure; decrease in differentials (demographic, economic, sociocultural) between strata, social groups, rural-urban, and regions (while decrease in differentials may affect the great bulk of the population, some higher cleavage may still persist or even increase at the top of the society, especially with the concentration of power, or at least certain forms of power).[2]

The distinctive trait of modern society is the permanent incorporation of appropriate mechanisms to originate and to absorb a continuous flow of change, while maintaining an appropriate degree of integration. In this respect one can introduce an analogy with economic development: social and political modernization are a transformation of the social structure involving mechanisms of "self-sustained social and political change." In fact, given the basic unity of the process of transition, "self-sustained economic growth" and "self-sustained political and social change" are different ways of perceiving the same concrete process. Failure to establish such mechanisms for continuous change may lead to a "breakdown" in the process of social or political modernization, in the same way as failure to establish the corresponding mechanisms in the economic structure is conducive to a "breakdown" in the process of economic development. Finally it must be stressed that the essential trait defining modernization is not the fact of continuous change but the capacity of originating and absorbing it.

Variations in Rates and Sequences Among the Component Processes

The interrelation between component processes must be conceived as one of reciprocal causation. That is, they affect one another and such reciprocal effects will determine the orientation and rate of the total transition, and may also produce inhibiting or facilitating effects on any single component process. In other words, processes of economic development (and, under given conditions, of economic expansion) condition processes of social and political modernization and vice versa. It may also be suggested that there exist minimum degrees (thresholds) of economic development (or economic expansion) which are required for the attainment of given degrees of social or political modernization, and vice versa, given minimum degrees of social or political modernization constituting necessary requirements for the attainment of given degrees of economic development or economic expansion. But a theoretical model suited to the analysis of such reciprocal relationships, and even an acceptable conceptual scheme, are still lacking. It may only be suggested that the types and forms of the interrelations and the various "thresholds" will vary according to the historical circumstances under which the transition of each nation occurs. Such historical circumstances cover a considerable range of factors — cultural, social, economic. And, most important, they regard not only the internal conditions of the society in transition, but also its external conditions, especially its relation to other societies. This is one of the reasons for the differences in rates and sequences among the various partial processes of economic development and social modernization. In this approach, economic expansion may generate effects on the social structure similar to those induced by economic development: it is in this sense that economic expansion may have a "modernizing effect."

The nature and consequences of this interrelationship between component processes are deeply affected by the historical and social circumstances under which the transition is taking place, including sociocultural differences at the "point of departure" for each nation or region. As already noted, one of the main sources of variation in the paths followed by the total transition is the variation in rates and sequences in which the component processes take place. And the variations themselves should be explained in terms of the different contextual conditions (economic, cultural, political and social), both at the national and at the international level. The asynchronisms noted in an earlier chapter may now be perceived as a result of these variations in rates and sequences. Coming back to the illustrations presented in analyzing some of the aspects of the "fusion effect," we may now consider them as side effects of deceleration or acceleration of rates, or as cases of retardation or of anticipation of sequences. Well-known illustrating cases of acceleration and anticipation (with regard to the "equivalent" degree of industrialization) are provided by the growth of urbanization (strictly defined as demographic concentration in urban areas), or by decrease in mortality rates, which tended to precede rather than follow or accompany economic development. Less universal, but often observed in different countries, are cases of acceleration of social mobilization, of political participation and diffusion of aspirations, which in the Western model have tended to occur at a lower rate and have advanced considerably only after the economy had reached a higher degree of economic development (especially in terms of structural change). But opposite phenomena of slower rates and retardation are also very common. It must be noted that acceleration and/or anticipation in certain processes may well coexist with retardation and/or deceleration in others.

It may be useful at this point to enumerate briefly other factors which are likely to intervene and to condition the nature, orientation and rate of the component processes and of the total transition:

• The nature and availability of human resources in each country (the country's "viability" and the necessary conditions for economic development according to its resources). These may originate different types of development and modernization, such as the expansionist or intrinsic development suggested by Hoselitz; or may impart a particular dynamics to the economic process as in the case of the "economy of the open spaces" in Argentina and other Latin American countries.

- The relative position (within the center-periphery dimension) of the country in relation to the international stratification according to political and economic power and consequently according to degree of political and/or economic dependence, and the specific (and changing) circumstances created by the international situation at the moment of and throughout transition.

- Historical and cultural traits and social structure of the country when initiating the transition, i.e. the type of society at the "point of departure." It may be observed that the concept of "traditional society" has often been used as a residual category including a great variety of social structures and cultural conditions. In fact, a typology of "points of departure" would be necessary.

- The state of knowledge in the natural sciences and the nature of the available technology at the initial moment of the transition and their further evolution and changes during the transition. (In many developing countries these changes are originated elsewhere; their exogenous nature will exercise a particular impact on the form of transition in the receiving country).

- The state of knowledge in the social sciences, especially in relation to the process of modernization and economic development. This is dependent not only on the development of the social sciences, but also on the degree of accumulation of historical experience, at the international level, at the initial moment of and during transition.

- The degree of "spontaneity," "awareness," "deliberation," and "planning" that characterize the social actions generating the partial processes of economic development and social modernization.

- The proportion and the nature of the exogenous or endogenous factors determining the transition.

- The different types of elite that lead, or in one way or another participate in, the initiation of the transition and its further stages.

- The changes which took place in societies which developed and modernized earlier, and the types of advanced industrial society which have emerged. These societies (especially the "central" and hegemonic nations) serve as models of transition and as such provide alternative goals for modernizing groups in developing societies, and, more generally, exercise the well-known "demonstration effect." It may be noted that this is how the different ideologies of development are originated. Such ideologies may turn out to be powerful factors in shaping the transition.

Some other general observations must be added. These categories of factors are not clearly separable — in fact there is considerable overlapping among them. The various factors are not independent, but are intercorrelated to different degrees. All the factors operate within an international system which moves toward greater unification and interdependence. While analyzing the process in a given national unit, one must always remember that such a process cannot be separated from the global context at the international level. Finally, all factors have a dynamic nature. In other words, they change continuously throughout time, thus originating at any given moment different configurations of circumstances affecting the transition while it is taking place.

An interesting example of the consequences generated by the variations in rates and sequences is the "modernizing effect" of economic expansion: an acceleration of certain processes of social modernization (often accompanied by retardation in others), in comparison with the rate of economic development (as defined here). This variation is particularly important in the case of many Latin American countries. Obviously the nature of economic expansion will determine its impact on modernization. Economic expansion which is based on a type of primary production, requiring the mobilization of a small part of the population, or with limited backward, lateral, or forward linkages on the rest of the economy, may not exercise a widely diffused impact on the social structure. Such may be the case of mining or plantation economies or other economic, foreign-oriented and integrated activities, which are relatively isolated from the national economy. A typical "dual" society and economy is likely to emerge with strong cleavage between "archaic" and "modernized" sectors. Social modernization may affect some aspects of behavior and institutions in some restricted areas and restricted social groups — usually the higher and middle strata in urban centers or more often in "primate" cities. However, even in these sectors some basic value-orientations may remain unchanged, coexisting with other manifest symptoms of modernization. But if economic expansion requires, or at least indirectly induces, the participation of large sectors of the population, both at the lower and intermediate occupational levels, an enlargement of the internal market and/or some other "spreading" effect (as well as other processes of social modernization) may occur at an accelerated rate and in advance of "corresponding" or "equivalent" degrees of economic development. These different forms of economic expansion may be considered as the extreme cases of a continuum admitting various intermediate types ranging from relatively "encapsulated" activities, more or less segregated from the rest of the economy and the society, to spreading activities which exercise an impact on a considerable proportion of the population and affect a wider range of social groups and institutions.

Stages in the Transition

One basic question which has not been solved theoretically is the definition of the "equivalencies," in comparing sequences and rates of the partial processes in different transitions. That is, some independent criterion for comparison is required in order to define the "equivalent" or "expected" degrees reached by the different partial processes. Two different procedures are usually followed: the historical experience of the Western model may be assumed as a general criterion or baseline for comparison (as in the examples given in the preceding paragraph) or equivalencies based on statistical averages and correlation of the indicators of the various processes in many countries may be used. Both procedures are useful, but inadequate theoretically to the extent that the criterion is assumed as a universal model of transition. There is no reason to believe that the "Western" model should be repeated; in fact the contrary is more likely. Statistical procedures are most necessary in order to discover correlations and associations between processes, but they cannot explain their causes, nor the existence of both statistically normal or deviating cases. Another problem with the statistical definition of "equivalencies" is that usually data are obtained from countries where transition has occurred at different historical periods, under rather divergent international conditions, and which find themselves at very different levels of transition.

The answer to this problem should be a theory of stages of modernization. This attempt, however, has not been successful so far.[3] In fact the differences in rates and sequences of the component processes as well as the other variations generated by the different sources already mentioned are likely to generate such a variety of "paths" so as to eliminate or greatly restrict the validity of any general or universal scheme of succession of fixed stages. Or perhaps the scheme of succession should be based on a theory able to integrate many relevant determinant and contextual factors, and to generate a whole typology of transitions (with "equivalent" stages along "diverging" paths) applicable to a great variety of historical processes. The social scientist is confronted here with a dilemma. On one hand, he lacks such a theory, at least at the moment. On the other, the use of notions of "levels," "degrees" and the like is very hard to avoid in any analysis of the transition. In fact they are implicit in it, and unless each case of modernization is considered as a unique instance and all comparisons (even implicit ones) are discarded, these notions are likely to be reintroduced in one way or another. That is why conventional and arbitrary external criteria (like the Western model or statistical correlations) maintain their usefulness, despite their obvious theoretical shortcomings. Another possibility could be suggested as a partial remedy to the lack of a satisfactory theory. I am referring to descriptive schemes of succession regarding a limited group of countries, perhaps a region, relatively more homogeneous in terms of their initial cultural and social structure and of the historical conditions under which the transition has occurred (or is occurring). It may be suggested that more valid generalizations could be formulated for limited geographical-cultural areas and for specific historical periods. This type of scheme would be no more than a convenient way of presenting a simplified overview of a series of similar (but not identical) historical processes, and not a theoretical construct. On the other hand it could have some analytical use in illuminating particular clusterings of traits and types of succession. In fact the use of stages could be linked to the idea that in the course of transition the variations in rates and sequences of the component processes and the impact of the other determining and contextual factors (at the internal and the international levels) may tend to crystallize in specific structural configurations. These in turn are likely to be incorporated into the process itself and to be transformed into key factors in explaining its further course. Perhaps this would offer a more objective basis for the selection of stages and the development of time periods of the transition.

Two main criteria may be suggested for the identification of stages: the emergence of a configuration of traits (in the economic, social and political structure) endowed with a certain degree of stability and duration, and clearly differentiated from the preceding and the succeeding structural arrangements) and second, its causal weight in shaping the further course of the transition. From another perspective the stage may be perceived as a "turning point" in the transition. Certainly any historical process is a concrete continuous flow and the notion of a "turning point" is always, to a great extent, an arbitrary or conventional device. However, its use may help to restrict a purely deterministic model of the transition. In this sense a "turning point" may be defined as a particular moment (of variable duration under different conditions) in which a reorientation is likely to occur. However, its actual occurrence as well as its nature, positive or negative, from the point of view of successful modernization and economic development, will be determined by the particular interrelationship of social and economic structural traits originated by the previous course of the transition, and the "decisions" assumed by the social actors (individuals and groups in key positions). It is suggested that the breakdown of modernization, economic stagnation, or (vice versa) further progress toward higher degrees of modernization and economic development, could be explained in terms of such "configurations" and "decisions." Two important questions must be noted here. In the first place, it is understood that configurations, or traits, regard not only the "internal" structure of the society, but also the external and international situation. Secondly, it is recognized that while the notion of "decision" is particularly difficult and theoretically imprecise, it is frequently used implicitly or explicitly in the analysis of historical processes and especially economic and political policies. In any case, the meaning of "decision" must be defined in terms of the range of "choices" concretely available to actors. Such a range will vary under different internal and external conditions (i.e. under given "configurations" of structural traits). Another important factor is the degree of scientific knowledge and technology (both in the natural and in the social sciences) available to actors. As mentioned earlier, the degree of "spontaneity," of "awareness," of "planning," under which the transition occurs, is an important factor which must be taken into account. These degrees have been increasing with time, and from this point of view the situation of the countries of earlier transition must be considered in a completely different way from that of the presently developing nations.

Notes

1. Among recent contributions to this discussion, see: A.S. Feldmann and W. E. Moore, "Industrialization and Industrialism," *Transactions of the Fifth World Congress of Sociology* (I.S.A. 1962), Vol. II; Raymond Aron, "La théorie du et l'interprétation historique de l'époque contemporariane" in R. Aron and B. F. Hoselitz, *Développment Social* (Paris, Mouton, 1965); Reinhard Bendix, "Tradition and Modernity Reconsidered," in *Comparative Studies in Society and History*, IX (1967), 292-346.

2. Some of the elements included in this definition are highly controversial. For instance, a number of economists challenge the idea of the predominance of industrial over primary production as a universal requirement for development; see for instance Peter T. Bauer and Basil S. Yamey in *The Economics of Under Developed Countries* (Chicago, University of Chicago Press, 1957), chap. XV. For an illustration of the opposite view, (which is also the most accepted one) see W. W. Rostow, "Industrialization and Economic Growth" in *Stockhom MCMLX. First International Conference of Economic History* (Paris, Mouton, 1960). The Latin American *communis opinio* among social scientists in the region is in favor of industrialization as a condition *sine qua non* of development. Most of them insist also on the key role of production goods industries as a necessary higher stage of industrialization. The "Latin American Thesis" is best expressed by the ECLA document on *Toward a Dynamic Development* Policy for Latin America New York, United Nations e/CN/12/680. Rev. 1). Statistical evidence confirms overwhelmingly the causal association between industrialization and economic development; see H. B. Chenery, "Patterns of Industrial Growth," in *American Economic Review*, (1960): 624-54.

3. The concept used here differs from the one currently employed. See G. Germani, "Social Change and Intergroup Conflicts," in I. L. Horowitz (ed.), *The New Sociology* (New York, Oxford University Press, 1964).

7.

Resistance to Change and Secularization

Resistances Implicit in the Industrial Structure Per Se, and Resistances Generated by Transition

Obstacles to changes connected with the process of secularization can arise in any of the areas discussed, and generally do in all of them, although with different degrees of intensity; these differences are due to the particular historical and cultural circumstances in which development itself takes place. Following the scheme presented up to this point, we can classify these obstacles in different groups:

a. Obstacles based on tensions implicit in the very structure of industrial society. We have seen at least three aspects of these possible "functional contradictions" to the impulse towards the expansion of secularization: the necessity of maintaining a minimal base of normative integration; the necessity of maintaining structures oriented towards "primary" relations; and other contradictions arising in the stratification system.
b. Obstacles originating in the preexisting structures. These in turn, can be classified in three groups: those rooted in each one of the structures subjected to modification (secularization); those which originate in the coexistence of secularized structures with others still persisting from previous stages; and obstacles arising from the disorganization provoked by the transition from one system to another (for example, the destruction of the traditional structures and the imperfection of nonexistent reorganization of the new "secular" structures.)
c. Obstacles originating in particular forms of transition and especially in the nature of the sequences between the various partial processes.

While the obstacles classified in the first group must be considered, on the basis of accepted hypotheses, as having a permanent character, and as being a source of permanent tension (and change) in industrial societies, the other two groups are typical of transition. It is also important to observe that, while the first are independent of the cultural type and historical circumstances of each country, the second and the third are tied much more closely to national peculiarities, so that these determine not only the importance of the obstacles but also the specific form assumed by development and by the limits of secularization.

It is obvious that the distinctions formulated above, although helpful in understanding the nature of the obstacles and the varying limits of secularization in each case, will only furnish this help when employed as a method of investigation, not as simple criteria of classification.

Empirically, the majority of obstacles seem to arise as conflicts among groups and, in a good many cases assume an ideological expression. In this respect, it is convenient to distinguish "total" from "partial" obstacles to development.

Total resistance to development and, in particular, to the adoption of the necessary attitudes in the spheres of natural science, technology and economic activity (in the strict sense), has received considerable attention from economists, sociologists, and anthropologists. Here the resistance to secularization arises directly from the persistence of internalized traditional patterns — for example, the prestige of certain traditional occupations, of certain forms of propriety, the absence of motivation for industrial work and the lack of "entrepreneurial" or "managerial" attitudes. These obstacles do not always assume an ideological form, although they tend to do so when they become open group conflict. To the degree to which they are a direct expression of a "social character," incapable of accomplishing the types of actions required by development, they are conducive to "disorganization," or "lack of adaptation." At other times they do assume an ideological character, while there are many forms that have both characteristics. For example, the first "protest movements" of workers faced with industrial work could be interpreted as ideological resistance based on attitudes rooted in a "traditional social character" inadequate for this type of activity. This type of resistance tends to reject the entire process and to cling to the existing situation in its preindustrial stage. This resistance can be more or less "blind" (i.e. more or less conscious of its real situation) but it should be distinguished from the types of resistance that accept in principle the necessity of economic development, while rejecting part of its conditions and implications or results.

Partial resistance to development and/or some of its consequences, especially that of the secularization of determined aspects of social organization, generally assumes ideological form and tends to rise from, or be directed by, groups at least partially secularized. Among the principle areas in which we encounter this type of resistance are the following:

- Social stratification: resistance to the modification of the system of closed strata.
- Political organization: resistance to the extension of the level of political participation.
- Familial organization: resistance to the acceptance of the degree of secularization of the family implied in development, and the tendency to maintain traditional forms inadequate to the new structure.
- Scientific knowledge: resistance to the extension of the type of natural scientific knowledge to the disciplines of social science.

- Education: resistance to the extension of education to all social strata; resistance to the acknowledgement of the importance of scientific and technical education.
- Central social values: resistance to the acceptance of some value changes implicit (or supposedly implicit) in development (rational individualism).

Many of the problems that are the source of conflict revolve around the consequences of development whose ties to it have been under discussion, and which can be interpreted as "unnecessary." As stated previously, these conflicts express, in part, implicit contradictions in all industrial society. The possibility of transcending the ideological level of the conflict depends, therefore, on a more penetrating investigation of that society.

A Particular Form of Conflict:
Ideological Traditionalism

Here I shall examine, as an illustration of the types of conflicts which arise from transition, a particular form that acquires considerable importance in countries where development has recently begun. I refer to what I have termed "ideological traditionalism" which especially expresses the position of groups belonging to the traditional elite of the preindustrial society. Often, in the recent period, these groups have not totally rejected development; rather they have accepted and promoted it. Nevertheless, if on the one hand they support specific changes in the economic sphere ("industrialization," "economic development"), especially inasmuch as these transformations are a basis for securing the independence of the country, then on the other hand they reject the extension of the other changes required or implied by such transformation.

The maintenance of the traditional is especially supported wherever the society does not take easily to technical-economic action. In this way there is a tendency to maintain "traditional" institutions such as the family, political institutions (or at least effective political power), education, and social stratification. The "electivity of action," emphasizing the capacity for self-determination and rationality, would be limited to the sphere of technical-economic action. Also the development of science would be subjected to the same limitations (for example, the development of the science of man would be discouraged inasmuch as it tends to relativize the content of tradition). It is precisely in this last form that the phenomenon of "ideological traditionalism" is introduced, a phenomenon which is a particular form of the "fusion effect."

To delimit this concept more clearly, it is necessary to state in what sense the terms ideology and tradition are being employed here. For that I must refer to the opposites of "elective" and "prescriptive" action, whose significance has already been explained. In "prescriptive" action there is no choice: consequently the attitudes that accompany and motivate actions of this type are not chosen; it is a question of forms of thought and feeling, of internalized affective contents, which are accepted without discussion although they present (in pure form) the possibility of discussion. They are naturally thought and felt. This notion of the naturalness which tradition possesses also lends it an absolute character; it is what elevates it to a criterion and leads us to consider as inferior, false, or ugly, as the case may be, all that is foreign to it. Ethnocentric forms of thought have exactly this absolute character, insofar as they assume the norm of the group itself as a universal criterion. The normative mark of elective action in change, corresponds to the alternatives between which the choice is prescribed and the opposed forms, contradictions of thought and feeling, contrasting attitudes or what is here called ideology. Agreement with such a definition of ideology can only occur in a situation of controversy and historically, such a situation introduces the phenomenon of public opinion. The ideology is therefore that which is debated, which is under discussion, which must be chosen, as an act of "free will." According to the enlightenment theory of public opinion, this action is of a rational type; according to other, later interpretations, it is a matter of irrational action.

In keeping with this distinction, it is not the content which determines the traditional or ideological character of a thought, but the way in which it is fixed in a particular group. To distinguish between the ideological and the traditional it is necessary to observe the type of normative pressure prevailing in the group, whether it is of an elective or a nonelective order. In other words, the degree of secularization and rationalization of a social group is found not so much in the content of the attitudes, but rather in the form by which one arrives at these attitudes. One can possess traditional beliefs and manifest traditional behavior through a choice in a situation of ideological controversy. In this case, if the traditional content is the result of an ideological choice then one should speak of "ideological traditionalism," which is a completely different phenomenon in which traditionalism is lived as the only reality possible and controversy neither exists nor is perceived.

In many developing societies the elite is connected with the traditional structure, which is frequently partially or entirely secularized. It is possible that through the progressive extension of elective action, the society in question may have already experienced internal changes and diffusion of attitudes which were introduced by cultural contact. In these cases it is frequently the elites who are found in the vanguard of the process. Nevertheless, if in one way they are part of this change, in another way they oppose it, especially those consequences which affect their privileged position in the traditional structure. In a situation where the elite is secularized and at the same time conflicts are arising from that secularization, there is a strong possibility that opposition may assume the form of ideological traditionalism. The content of tradition is supported by these groups, but like an ideology, it is in a certain sense used in the ideological struggle, so that, for example, "progressive" ideologies oppose them. The tendency to revive traditions and many aspects of folklore, part of the ideological content of right-wing totalitarian movements, undoubtedly has this character (and in a lesser way, the left as well). To the extent that there are behavior patterns in family institutions which can express this ideological traditionalism, in the sense that while they are a faithful complement of traditional patterns, underlying motives fall into the sphere of elective action; they are deliberate forms of traditional behavior. For example, many old families of the upper class maintain a very high birth rate.[1] At the same time the large family becomes a status symbol and an ideological affirmation of tradition, but in no way represents a natural attitude or a deliberate one (nonelective), in keeping with a traditional life style.

Ideological traditionalism can appear especially in societies which, aside from the process of rapid change, are moving toward the stage of fundamental democratization; that is, they are characterized by massive incorporation of great sectors of the popular classes, which until now had been excluded from most aspects of industrial-urban life, particularly the effective practice of political rights. In these cases the objective of the traditional elites can no longer be the clear-cut rejection of development, but rather a partial acceptance of it in order to limit its sociocultural effects to the technological-economic sphere. The ideal situation, as seen by these groups, would be a society which, while it may value the development of economic organization, keeps the rest of the society within the traditional structure. Frequently this traditionalist position is infused with ideological positions historically corresponding to previous stages. Thus the nationalism of such groups rests upon, and is fused with, traditional content, which at some other time was bound up with loyalty to the local community or other forms of loyalty bound to traditional structures. It is obvious that the rupture of the local community and the substitution for it of a unit at least at the national level is an indispensable requirement for all economic development; here there is a need for a strong nationalist emphasis. But in groups among the traditional elite, such nationalism aquires particular forms which are quite distinct from the traditions of thought with characterized bourgeois nationalism in the last century, or countries advanced in development.

Anti-Semitic attitudes furnish another example. Research in different countries has shown an inverse correlation between socioeconomic level and anti-Semitism and also (and especially) between education and anti-Semitism. The poorest, least educated groups, those of manual or unskilled occupations showed the highest proportions of persons with anti-

Semitic bias. It has also been proven that this bias (mediated by verbal reactions to face-to-face questionnaires) depends on the type of culture and greater or lesser proximity to the traditional society. At the same time, many of the psychological researchers of Adorno and the considerations of other observers (such as Sartre) tend to show an "authoritarian syndrome," which is expressed in anti-Semitism and manifestations of neurotic tendencies.

I may formulate the hypothesis that we are confronted by two types of anti-Semitism: the first of a traditional character, and of a special psychological significance (this would be the anti-Semitism which diminishes with an increase in education and with greater participation in modern culture, aside from elevation in the social scale); and the second of an ideological type, which tends toward the psychological correlates described by Fromm, Adorno, and others.[2] Here too would lie the possible ideological advantage of traditional anti-Semitism. Where development was later and began through cultural contacts, groups from the traditional elite may frequently take the initiative or at least collaborate closely with other sectors; here is where the ideological use of tradition is revealed in all of its possibilities. In effect, it is an instrument rich in possibilities for the manipulation of the popular masses recently incorporated into industrial society, still bearing traditional attitudes, and who, above all, continue moving for the most part within the norms corresponding to this type of society. The problem naturally remains open — if it is effectively possible to circumscribe the functionality of normative points of the elective type to the technical-economic sphere, leaving aside the other structures. Here historical experience shows that, while there are certain intrinsic limitations to this extension, the progressive broadening of the elective norm can be definitively defined.

Notes

1. Cf. A. Bunge, *Una Nueva Argentina* (Buenos Aires: Kraft, 1940).
2. Cf. T.W. Adorno, et al., *The Authoritarian Personality* (New York, Harper & Row, 1950) and the following three volumes; at the Institute of Sociology of the University of Buenos Aires there was an inquiry completed which confirmed the correlations found in other countries for Argentina as well. This work permits us to explore the distinction between ideological anti-Semitism and traditional anti-Semitism.

8.
Social and Political
Consequences of Mobility

Only one conclusion about the social consequences of mobility is likely to encounter general agreement: an enormous variety of social and individual consequences can be imputed to social mobility. Not only will different kinds of mobility produce different consequences under different circumstances, but the number and variety of processes that can be distinguished under the general concept of mobility (even limiting this to vertical mobility), and above all the complexity and diversity of historical circumstances that may affect mobility and of course its consequences, make it extremely difficult to formulate even a few valid empirical generalizations.

An adequate analysis of the consequences of mobility — either social or individual — requires both a theory, that is, a series of clearly specified, logically interrelated hypotheses, and relevant data. Unfortunately neither theory nor empirical evidence is adequate at present. Most of the empirical material consists of impressionistic studies, vague historical generalizations, indirect inferences and sheer guesses, and though many interesting theoretical suggestions have been made, few specific hypotheses and certainly no systematic theory has been formulated.

Among the many possible consequences of mobility[1] the present paper will be concerned only with its impact on the attitudes of accepting or rejecting the existing social and political order, with special reference to the effects of mass mobility in the lower strata.

The General Social Context of Mobility

"Individual" and "social" consequences of mobility stem from the same basic social processes. The former affect individuals qua individuals, whereas the latter affect the social structure, or some of its aspects through the individuals and groups involved. Thus, some of the "individual" effects of mobility play a role as intervening variables in the causation of social consequences. The impact on individuals, however, is not to be considered a purely psychological phenomenon; in fact, the "individual effects" are themselves the outcome of socially and culturally patterned processes.

In Tables 1 and 2 I have summarized the main categories of variables which should be taken into account in analyzing the consequences of mobility. Their relevance depends on the kind of impact being studied. The list is by no means exhaustive; it should be considered only an illustration of the kind of factors that determine the social effects of mobility.

"Objective Mobility" as an Independent Variable

The notion of "objective" mobility is based on the procedures commonly used to measure positional changes in the manifest status of individuals (or other units, such as families or groups) along one or more

TABLE 1
Relevant Factors in the Analysis of the
Social Consequences of Mobility

1. INDEPENDENT VARIABLE:	"OBJECTIVE" MOBILITY
1.1 Nature of the movement	Direction (up or down). Distance. Starting point. Dimensions (occupation, power, wealth, prestige, consumption, social participation, etc.) Time (number of years or generations required to complete movement).
1.2 Characteristics of the individuals (or other units) involved both (mobile and nonmobile)	Criteria for selection (intelligence, personality traits, ethnicity, rural/urban origin, etc.).
1.3 Quantitative importance of the movement	Proportion of mobile and nonmobile individuals (or other units), by specific kind of mobility as defined by factors mentioned in 1.1 and with regard to (a) sending stratum; (b) receiving stratum.
2. INTERVENING PSYCHOSOCIAL VARIABLES:	"SUBJECTIVE" MOBILITY AND IMPACT ON INDIVIDUALS
2.1 Gratification/frustration of individuals (mobile and non-mobile) involved in the process	Balance between level of aspiration and actual mobility.
2.2 Acculturation	Acquisition of cultural traits of the receiving stratum; varying from overconformity to retention of the traits of the sending stratum.
2.3 Identification	Degree of identification with receiving stratum (or retention of identification with sending stratum).
2.4 Personal adjustment	Capacity to bear psychological stresses (if any) caused by movement into a different sociocultural and interpersonal setting.

TABLE 1 (Continued)
Relevant Factors in the Analysis of the
Social Consequences of Mobility

3. INTERVENING CONTEXTUAL VARIABLES:	SOCIAL STRUCTURE AND RATE OF CHANGE
3.1 Structure of the stratification system and degree and rate of modernization of the society	
3.2 Degree and rate of economic growth	
3.3 Configuration of mobile and non-mobile sectors	Various possible combinations originated by the simultaneous occurrence of different types of mobility and its coexistence with nonmobile sectors.

stratification dimensions. A large number of types of "objective" mobility can be constructed on the basis of the traits indicated in Table 1; some of them may not be empirically relevant or even theoretically important, but it is obvious that the social impact of mobility should be specifically related to specific types of objective mobility.[2]

"Subjective" Mobility and "Individual" Effects as Intervening Variables

Objective mobility requires an interpretation in terms of social action. How mobility is perceived by both mobile and nonmobile individuals concerned, and how they react, is determined not only by the specific type of "objective mobility," but also by a number of psychosocial processes.

The relevance of reference group theory for the analysis of mobility is well known:[3] whether an individual experiences gratification or frustration depends on his reference groups, his aspirations, and the discrepancy between such aspirations and the actual opportunity for mobility perceived. Not the kind or amount of objective mobility, but the balance between aspirations and mobility is the dynamic factor (among others) in determining individual and social consequences. And, as others have observed, more objective mobility may increase the level of aspiration, or create aspirations that previously did not exist in both mobile and nonmobile persons. Thus, the notion of relative deprivation (and relative gratification) is highly relevant in this context.

Although level of aspiration and choice of reference groups may be in part the result of idiosyncratic factors, they are to a much greater extent the result of the socially and culturally patterned experiences in early socialization and in later stages of individuals' lives. Intervening contextual variables in such patterning include the structure of the stratification system and the impact of particular events during the life of coexisting generations.[4]

Displacement from one stratum to another may involve acculturation, change of class identification and adjustment to a different social environment. Most research on the consequences of mobility and on its "cost" is concerned with precisely such processes. Here the available empirical evidence reveals different "effects." For instance, "normative" mobility,[5] that is, mobility involving a change in class subculture, may result sometimes in "overconformity," sometimes in "assimilation" or average conformity, and in other cases in "retention" of the older norms characterizing the original or sending stratum.[6] Fairly similar alternatives have been observed with regard to class self-identification.[7] And, finally, for individuals and groups displaced from one sociocultural and interpersonal environment to a different one, the conflict between internalized norms and the requirements of the new situation result in personal or collective disorganization, or anomie.[8] Other important effects have been imputed to the conflict between culturally favored aspirations and socially permissible means.[9] These processes — acculturation, identification and personal adjustment — may play an important role in shaping the impact of mobility on social structure and social processes.

Intervening Contextual Variables

My concern here is with the general social context not as a cause of mobility but only as it conditions its social consequences. The general framework in which mobility occurs is the system of stratification, which conditions the impact of mobility not only through specific mobility norms and values, and the actual distribution of real life-chances, but also through the other characteristics listed in Table 2.[10] A few remarks will illustrate their relevance in this respect.

The profile of stratification is very important in determining the quantitative impact of mobility: given the same proportion of mobile or nonmobile individuals, the impact depends on the relative sizes of the sending and receiving strata. When the middle and higher strata are relatively small, even complete permeability (i.e., an empirical mobility approaching the "perfect" mobility formalized in certain indexes) means very little in terms of actual chances for individuals in the lower strata. The opposite effect may occur when the middle strata are larger and include at least a proportion of the population not much smaller than the proportion located in the lower strata.

Given the direction, distance, starting point, etc., of "objective" mobility, and the level of aspirations and anticipatory socialization, acculturation, identification, and personal adjustment will be more traumatic and more conducive to anomic reactions when a high degree of discontinuity

TABLE 2

Characteristics of the Structure of the Stratification System
Relevant to the Analysis of the Consequences of Mobility

1. Profile of stratification: proportion of the population located in each stratum.

2. Degree of discontinuity between strata: ranges from maximum discontinuity, with clear cleavages between strata coupled with gross differences and inequalities in all dimensions, to minimum discontinuities in all the dimensions and a "stratification continuum."

3. Degree of hierarchization of interpersonal relations: ranges from maximum to minimum emphasis (overt or covert) on status inequalities in most or all social situations.

4. Degree of institutionalization of the "image" of the stratification system: ranges from maximum to minimum degree of institutionalization involving also maximum to minimum clarity of the "image" of each stratum, and of "ideal" congruence.

5. Mobility norms: predominance of inheritance or of achievement among the stratification dimensions, with various intermediate possibilities.

6. Mobility values, beliefs and attitudes: ranges from a maximum emphasis on stability and inheritance to a maximum emphasis on mobility and achievement (combined with varying degrees of consensus in the different strata).

7. Real possibilities of mobility: ranges from very few, unequally distributed among the strata, to many, equally distributed among the strata.

---

exists between strata. Hierarchization of interpersonal relations may be considered a particular kind of discontinuity, and in this sense it may have similar effects. At the same time, however, its impact on mobility may be indirect, with different social consequences. Under conditions of a high degree of hierarchization, individuals in the lower strata feel segregated: the cleavage between strata is highly visible. Although the actual chances of mobility may be the same, upward mobility is likely to be less visible under these conditions. Downward mobility, or relative deprivation for the nonmobile, may be expected to have more severe effects where discontinuity and hierarchization are high.[11] In addition, these characteristics are usually accompanied by a highly institutionalized image of stratification, which may be quite important in determining the nature and the impact of status congruence. With a clear image of congruence, the psychosocial effects of incongruence should be much stronger than they are in a society where class lines are blurred and a clear notion of the "equivalents" in each stratification dimension is absent.

The probability of incongruence is related, of course, to the degree of homogeneity of mobility norms and to actual chances in the various dimensions. Where the mobility norms and empirical chances are the same in all dimensions, mobility is not likely to produce status incongruence; but if inheritance is the dominant norm in some dimensions, while other channels are open according to achievement criteria, incongruence will be a frequent outcome of mobility. This situation is particularly important for the social effects of mobility: partially blocked mobility is usually considered one of the more powerful sources of resentment and social tension. Mobility values, attitudes and beliefs condition the level of aspiration, and together with mobility norms and the real chances open to individuals, determine the degree of satisfaction or frustration induced in both mobile and nonmobile persons. Also, as suggested above, beliefs and attitudes may alter the visibility of actual mobility.

With the characteristics listed in Table 2 a typology of stratification systems could be constructed. The most widely used — either explicitly or implicitly — is the dichotomous classification (or, better, the continuum) in which the polar types are the "traditional" and "modern" patterns. The first is frequently described as a two-class system, with the great majority of the population in the lower stratum. It is characterized by high degrees of discontinuity and hierarchization and a highly institutionalized image of stratification, in which inheritance norms, values and attitudes are dominant and real chances for mobility are slight. The second, the "modern" pattern of stratification, is defined by the opposite traits: multiple strata, or even a "stratification continuum," low degrees of discontinuity and hierarchization, an unclear image of the system, frequent status incongruence, predominant achievement norms, values and attitudes and high chances for effective mobility. As is well known, this typology does not describe concrete systems: on the contrary, various mixtures of "modern" and "archaic" traits exist not only in transitional societies — because of their transitional character — but in more stable societies as well. In fact, "modern" traits have been observed in many preindustrial societies, and vice versa; the degree of compatibility between "traditional" traits — including aspects of stratification — and urban, industrial, modern structures seems to be quite large. On the other hand, many traits enumerated in the table are not completely independent of one another. They tend to cluster, and the combinations in which "modern" traits prevail are more frequently observed in industrial urban societies, while more "traditional" configurations seem fairly common in preindustrial ones. At the same time, however, many important social consequences of mobility can be understood only in the context of a "mixed" stratification system.

Other aspects of modernization also affect the results of mobility: urbanization, literacy, diffusion of communication media, mobilization, political participation, secularization of the family, the church and other institutions, and so on. Many of these traits are somewhat related to the stratification system and exercise their influence mostly through it; some aspects of modernization, however, such as attitudes toward change, ability to adjust to new situations and especially to social and ecological displacement, and various others intervene more directly in determining the social consequences of mobility.

The level and rate of economic growth (as distinguished from degree and rate of modernization) are also likely to modify the impact of mobility. I am suggesting here that at a given level of modernization, the same type of "objective" mobility may produce one set of social consequences under conditions of economic growth and another during an economic depression, and that the stage of economic development reached by the society comprises analogous modifying conditions.

Finally, different types of mobility may occur at the same time, and the particular configurations resulting from simultaneous processes may introduce new conditions relevant to the effects of mobility.

Mobility as a Factor in Radical Opposition

Mobility has its most disruptive effects on the social order when it is noninstitutionalized mobility and when there is an imbalance between aspirations and actual chances of mobility, that is, a lack of mobility when it is expected and institutionalized. In this sense mobility is disruptive in a "traditional" society with an "ascriptive" system of stratification, while in an "industrial" society that approaches the opposite ideal type, it is a normal recurrent process favorable to (or even required for) the maintenance of system equilibrium.

Noninstitutionalized mobility by definition introduces status incongruencies: it involves opening some dimensions while the dominant norms and values (or at least the norms and values of the dominant groups) remain geared to the requirements of the previous structure. This situation is a powerful potential source of social tension because the groups involved tend to reequilibrate their status.[12] I shall consider two types of situations: upward partial mobility, and downward partial mobility.

Upward Partial Mobility: The Case of Developing Countries

Typically, in this situation, the groups affected try to remove the obstacles blocking their social ascent and in doing so become innovating or revolutionary groups. The well-known theory of the strategic role of the "partially deprived group" in the earlier stages of development is based precisely on a hypothesis of this kind.[13] According to this theory, if complete mobility had been possible (that is, if the possibility of status equilibration had existed), no innovating or revolutionary attitudes would have developed. Analogous consequences have been attributed to the partial mobility created by the diffusion of education. The rising expectations of newly educated groups remain unsatisfied because other groups — foreign or domestic — virtually monopolize the higher positions available in the society, or because the new supply of educated persons exceeds the demand or fails to correspond to the specific technical or intellectual skills required. Thus the formation of a "rootless intellectual proletariat" has been counted as one factor in the development of communism in Asia.[14] "Distinct ideological polarization" between "old" and "new" (educated) elites, giving rise to similar innovating movements, has been observed in Africa and elsewhere. Their sense of superiority, born of acquaintance with modern ideas and methods, supports their ambition to achieve power through revolution or reform.[15]

In Latin America, extremist or at least radical movements have been promoted by groups whose ascent was partially blocked by the persisting rigidities of the stratification system. The rising middle strata created by the first steps toward economic development and social modernization, were led by their newly acquired class identification and their desire to gain political power and prestigious positions to oppose the political and social order that gave the traditional elites a virtual monopoly on power and prestige. Supported by recently mobilized sectors of the lower strata, which usually lacked political experience, intellectuals, professionals, industrial entrepreneurs and similar groups organized the "national-popular" movements that have appeared in most of the Latin American countries in the last few decades. These include, among others, the APRA in Peru, the National Liberation party in Costa Rica, the Venezuelan Acción Democrática, the MNR in Bolivia, the radical parties in Chile and Argentina, at least at an earlier stage of their political evolution, and the PRI in Mexico. Peronism and Varguism (which I will examine later) must also be classified in this broad category, so far as they included middle class sectors, partially blocked in their political and social ascent, as an important dynamic element.[16]

These political movements did vary a great deal, and for the purposes of a more specific analysis more refined distinctions should be introduced, but all of them were multiclass parties with an ideology favoring basic social changes, and all of them were equally and emphatically nationalistic, antiimperialist and antioligarchic. From country to country, and from time to time within the same country, the extent of their real opposition to the status quo also varied, however, according to the success of the leading middle-class components in their efforts to equilibrate their status. The typical evolution of these movements has been from revolutionary and radical opposition to the political and social order to a more moderate orientation. Such change seems to correspond to the level of integration of the middle-class groups. The Radical Party in Argentina, for example, maintained its revolutionary impetus until the beginning of the century. But an unusually high rate of mobility and very rapid modernization produced an independent urban working class, and the party became a typical centrist party more homogeneously based on the middle classes. In Chile a similar evolution occurred.

The Peruvian APRA started with a more extremist orientation characteristic of the rigid stratification system, but later increased its political participation, and — probably — the increased legitimacy of its leaders moderated the APRA position.[17] The national revolution in Bolivia was a more extreme consequence which may be attributed largely to the severe deprivation of the leading middle-class sectors, combined with the more complete mobilization of the lower strata, which made available for the MNR far more popular support than the Peruvian party achieved.

Downward Partial Mobility: A European Example

One of the most impressive symptoms of major social tension created by downward partial mobility was the middle-class support of rightist totalitarian movements in the interwar period, in Europe. Downward mobility resulted from the accumulation of various factors: inflation drastically reduced the savings and real income of the majority of the middle strata, their relative position was deeply affected by the substantial gains the workers were obtaining at that time, both in income and in political power, and finally unemployment among professional people contributed to their "proletarianization." Under the impact of this process, the intellectuals provided the leadership for both radical extremes of the political spectrum, but mostly for the rightist totalitarians.[18]

This European example suggests that when downward mobility affects a high proportion of the individuals in the middle or higher strata, the anomic effects of the displacement are likely to be transformed from an individual to a mass phenomenon. Mannheim and others have suggested that individual insecurity caused by inflation, status panic, or mass unemployment may stimulate collective insecurity, thus creating the conditions for the acceptance of totalitarian solutions.[19] In a similar general climate of depression, analogous consequences have been observed in lower-class groups at the individual level.[20] In the European example, another essential factor in this process was the high discontinuity and high hierarchization of the stratification system of the time, which increased the anomic consequences of the displacement and rendered intolerable the threat of the rising working class, especially for the lower middle groups. A similar process of decreasing differentials, occurring in the same countries after the Second World War, did not have mass effects. As I shall suggest in the next section, recent changes in the stratification system are one important source of this difference.

The preceding illustrations have shown that the direction of mobility may be correlated with specific ideological orientation: blocked upward mobility creates a propensity for "progressive" ideology, while a reactionary orientation expresses the experience of downward mobility. The relationship is much more complex, of course, because many other factors intervene. For instance, the specific configuration of mobile and non-mobile groups, and their availability for political action comprised another condition that promoted the "national-popular" parties in Latin America, and the rightist totalitarian movement in Europe. In Latin America the incongruent sectors of the middle-class were small, but the support of recently mobilized lower groups was available to them, and this required a "populist," "social justice" ideology. Even the downwardly mobile elements in the traditional elite (which had failed in their previous attempts to produce Fascist-like movements) joined the mass national-popular Peronist and Varguist parties in Argentina and Brazil. In Europe the working class had been politically organized for a long time and was historically associated with a progressive ideology: the only "available" masses were the displaced middle-class groups, which included enough people for a mass movement, though less than a majority of the population.[21] Available elites, available masses and available ideologies are the important conditions shaping the specific ideological orientations of the movements originating in partial downward or upward mobility.

Mobility as a Factor in Political and
Social Integration

Implicit in the foregoing discussion are the general conditions under which mobility is likely to be an integrative force in the society. Such conditions may be summarized as follows: Mobility aspirations are of some importance for individuals and are widely diffused in the population; aspirations and actual mobility are balanced[22] in all strata and for the great majority of individuals (failures being perceived as "deviant") with respect to the institutionalized mobility norms; mobility is equally possible along all the relevant dimensions (that is, serious incongruencies are rare); hierarchization and cultural and interpersonal discontinuities (or at least their visibility for the majority of the individuals) are minimal; and finally, individual and social mechanisms of adjustment to mobility are effective. Under these conditions the individual "costs" of mobility are likely to be negligible, while the balance between aspirations and actual chances tends to increase (or at least to maintain) a strong feeling of participation in the society and to promote, as a consequence, a high degree of involvement in and acceptance of its social and political order.

The historical experience of the presently advanced countries, as well as certain developing nations, indicates that under the cumulative impact of some of the processes typical of economic development and social modernization, the contextual factors that made mobility disruptive or neutralized its integrative consequences in an earlier stage tend to be replaced by the opposite conditions. These processes include changes in the profile of stratification — broadening of the middle strata and a resulting "structural" mobility; additional mobility created by demographic differentials; greater "fluidity"[23] stemming from the "exchange" mobility produced by a wider application of achievement criteria; continuous transference of status symbols from top to bottom through increased participation in the "higher" consumption patterns and styles of living, or mobility by increasing participation.

This entire process is powerfully reinforced by mobility itself, once it reaches a relatively high quantitative level and has achieved a certain duration. First, as a reinforcing factor in structural change, mobility helps to modify the psychological meaning of incongruence and to diminish its effects. During the initial stages of the transition the "incongruence" continues to be perceived because the traditional stratification pattern provides an "ideal image" of congruence. This situation may last for a long time, and it may coexist with more modernized aspects. But once a persisting high mobility rate increases the proportion of incongruent individuals beyond a certain level, the "ideal image" is likely to lose much of its validity as a criterion of evaluation. Except in certain special cases where castelike elements exist, the higher the proportion of the incongruent individuals in a population, the weaker the previously institutionalized image. At a given point, as has occurred in advanced areas, congruence becomes either a matter of opinion (one polls the population to discover what the image is in that society), or a statistical fact, based on the frequency distribution of stratification indicators.[24] A high frequency changes incongruence into a property of the stratification system, and its psychological meaning, its individual and social effects, and the very possibility of being aware of it tend to decrease. A second consequence of an enlarged proportion of incongruents, when the rates of downward and upward mobility are high is that the internal homogeneity of classes is decreased and, consequently, the gap between them is diminished, thus tending to blur discontinuities. This observation is far from original,[25] but the phenomenon does not seem to have stimulated studies of the extent to which this process may alter the structure of the stratification system.[26] It is unnecessary to insist on the immediate effects its tendency to weaken class solidarity[27] has on political orientations; what I want to emphasize here is the structural impact of fluidity, once it reaches a high, fairly constant level.

Finally, the experience of mobility shared by a wide and increasing proportion of the population through many generations contributes to the diffusion of more equalitarian values and beliefs, and to less hierarchical attitudes, manners, interpersonal relations.

This self-reinforcing process may be associated with the process of economic growth. "Self-sustained" mobility is possible only after a number of strategic aspects of the social structure have been modified, and the time this transition takes depends on the structural characteristics of the society at the "starting point." When the positive feedback of the self-sustaining stage is achieved, mobility becomes a normal, permanent process. The changes required by industrial development begin to broaden the stratification profile and bring about other modifications of the occupational structure, causing an initial mass mobility. At the same time the changing requirements for allocating personnel — especially educational requirements[28] — tend to increase "exchange" mobility, while the growth of the national product and its more equalitarian distribution increases consumption. On the other hand, the mobility so originated eventually reacts on the new structural conditions, reinforcing the previous changes. Technological innovation as a normal process seems to be a basic mechanism in maintaining the rate of mobility needed to produce the integrative effects. ("Exchange" mobility alone is insufficient, because the maximum degree of fluidity possible in any society has a definite limit.) Technological innovation increases mobility in two ways: it produces a continuous occupational upgrading by transferring "lower" tasks to machines, and at the same time creates new needs and new products to satisfy them. Thus, a constant flow of new status symbols is circulated from top to bottom.

Massive Mobility in Advanced Countries in Recent Years

The changes that have taken place in Europe seem to have made the European countries more similar to the kind of industrial society typified by the United States. In spite of remarkable differences among such countries, all of them have been approaching the various conditions under which mobility has an integrative impact: decreasing interclass tensions, greater acceptance of the social order by the lower strata and a substantial reorientation of their political parties. The two basic aspects of the process are mass "individual" (exchange and structural) mobility and mobility by increasing participation.

On the mass character of individual occupational mobility, a number of points are relevant. Using a manual/nonmanual dichotomy Miller showed that in the nine most industrialized countries, upward intergenerational mobility out of the manual strata was twenty to thirty percent.[29] Now, whether these figures are "high" depends on one's expectations concerning this process in the type of society in question. In any case, however, rates of this size must leave unsatisfied a majority of the people belonging to the manual strata, assuming that all of them really aspired to the nonmanual level. On the other hand, it has been observed that the manual/nonmanual categorization, though very useful for international comparisons, may grossly underestimate the extent of psychologically meaningful mobility.

The rate of mobility certainly depends on the number and kind of categories employed. For instance, when one discriminates within the manual stratum, separating the skilled from the unskilled workers, the rate of movement out of the unskilled includes, in many industrialized countries, a majority of the people.[30] Moreover, there are indications that upward (or downward) short-distance mobility may be perceived and experienced as deeply important by the mobile subjects,[31] especially in the case of intra-generational mobility. One's ability to discriminate on the basis of prestige is higher when comparing occupations in the proximity of one's own than it is when the occupations are more distant. More important, individual aspiration levels may usually be restricted to a very small range of the social hierarchy.

Thus, many mobility studies based on a set of broad occupational categories probably underestimate the extent of psychologically and socially relevant mobility. More precise knowledge of modal and deviant levels of aspiration and reference groups characteristic of each stratum, and the factors determining these characteristics, is needed. Data now available show that even in the United States, which could be taken as an extreme example of a culture emphasizing occupational and economic success, workers' levels of aspiration are much lower than those of the middle and upper classes. Social values that emphasize individual success tend to be seen in realistic terms, according to the possibilities actually available.[32]

Other general tendencies also transform the work situation, shaping mobility aspirations in terms of an ordered sequence of steps: this is the so-called professionalization of work. This process itself results from a series of other technological and economic factors, but in turn one of its general consequences is to introduce "career" mobility. Even when it is limited to the range of "working-class" positions, individuals nevertheless experience it as an orderly process of advancement conforming to a series of expectations.[33]

True, orderly careers during the larger part of the individual's life are probably still a small portion of all careers, according to recent studies by Wilensky.[34] But, as he point out, the psychological effects of the "career" depend on other circumstances, including among others, the generational experience, which affects the aspiration levels of individuals of different ages according to the different historical circumstances through which they have lived.

One of the most important aspects of mass mobility hardly needs mentioning: the great rural-urban migrations and the successive displacement from primary to secondary and tertiary activities. Although the interpretation of these movements in terms of mobility is far from simple,[35] the indisputable long-run result — whatever the difficulty of adaptation and whatever the internal contradictions — is the massive upgrading of great strata of the population.[36] In the past century through part of the present one, in the United States and several other countries, rural-urban migration was combined with great international migrations. Most European countries, and especially the less advanced ones, have experienced great changes in this respect.[37]

Downward mobility seems to have been quite considerable in Europe in recent decades.[38] Although not much attention has been devoted to this phenomenon, it is known that mobile individuals tend to maintain for a time their original attitudes and even their original class identification. But this is in advanced industrial societies in a period of economic growth. Mobile individuals' retention of cultural traits related to their class origins may increase heterogeneity within each stratum, but the "cost" of mobility may at the same time be reduced by the decreasing class differentials. Also, for contemporary generations, socialization in a period of rapid change and widespread ecological and vertical mobility may encompass mechanisms for adjustment to what seems to be a normal occurrence.[39] The frustrating effects of downward mobility may be partially neutralized by a widespread sense of increasing opportunities, as already noted. In any case, this climate may have prevented individual cases of downward mobility from creating a mass phenomenon.

To what extent is the progressive participation of growing sectors of the population in the consumption patterns, the style of life and the education levels were once symbols of upper-class status, experienced as personal mobility? In other words: when do such elements lose their psychosocial value as status symbols? For example, new items of consumption tend to be included in the family budget very soon, on a permanent basis, as normal expectations.[40]

Nevertheless, at least at present, many of the new consumption patterns are still viewed as symbols of personal success.[41] In any case, we do not need to belabor the fact that this process has narrowed considerably the distance between the working-class style of life and that of the middle classes, giving rise in the working population to a certain degree of "embourgeoisement." The progressive elevation of education, so that each new generation has access to levels that were out of the reach of the preceding one, not only promotes opportunities for individual betterment, but also permits fathers to transfer to their children their mobility aspirations. Thus, what is in fact a generalized improvement for the whole population may be felt by the subjects themselves as an individual attainment.

Two very important elements of this type of collective mobility are its continuity and its relative rapidity, so that most members of the present generations have experienced a progressive expansion of the possibilities of the individual. The expansion of aspirations has been simultaneous with the expansion of the possibilities of their satisfaction.

In a well known hypothesis, Lipset and others have suggested that "high" rates of individual mobility are equally characteristic of all industrial societies and that some consequences attributed to this process with respect to the United States, particularly the greater integration of the lower classes and the absence of typical class movements, are due not so much to mobility but rather to other aspects of social structure: equalitarian values and associated attitudes, especially the "equalitarianism of manners" which undoubtedly has helped to conceal or diminish class differences in power and prestige. In many European countries these differences are (or were) much more visible and exerted a much greater influence in accentuating the isolation of the working class. Other factors linked to the persistence of archaic traits in the stratification system, and some of the main conditions blocking mobility and facilitating the radicalization of the subordinated or isolated groups, were typical of the Western European situation. But as European countries approached the conditions required to facilitate the integrative effects of mobility, the integration of the working class increased considerably, as Lipset and others have observed. This change was clearly expressed in the substantial modification of working-class political and ideological attitudes, even though the old labels and party organization remained unchanged.[42]

The hypothesis that mobility occurs at an equally high rate in all industrial societies is limited, in any case, to "individual" mobility and mainly to the manual/nonmanual distinction. But this kind of mobility is only one of several forms that may create the mass mobility conditions needed to break the isolation of the lower strata and ameliorate their feelings of inferiority and rejection. Values, attitudes and ideologies are indeed determining factors in the consequences of mobility, but we must recognize that under conditions of mass mobility these same values, attitudes and ideologies are likely to be substantially modified. This is, in fact, the process that occurred in Europe in the postwar decades.[43] The contrast between the American and the European experiences indicates that a rather long period of isolation under a highly hierarchical and discontinuous stratification system is a necessary condition for establishing political organizations of a predominantly or exclusively working-class composition. Such organizations evidently are stable enough to persist after the conditions of isolation have disappeared or greatly diminished, although the ideological orientation of their political actions will be deeply modified as the lower strata they still represent become integrated with the national society. In the United States the integration occurred much earlier, and the greater and more diffused acceptance of the existing social order evidently inhibited the formation of specifically working-class parties of any importance.

Mass Migrations, Mass Mobility and Social Consensus in Argentina and Brazil

Argentina in two stages of its socioeconomic development and Brazil, more recently, in its rapidly industrializing regions have approached the conditions most conducive to the integrative effects of mobility.

The Argentinian experience during six decades of mass international migration (1870-1930) involves an almost complete transformation of the stratification system, and remarkable changes in values and attitudes, under the impact of mass mobility. At the beginning of the period the social structure and predominant values of this society were fairly similar to those of other Latin American countries, with the traditional Spanish emphasis on ascriptive norms and values, family origin and stability. At the national level the socio-occupational structure exhibited the typical two-class pattern,[44] with the bulk of the population in the lower stratum and the usual high discontinuity and high hierarchization prevailing between classes. In the decade 1860-1870 an accelerated process of economic growth and modernization was initiated, which in little more than forty years completely transformed the social structure and the economy of the country, at least in its "central" region where two-thirds of the population live. The innovating agent was the liberal elite, composed mostly of big landowners, who undertook the task of organizing Argentina as a modern nation, within the limits of the economic conceptions of the time and in accordance with their own political and economic interests. Their program involved mass foreign immigration, massive imports of foreign capital, building railways, roads and means of communications, establishing and diffusing modern education at all levels, creating modern bureaucratic organization and a stable representative democracy, occupying all the available land, incorporating all the national territory in the market economy, and finally integrating the national with the world economy by modernizing agriculture and cattle breeding, changes that turned Argentina from an importer nation into one of the main exporters of cereals, meat and other food products. The amazing growth of the society in the first three of four decades of the process is illustrated in Tables 3 and 4.

The conditions of mass mobility were created chiefly by the rapid expansion of the middle-class, whose proportion more than doubled in the twenty-five years before the turn of the century and has continued to grow at a very high rate ever since. This increase involved mass recruitment from the lower strata: during the period from 1890 to the end of mass immigration in 1930, more than two-thirds of the middle-class were of lower-class origin and in many cases the mobility was intragenerational.[47] In fact, most of the recruitment took place among the foreign immigrants who long formed the majority of the adult male population in the "cen-

TABLE 3
Some Indicators of Growth and Social Modernization
in Argentina: 1869-1960[45]

	1869	1895	1914	1947	1960
Population (000's)	1,700	4,000	7,900	15,900	20,000
Crude Birth Rate (0/000)	°	°	38	25	23
Crude Death Rate (0/000)	°	°	19	10	10
Mean No. Persons per Household	6.05	5.48	5.24	4.32	†
Percent of Population in Cities of 2,000 or More	27	37	53	62	†
Percent of Population in Cities of 20,000 or More	14	24	36	48	58‡
Percentage Foreign-Born	12	26	30	15	12
Percentage of Active Population in:					
Primary Activities	41 ‡	39 ‡	28 ‡	25	23
Secondary Activities	31 ‡	25 ‡	34 ‡	32	33
Tertiary Activities	28 ‡	36 ‡	38 ‡	43	44
Percentage of National Product: §					
Agricultural	°	37	25	18	°
Industrial	°	13	16	24	°
Percentage of Active Population in Middle Occupational Level ‡	11	25	30	40	45
Percentage Literate	22	47	65	84	92
University Students Per Thousand Inhabitants	°	°	1	3	7

° Data not available or not published.
† 1960 Census: data not yet available.
‡ Estimates based on census and other information.
§ Information refers to an approximate date, not precisely the year of the census.

TABLE 4
Percentages of the Active Population in Different
Socio-occupational Strata: Argentina, 1869-1960[46]

	Middle and Higher Occupational Levels		Lower Occupational Levels		
Year	Secondary and Tertiary Activities	Primary Activities	Secondary and Tertiary Activities	Primary Activities	Total
1869	5.1	5.5	53.5	35.9	100
1895	14.6	10.6	46.2	28.6	100
1914	22.2	8.2	50.0	19.6	100
1947	31.0	9.2	43.8	16.0	100
1960	37.3	7.9	39.7	15.1	100

tral" regions of the country.[48] Until 1900, more than ninety-five percent of the foreigners who arrived in Argentina were lower-class, mostly rural laborers, and in the following decades the proportion of middle-class immigrants increased a little but never exceeded ten percent during the period under consideration.[49]

As one of the consequences of this process, "open society" attitudes came to prevail in Argentina, including equalitarian values, manners and interpersonal relations, with diffused beliefs in the possibilities of individual success conceived in material terms, and less formalism and less tendency to make hierarchical distinctions than in the other Latin American countries.[50] This change (with respect to the original situation) was much less marked or even absent in the "peripherial" areas not affected by the developmental process, which was concentrated mainly in the *litoral* region.

With regard to the acceptance of the social and political order, the impact of mobility during this period (1870-1930), seems to be analogous to the European experience. The innovating elite — the so-called "oligarchy" — conceived its political regime as a liberal democracy, with limited popular participation. The radical changes the elite itself had promoted, in fact, initiated the social and political forces that would in time challenge its monopoly of power and prestige. As indicated earlier, the outcome of this situation of "partial mobility" was a "populist" reform movement led by the middle-class, but its relatively easy political success — enlarged political participation and access to power, coupled with a persisting high rate of mobility — evidently dissipated a great deal of its reformist zeal. In the lower strata the newly formed urban proletariat originated, in the first decade of the century, extreme radical protest movements, prone to violence but of relatively short duration as they were rapidly absorbed in the unions and in the very moderate socialist party that emerged in the twenties and thirties as a left-of-center alternative to the middle-class parties. Communism in its different varieties has remained an extremely limited group in Argentina, both before 1930 and afterwards.[51]

The relatively rapid integration of the urban proletariat in the "central" region can be explained partly as a consequence of individual mobility from the manual strata. This mobility rate was high,[52] but even if it had been low, similar effects would have been produced by complementary mechanisms. Certainly the country did not reach the stage of mass consumption at that time, but the process of uninterrupted economic growth may have contributed to satisfy the modest aspirations of the majority. However the most effective "multiplier" of the effects of individual mobility was the continuous renewal of a high proportion of the lower strata, by the constant flow of new immigrants into the lowest level, replacing those who were upwardly mobile. When this well-known mechanism of replacement from the bottom occurs fairly quickly, as it did in Argentina, there is not enough time to form a real "proletarian tradition," which requires, as in the European experience, a long period of isolation and class homogeneity.

The seventy-year period under consideration was quite stable, with a succession of civilian governments and no military intervention, and with popular participation in elections and normal political activity increasing. The large foreign population did not vote,[53] and in the "outer" underdeveloped regions the political influence of the lower strata remained fairly low.

A second stage in the modernization and economic development of Argentina, and similar changes in Brazil, illustrate the integrative effects of mobility in presently developing countries. In both countries mass mobility approaching the required conditions seems to have attentuated the tensions generated by the very rapid process of "social mobilization" through which large elements of the population are incorporated in the national life. The process is similar to what occurred in many European countries during the past century, but the much faster uprooting from traditional or rural milieu, coupled with the higher aspirations created by the "demonstration effect" in an age of mass consumption, introduced important differences.

In Argentina the recently mobilized masses came chiefly from the "peripheral" relions still largely underdeveloped and more traditional, but they also came from the "central" modernized areas where large sectors had been economically and socially uprooted as a result of the drastic reduction of exports during the world crisis and the long depression of the early thirties. The interruption of world trade set in motion a new cycle of industrialization, much more intensive and faster than the first one,[54] and the mobilized and displaced sectors of the population provided the necessary labor. Mass internal migrations replaced foreign immigration, which had completely stopped in 1930; the Buenos Aires metropolitan area received an average of nearly 100,000 migrants annually, from the middle thirties to the fifties. The growth of internal migration also affected the other large cities, and by 1947 nearly one-fourth of the population was living in a state different from the one in which they were born.[55] A large mass of rural and small-town laborers, small farmers (mostly tenants), petty artisans, peddlers, small shopkeepers and the endemic unemployed from the underdeveloped provinces, became industrial workers in the large cities and in the Buenos Aires area,[56] with the usual impact on housing and general social conditions. Labor turnover was higher and productivity was probably lower than for urban workers previously,[57] personal and family relations were disorganized, and workers were more isolated, more alienated and less likely to participate in voluntary associations, less rational in economic behavior and so forth.[58] But reorganization according to the urban pattern also occured very quickly,[59] and the social tensions caused by the large influx of migrants and the new industrial situation, though serious, never reached the high intensity of the similar situation that occurred at the beginning of the century.[60]

More recent tensions were reduced by mass mobility in its various forms, better living conditions, general upgrading through increased exposure to education, material and immaterial culture, and by individual mobility. In the Buenos Aires area upward mobility out of the manual strata was even more intense than at the turn of the century, and it was based on the same mechanism of upgrading the successive generations who immigrated to the city.[61] Even when individual chances deteriorated the newcomers did not feel frustrated in their hopes;[62] after ten years of economic stagnation and a decreasing level of living, most of the urban proletariat still believed in success through hard work and personal initiative.[63] On the whole, the workers seemed quite willing to accept the existing economic and social order, even if they wanted moderate reforms.

In any case the political instability of the last three decades cannot be imputed to overwhelming social pressure from a revolutionary lower class; these political troubles resulted from other historical circumstances, although they also reflected the impact of the sudden political incorporation of recently mobilized groups and the beginning of democracy based on total participation. That incorporation occurred through an authoritarian "national-popular" movement was mostly the result of the severe limitations under which the political system had functioned since 1930. To accommodate the recently mobilized groups and adapt to the changing composition of the urban lower strata, either the existing political parties had to be altered or a new one created, within the framework of representative democracy. But, on the one hand, the attempt to reestablish a "limited" democracy on behalf of the old "oligarchy" added new rigidities precisely at the moment when maximum flexibility was deeply needed.[64] On the other hand, the political elite was unable to understand the economic and social changes that were occurring so rapidly and the Socialist Party especially, as well as the unions, did not effectively take advantage of the political potential offered by the new industrial workers.[65] The Communists and other leftist groups were active, but failed to win their support, which was given instead to Perón.

The success of Perón can only partially be explained as an expression of the need for charismatic leadership, except with regard to the most traditional sectors of the lower class. For most workers Peronism presented the only realistic opportunity for moderate reform under the existing social order, which they basically accepted. In supporting Peronism they chose a moderate alternative: beneath the anti-imperialist, anti-oligarchic proclamations usually emphasized in Latin American populism, Peronism was much more conservative than most movements of this type. It never contested the basis of the existing economic order — private property and private enterprise — it only insisted on "social justice," social legislation, industrialization, agrarian reform, planning and other changes compatible with the interests of some sectors of the middle classes.[66] Its leaders' undemocratic and authoritarian orientation had a very different meaning for the followers or the union members.[67]

Political events of the post-Peronist years have shown that the majority of workers, while maintaining their organizations and their readiness to defend their economic and social interests through the normal pattern of industrial conflict, were not available for extreme solutions. In the various recent elections most of the previously Peronist votes were given to democratic parties, and the Peronist movement itself, profoundly divided, seemed ready for an analogous reorientation.[68]

The process that occurred in Brazil since 1930 is similar in many ways to the one just described. A cycle of intense urbanization and industrialization has deeply modified the social structure in some regions, creating a more modern pattern of social stratification with a new urban proletariat and a new middle class. This change has not affected large areas of the country: Brazil is still mostly rural, with marked contrasts between the highly industrialized and urbanized areas and the large underdeveloped regions, highly traditional, and economically marginal.[69] But internal migration and the absorption of an increasing proportion of the population into the new urban and industrial environment have occurred under conditions of rapid economic growth and mass mobility. Compared with Western Europe and the United States, the emergent groups are more traditionalist, the stratification system is less modern, even in the more advanced regions, and the society is characterized by marked internal discontinuities in modernization, but other factors have compensated for these differences and the impact of mass mobility has produced similar integrative mechanisms in the rapidly changing areas.

A number of studies describe the role of mobility in the assimilation of rural migrants. In this transition two main phases have been distinguished. The first one consists of the simple transposition of traditional patterns to the new situation; the second one involves a new definition of the situation, with new attitudes and new modes of action.

In the first stage of the specific tasks associated with the job are identified with traditional "obligations" to the "Patrão," which were "reciprocated" with a "fair" salary. The enterprise is expected to give the same particularistic "protection" as the landowner. Although a diffuse feeling of solidarity is not absent, it expresses the traditional distinction between the "poor people" and "the rich" rather than the solidarity of the workers'

group as such.[70] As a result, the new workers either lack a basis for organized collective action, or depend exclusively on the primary relations of
kinship and friendship. A union may initiate and organize collective
action, but even when it succeeds in imposing the discipline required for a
strike, it is still perceived as an external factor, lacking the active and
psychological participation of the migrant workers. They view the union as
a provider of services; often they make no distinctions between the State
and the union. Aspirations are predominately oriented toward escape from
the industrial situation itself.[71] Nevertheless, adaptation to the new urban
industrial culture does take place: at least some of the migrants develop
new modes of interaction and a clearer consciousness of being an industrial worker facing a new set of social relations. But even if these changes
do involve a higher level of political awareness, and more conscious and
mature union participation, they do not involve more readiness to accept
ideological radicalism. Cardoso believes that the behavior of workers who
have reached this stage is determined

> more by their demands of better conditions within the capitalist system then
> by a political action addressed to transform the total social system. Such an
> evaluation of the future is based on the fact of the existence of career posibil-
> ities within the industry, on the fact of economic growth and of the reason-
> able level of skilled workers' salaries.

At present, the Brazilian urban proletariat has little revolutionary potential. On the contrary, Cardoso thinks that workers' action will probably be
increasingly oriented toward movements demanding better working and
living conditions more than anything else.[72]

Individual mobility assumes a central role in this transition. Touraine
has applied a typology to it based precisely on different levels of aspiration
and different mobility experiences. At the lowest level there are no aspirations and no mobility, and we find a simple denial of the industrial situation, leading to a kind of apathetic adaptation — perhaps the condition
most favorable to *populismo;* on the other hand, when aspirations are
higher the experience of some measure of upward mobility within the
industrial situation will produce a higher level of integration and increase
political and union participation. Under conditiona of economic growth,
and if this individual mobility is part of a general process of national development, the workers' political orientation is likely to be more moderate
than revolutionary.[73]

The political evolution of Brazil reflects the reformist and moderate orientation of the new urban proletariat. In this sense, Varguism is similar to
Peronism with respect to its moderate character and the composition of its
leadership, as well as its authoritarianism.[74] Given the more traditional
element in the mobilized sectors, the paternalistic and charismatic factor

must have been stronger,[75] but Varguism also represented a moderate choice when other more extreme possibilities were available.[76] President Goulart's failure to win the support of the industrial workers at a crucial moment may be considered another expression of the absence of revolutionary potential in the urban lower class.

While moderation may in part reflect the passivity of a still traditional (and submissive) population, it is also the result of an evolution of working-class consciousness which is remarkably different from the European experience. In Europe the awakening of class consciousness in the traditional groups involved an intermediate stage of predominant alienation and extreme radicalization (which could last many decades), and only later did a third stage take place in which workers were progressively integrated and increasingly apt to accept the existing social order. In Brazil and in Argentina only two stages have occurred: the lower strata moved from traditionalism directly to integration and moderate reformism. Mass mobility and other conditions eliminated or considerably reduced the period of working-class isolation and segregation of the working class: at the same time they eliminated the possibility of an intermediate radical stage.

Given the other necessary intervening conditions I have described, these are the specific consequences of mass mobility in developing countries.

Notes

1. For a general review see Pitirim A. Sorokin, *Social Mobility* (New York: Harper & Row, 1927), Ch. 21.

2. This degree of specificity is not usually achieved in empirical studies of the effects of mobility.

3. Robert K. Merton, *Social Theory and Social Structure* (New York: Free Press of Glencoe, 1957), pp. 262-80.

4. Harold L. Wilensky, "Orderly Careers and Social Participation," *American Sociological Review*, 26 (August, 1961), pp. 521-39.

5. Arnold S. Feldman, "The Interpenetration of Firm and Society," in International Social Science Council (ed.), *Les implications sociales du progrès technique* (Paris, 1962), p. 192.

6. See Peter M. Blau, "Social Mobility and Interpersonal Relations," in *American Sociological Review*, 21 (June, 1956), pp. 290-95.

7. The tendency seems to be "retention" of father's status; this effect was quite clear in the author's Buenos Aires study: Gino Germani, "Class Social subjectiva e indicadores objetivos de estratificación" (Buenos Aires: Instituto de Sociologia, 1963). Effects of mobility on self-affiliation were also observed by Bertram A. Hutchinson, "Class Self-Assessment in a Rio de Janeiro Population," *América Latina* 6 (1963), pp. 53-64, and by F. M. Martin, "Some Subjective Aspects of

Social Stratification," in David V. Glass (ed.), *Social Mobility in Britain* (London: Routledge and Kegan Paul, 1954), Ch. 3.

8. Emile Durkheim, *Le Suicide* (Paris: Alcan, 1897), Ch. 5; Maurice Halbwachs, *Les causes de suicide* (Paris: Alcan, 1930), Ch. 15 (an interesting early reformulation of the classic Durkheimian hypothesis by a prominent member of the school); Merton, *op. cit.,* p. 188. On the disorganizing effects of social mobility, see the summary and bibliography in Seymour M. Lipset and Reinhard Bendix, *Social Mobility in Industrial Society* (Berkeley: University of California Press, 1959), pp. 64 ff., 252, and *passim.* See also Morris Janowitz, "Some Consequences of Social Mobility in the United States," in *Transactions of the Third World Congress of Sociology* (London: International Sociological Association, 1956), pp. 191-201. More recent contributions to this topic are Robert J. Kleiner and Seymour Parker, "Social Striving, Social Status, and Mental Disorder: A Research Review," *American Sociological Review,* 28 (April 1963), pp. 189-203 and Warren Breed, "Occupational Mobility and Suicide Among White Males," *American Sociological Review,* 28 (April, 1963), pp. 174-188. For a review of earlier literature, see Sorokin, *op. cit.* Ch. 21.

9. Merton, *op. cit.,* pp. 135 ff.

10. See also Melvin Tumin, "Competing Status Systems" in Wilber E. Moore and Arnold S. Feldman (eds.), *Labor Commitment and Social Change in Developing Areas* (New York: Social Science Research Council, 1960), pp. 279-80.

11. Lipset and Bendix, *op. cit.,* esp. Ch. 3.

12. Lipset and Bendix, *op. cit.,* consider status incongruity one of the major intervening factors in conditioning the social consequences of mobility. Some effects of low crystallization on political or ideological orientation were found by Lenski, who also formulated a statistical definition of incongruency; see Gerhard E. Lenski, "Status Crystallization: A Non-Vertical Dimension of Social Status," *American Sociological Review,* 19 (June, 1954), pp. 405-13. Analogous results were found by Erving W. Goffman, "Status Consistency and Preference for Change in Power Distribution," *American Sociological Review,* 22 (February, 1957), pp. 275-81. Lenski also studied effects on social participation: "Social Participation, Status Crystallization and Class Consciousness," *American Sociological Review,* 21 (June, 1956), pp. 458-64. Degree of status congruence also seems to affect self-affilation to class: see Werner S. Landecker, "Class Crystallization and Class Consciousness," *American Sociological Review,* 28 (April, 1963), pp. 219-29. Similar results were obtained in Buenos Aires by Germani, *op. cit.*

13. Marion Levy, "Contrasting Factor in the Modernization of China and Japan," in Simon Kuznets, Wilbert E. Moore and Joseph J. Spengler (eds.), *Economic Growth: Brazil, India, Japan* (Durham, N.C.: Duke University Press, 1955); Everett E. Hagen, *On the Theory of Social Change* (Homewood, Ill.: The Dorsey Press, 1962).

14. Morris Watnick, "The Appeal of Communism to the Peoples of Underdeveloped Areas," in Seymour M. Lipset and Reinhard Bendix (eds.), *Class, Status and Power* (New York: Free Press of Glencoe, 1953); Myron Weiner, "The Politics of South Asia," in Gabriel A. Almond and James S. Coleman (eds.), *The Politics of the Developing Areas* (Princeton: Princeton University Press, 1960); Jerome M. v.d. Kroef, "Social Conflict and Minority Aspirations in Indonesia," *American Journal of Sociology,* 55 (1950), pp. 450-63.

15. Richard F. Behrendt, "The Emergence of New Elites and New Political Integration Forms and their Influence on Economic Development," in *Transac-*

tions of the Fifth World Congress of Sociology (Louvain: International Sociological Association, 1962). An interesting example of the contrasting effects of modern education in a traditional setting when accompanied or not accompanied by status discrepancies is mentioned in a study on the political evolution of Uganda: David E. Apter, *The Political Kingdom of Uganda* (Princeton: University Press, 1961), pp. 199 ff. and 313 ff.

16. On the populist alliance of the rising middle class and the lower strata, see Víctor Alba, *Historia del Movimiento Obrero en América Latina* (México: Liberos Mexicanos Unidos, 1964), Ch. 7; Armando Villanueva-del-Campo, "Partidos Democráticos Revolucionarios en Indoamérica," *Combate* (September 1961 and February 1962); Mario Monteforte-Toledo, *Partidos Políticos de Iberoamérica* (México: Instituto de Investigaciones Sociales de la Universidad Nacional Autónoma, 1961). Torcuato Di Tella has analyzed the role or partially blocked mobility in the anti-status-quo attitudes of Latin American intellectuals and middle-class groups: "Los Procesos Políticos y Sociales de la Industrialización," *Desarrollo Económico*, 2 (1962), pp. 19-48 and *El Sistema Político Argentino y la Clase Obrera* (Buenos Aires: Eudeba, 1964), Ch. 9.

17. The typical evolution of the APRA and other similar Latin American movements is examined from a leftist standpoint by Álvaro Mendoza-Diez in *La Revolución de los Professionales e Intelectuales en Latinoamérica* (México: Instituto de Investigaciones Sociales, Universidad Nacional Autónoma, 1962).

18. Social status and degree of modernization of the region of origin have been important in determining political orentation. In Germany, intellectuals of higher status and from more traditional and peripheral regions most frequently adopted the Nazi ideology, while the opposite was true for the "cosmopolitans" and those of lower social origins. In Argentina, extreme right-wing nationalism, during the thirties, was supported by a downwardly mobile traditional elite drawn disproportionately from the backward rural regions.

19. Karl Mannheim, in *Man and Society in an Age of Social Reconstruction* (New York: Harcourt, Brace & World, 1940), aptly describes the difference between the effects of *individual* unemployment and mass unemployment: "If in normal times an individual loses his job, he may indeed despair, but his reactions are more or less prescribed and he follows a general pattern in his distress. The panic reaches its height when the individual comes to realize that his insecurity is not simply a personal one, but is common to masses of his fellows, and when it becomes clear to him that there is no longer any social authority to set unquestioned standards and determine his behaviour," p. 130.

20. See Harold L. Wilensky and Hugh Edwards, "The Skidder," *American Sociological Review*, 24 (April, 1959), pp. 215-31, on the different consequences of downward mobility in a climate of depression as compared with a period of prosperity.

21. For a comparison between Italian Fascism and Argentine Peronism, see Gino Germani: "La Integración Política de las Masas," *Cursos y Conferencias*, 42 (June, 1956).

22. That is, specific aspirations are related to specific kinds of actual mobility; relative deprivation is minimized and optimum relative gratification ensured.

23. The term fluidity is used by S.M. Miller: "Comparative Social Mobility," *Current Sociology*, 9 (1960).

24. See, for example, the procedure used by Lenski, *op. cit.*

25. Sorokin, *op. cit.*, Ch. 22.

26. In the Buenos Aires metropolitan area a sample survey showed that the occupational origins of the present generation were quite mixed. In the two lower (manual) strata, taken together, only 34.7 percent had remained stable (within either stratum); within the two manual categories 21.7 percent had moved up, and 6.6 percent down; finally, 37.0 percent had fathers who were nonmanual. In the three middle categories only 23.8 percent had remained in the same middle category as their fathers; another 20 percent had moved up or down within the middle strata; 17.4 percent were born in the two upper most strata; and finally 38.7 percent were of lower-class origin. In two higher strata, 29 percent were stable, 8.5 percent had been mobile within the two strata, and the majority — 62.5 percent — had lower origins (42.0 percent were born in the middle strata and 20.5 percent in the manual strata). While this situation seems rather common in urban areas, it is still important here to clarify the psychological and cultural meaning of the occupational classification. (In this example it was based, as usual, on occupational prestige.) Gino Germani, *La Mobilidad Social en la Argentina* (Buenos Aires, Instituto de Sociología, P. Interna 60, 1963), p. 21.

27. Sorokin, *op. cit.*, Chs. 21-22; Lipset and Bendix, *op. cit.*, pp. 66 ff; Wilensky and Edwards, *op. cit.* Ralf Dahrendorf expresses the same opinion but he notes that "mobility within classes is entirely irrelevant" in the context of class conflict: *Class and Class Conflict in an Industrial Society* (London: Routledge and Kegan Paul, 1959), pp. 220-21. But then one may ask where class boundaries are in metropolitan urban society.

28. The rate of downward mobility is likely to increase with the growth of occupations to which acess is based on educational requirements rather than inheritance of wealth, because there is the risk that an individual will fail to achieve the education level required to maintain his family position while virtually no such rish is involved in inheriting property. In the stratification and mobility survey in Buenos Aires (already quoted), and in a similar survey in Sao Paulo (Brazil), a considerable proportion of downward mobility was associated with failure to achieve the educational level "required" at any given occupational level (the "requirement" being defined statistically). See Gino Germani, *La Mobilidad, op. cit.*, and Bertrand Hutchinson: "A Educação e a Mobilidade Social" in Bertrand Hutchinson (ed.), *Mobilidade e Trabalho* (Rio de Janeiro, Centro Brasileiro de Pesquisas Educacionais, 1960).

29. Miller, *op. cit.*

30. Published data show that mobility from the unskilled or lowest level may be very high in some countries: 79.6 percent in the Netherlands; 80.0 percent in the U.S., 72.6 percent in Great Britain, 54.6 percent in Denmark, and lower in Japan (36.2 percent) and Italy (34.0 percent). In the former countries, however, upward mobility from the semiskilled level includes the majority of those born in the stratum (53.7 percent); high mobility is also observed when one takes into account only movement from the lower urban stratum: Puerto Rico, 86.0 percent; U.S., 63.0 percent but in West Germany only 38.5 percent. Cf. Miller, *op. cit.*

31. The possibility of an inverse relation between distance and the effects of downward mobility has been mentioned by Seymour M. Lipset and Joan Gordon, "Mobility and Trade Union Membership," in Lipset and Bendix (eds.),*Class, Status and Power, op. cit.*

32. Leonard Reissman, "Level of Aspiration and Social Class" in *American Sociological Review,*18 (April 1953), pp. 233-242 and the bibliography in his *Class in American Society* (New York: Free Press of Glencoe, 1959), Ch. 6. In his

research on automobile workers Chinoy found that a stable job was experienced as mobility or "getting ahead." Ely Chinoy, *Autombile Workers and the American Dream* (Garden City, N.Y.: Doubleday & Company, 1955), p. 125. According to Zweig, the worker "wants to better himself not so much by promotion, but by higher wages," and he wants security more than anything else. Ferdynand Zweig, *The Worker in an Affluent Society* (London: Heinemann, 1961), pp. 205-06.

33. Nelson N. Foote, "The Professionalization of Labor in Detroit," *American Journal of Sociology*, 58 (1953), pp. 371-80. For the same trend in France, see Serge Mallet, *La Nouvelle Classe Ouvrière* (Paris: Editions du Seuil, 1963), pp. 56 ff.

34. Wilensky, *op. cit.*

35. Arnold S. Feldman, "Economic Development and Social Mobility," *Economic Development and Cultural Change*, 8 (1960), pp. 311-20; see his remarks on the interaction between status and situs mobility.

36. International data on mobility connected with rural-urban migration have been summarized and analyzed by Lipset and Bendix, *Social Mobility . . . , op. cit.*, pp. 216 ff. While the circumstances of migration, the selection of the migrants, the distribution of occupational opportunities, and so on, condition the consequences of migration, in a time of industrial growth and in the contemporary work situation, rural-urban displacements are likely to be experienced as upward mobility. In a recent research on French workers of rural origin, Touraine says: "Their presence in the factory is the proof — for them — of mobility, if not of an achieved mobility at least of a first step, of a first victory: their entrance into urban economy and into urban life." Alain Touraine and Onetta Ragazzi: *Ouvriers d'origine Agricole* (Paris: Editions du Seuil, 1961), p. 117.

37. Italy is probably one of the most extreme among Western European countries: in 1951 forty percent of the labor force was concentrated in agriculture; in 1961, this proportion had been reduced by half, i.e., to twenty percent. This process will probably continue in many European countries: the European Parliament has estimated at many millions the labor force to be transferred from the primary sector to the others. See Gaston Beijer, *Rural Migrants in an Urban Setting* (The Hague: Martinus Nijhoff, 1963), p. 23.

38. Miller, *op. cit.;* the published figures show a minimum of approximately twenty percent to a maximum of forty-three percent percent moving out of the nonmanual into the manual strata.

39. Mobility seems not to be disruptive for those who are trained for it; this provisional conclusion refers to ecological mobility, but may have some application to vertical mobility as well. See Phillip Fellin and Eugene Litwak, "Neighborhood Cohesion Under Conditions of Mobility," *American Sociological Review*, 28 (June, 1963), pp. 364-76.

40. This process of progressive change in the normal expectations of consumption was observed and described more than thirty years ago by Maurice Halbwachs, *L'Evolution des besoins dans les Classes Ouvrières* (Paris: Alcan, 1933), pp. 148 ff.

41. Conspicuous consumption is becoming common among workers. "He (the worker) wants to show something for his labor, something tangible which can be seen by everybody and speaks clearly the language of success. He wants to show that he has not wasted his life, but achieved something which does not fall behind the standard of others. In this way a large section of the working-class population becomes a property-owning class." (Zweig, *op. cit.*, p. 206). Durable goods, cars

and home ownership retain their value as status symbols, even if increasingly common ("My neighbours would call me middle class because I have my own house." *Ibid.*, p. 138).

42. Seymour M. Lipset, "The Changing Class Structure and Contemporary European Politics," *Daedalus* (Winter, 1964), pp. 271-303; see also the articles by Ralf Dahrendorf, Alessandro Pizzorno and Alain Touraine in the same issue.

43. It is interesting to compare the necessary conditions for a distinct working class consciousness as summarized by de Man some thirty years ago on the basis of a survey among workers, and Zweig's observations on the contemporary English working class. According to de Man, the conditions are: (i) membership in a class deprived of any property; (ii) insecurity; (iii) low status, lack of consideration; (iv) lack of mobility. Henri de Man, *La Gioia nel Lavoro* (Bari: Laterza, 1931), p. 393. According to Zweig, (i) "the working-class population becomes a property-owning class," (ii) has "security mindedness," (iii) "has a recognized niche and social position; (iv) even apart from those who are mobile within the working class, "a quarter of the boys coming from factory workers' families are reaching middle-class levels," Zweig, *op. cit.*, pp. 146-47; 205-06.

44. Di Tella has observed, in Chile, Argentina and elsewhere, an "intermediate" stratum of a traditional nature (artisans, small shopkeepers and the like) which includes a considerable proportion of the urban population even if in the national average it is very small. Downgraded by the "first impact" of economic development it could have some political role. This hypothesis, however, does not alter the basic assumption of a two-class system at the national level. See Torcuato Di Tella, Economía y Estructura Ocupacional en Un País Subdesarrollado," *Desarrollo Económico*, 1 (1961), pp. 123-53.

45. Sources for the data are the national censuses and other official statistics; estimates and analysis in Gino Germani, *Estructura Social de la Argentina* (Buenos Aires: Raigal, 1955), and Ruth Sautú, "The Socio-occupational Structure of Argentina, 1869-1914" (Buenos Aires, Instituto de Sociología, 1961) (unpublished paper).

46. Same sources as Table 3.

47. Germani, *La Mobilidad Social, op. cit.*, p. 10.

48. More than seventy percent in the Buenos Aires area and more than fifty percent in the Litoral, Gino Germani, "La Asimilación de los Inmigrantes en la Argentina," *Revista Interamericana de Ciencias Sociales* (Washington), 1 (1961), no. 1.

49. Germani, *La Mobilidad Social, op. cit.*, p.7.

50. Except for Uruguay, where development took a form closely similar to Argentina's.

51. In the twenties Argentine Communists numbered fewer than 3,500. See Rollie Poppino, *International Communism in Latin America* (New York: Free Press of Glencoe, 1964), p. 64. The maximum vote obtained by Communists, in a coalition with democratic noncommunist groups, was less than five percent in 1946, in the Buenos Aires area. In the rest of the country they were nonexistent.

52. The national average may be estimated at some twenty to twenty-five percent as a minimum. But since the process was concentrated in the central areas the actual upward mobility rates in this region must have been much higher, especially in Buenos Aires and other large urban centers.

53. Only two percent of the foreigners had Argentine citizenship; the procedure

was open to all, and relatively simple, but nobody really cared since the legal situation of foreigners was quite favorable in every respect.

54. During this period the share of the national product contributed by industry became larger than the portion generated by agriculture and cattle breeding; see Table 3.

55. Gino Germani, "El Proceso de Urbanización en la Argentina," *Revista Interamericana de Ciencias Sociales* (Washington), 3 (1963), no. 3.

56. The industrial demand for labor far exceeded the total annual increase in the labor force. The internal migrants, who comprised only eleven percent of the population of the Buenos Aires metropolitan area in 1914 and still did not exceed this percentage in 1936, had increased to twenty-six percent in 1947. At the same time the foreign population was rapidly decreasing. The same process took place in the majority of the urban centers.

57. Knox found much higher labor turnover and absenteeism among the internal migrants than among the foreign born workers or those born in the city. John B. Knox, "Absenteeism and Turnover in an Argentine Factory," *American Sociological Review*, 26 (June, 1961), pp. 424-28.

58. Gino Germani, "An Inquiry into the Social Effects of Industrialization and Urbanization in Buenos Aires," in Phillip Hauser (ed.); *Urbanization in Latin America* (Paris: UNESCO, 1962).

59. Living in a shanty town was an effective barrier to the acculturation of the migrants to urban life, though only some two percent of the total population lived in such conditions. Even a slum was a more favorable situation for the rapid adjustment of the migrant.

60. Germani, "El Proceso de Urbanización," *op. cit.*

61. In 1960, in Buenos Aires among sons of unskilled fathers, more than eighty percent of those born in the area, and some seventy-five percent of the internal migrants, had achieved some upward mobility. Mobility into the nonmanual categories was also high, and it revealed larger differentials among the city-born, the migrants and the foreigners. Germani, *La Mobilidad Social, op. cit.*

62. Only three percent of the migrants with longer residence in the city said that their hopes had been frustrated. For those with shorter residence the proportion was higher (twenty percent) but they had arrived in a period of economic decline. (See Germani, "An Inquiry into the Social Effects," *op. cit.*)

63. Germani, *La Mobilidad Social, op. cit.* The rapid increase of per capita income (more than six percent per year) had ceased in 1950-52.

64. This attempt took place in 1930, when a military coup put an end to seventy years of political stability. Widespread electoral fraud limited the functioning of the representative system. From 1943 to 1945 another military coup attempted to establish a fascist dictatorship of the European type. In 1946 the Constitution was reestablished and Peronism won some fifty-five percent of the vote in regular elections.

65. The periodicals of the Labor Confederation and the Unions gave no attention to the mass of new industrial workers, and they remained largely unorganized until mass unionization occurred under the Peronist Unions.

66. Especially the new industrial middle class, which probably had experienced partially blocked mobility; Peronism was not fully accepted by the older middle class.

67. For a specific analysis of the meaning of freedom and authoritarianism for the lower class under Peronism, see Germani, "La Integración Política," *op. cit.*

68. From the high mark reached by the Peronist vote under the regime (some sixty-five percent of the vote), the "blank" (Peronist) vote was reduced to some eighteen percent in the 1963 election, in spite of Perón's "order." Survey data on the political attitudes of the population of the Buenos Aires area (in 1960) seem also to indicate wide support for political pluralism as against the one-party system:

Socioeconomic Status	Percent Preferring One-Party System
1 (low)	20.1
2	17.1
3	13.4
4	13.7
5	6.3
6 (high)	3.2

(The two lower groups contain forty-one percent of the total population.) See Gino Germani, "Authoritariansim and Prejudice in Buenos Aires" (unpublished). Many indications suggest that these authoritarians are of the "traditional" type. Another survey (1962) showed that the rest of the hard-core Peronists came disproportionately from the migrant sector of the population, and that their orientation was mostly determined by their "loyalty" to the charismatic leader: José L. de Imaz, *Motivación Electoral* (Buenos Aires: Instituto de Desarrollo Económico-Social, 1962).

69. See Charles Wagley, "The Brazilian Revolution: Social Changes since 1930," in Richard N. Adams and others, *Social Change in Latin America Today* (New York: Harper & Row, 1960); Fernando H. Cardoso, "Le Proletariat Brésilien," *Sociologie du Travail,* 4 (1961), pp. 50-65; Bertrand Hutchinson, "The Migrant Population of Urban Brazil," *América Latina,* 6 (1963), pp. 41-71. According to this survey, conducted in six of the most important Brazilian cities, some sixty-five percent of the population were internal migrants.

70. The change of class-identification from "poor" to "worker" decreases with education and seems also to be inversely correlated with political awareness; Glaucio A. Dillon Soares, "Classes Sociais, Strata Sociais e as Eleições Presidenciais de 1960," *Sociologia* (1961), pp. 217-38.

71. Brandao Lopes, *op. cit.* and Relations Industrielles dans deux Communautés Brésiliennes," *Sociologie du Travail* (1961), pp. 18-32. Fernando H. Cardoso, "Atitudes e Expectativas Desfavoráveis a Mudança Social," *Boletin* (Rio de Janeiro: Centro Latino Americano de Pesquisas em Ciencias Sociais, 1960), No. 3, pp. 15-22.

72. Cardoso, "Le Proletariat . . ." *op. cit.,* p. 377.

73. Alain Touraine, "Industrialisation et Conscience Ouvrière à São Paulo," *Sociologie du Travail* (1961), pp. 389-407.

74. Wagley, *op. cit;* John Johnson, *Political Change in Latin America* (Stanford: Stanford University Press, 1958), p. 171.

75. Andrew Pearse, "Algunas Características de la Urbanización en Río de Janeiro," Hauser (ed.), *op. cit.,* pp. 194-207.

76. The Communist party won eight percent of the vote; it was well organized with a prestigeful leader.

9.

Urbanization in the Advanced and Developing Countries

The Demographic and Sociological Definitions of Urbanization

The term urbanization refers to the process by which a determined area and its population become urbanized, as well as the stage reached by the process at a given moment. In its dynamic and static sense, the definition will depend on the criteria used to characterize what is "urban." These criteria vary considerably and in reality there does not exist a definition which is accepted universally. What makes the analysis and definition of this term so complex is the intimate connection between the process of urbanization and other processes of change, in modern times as well as in the paet. This connection is such that often the concept of urbanization tends to indicate the global process, or rather, is identified with the totality of these changes. Our purpose here is very limited: We are attempting to point out in very brief and general terms to what extent the process of urbanization, understood purely as a phenomenom of ecological concentration, should be considered in connection with the other component processes of economic development and the subprocesses of social modernization.

In the census and other official statistics, criteria which are relatively simple and easily determined quantatively are usually used. The criteria of the numerical size of inhabitants, and the density of population, are usually employed. According to these criteria, what is defined as urban is the center and the identifiable agglomeration, (for example, on the base of a given level of density), which contains a certain minimum number of inhabitants. This minimum usually varies: 2,000, 5,000, 10,000 and 20,000 are numbers often used to mark the difference between urban and non-urban entities. Another less used criterion, which is sometimes combined with the preceding ones, is based on the type of political-administrative organization of the area under consideration. This is possible especially in those countries where the urban areas have a different form of administration than that of the rural areas. Finally, also for purposes of the census, a third criterion has been proposed, based on the occupation, agricultural or nonagricultural, of the inhabitants under consideration. The International Institute of Statistics, which has made this proposal, suggests that those minimum administrative divisions be considered as urban in which at least sixty percent of the population are employed in nonagricultural work.[1]

All these criteria are obviously only indicators of a certain social reality under study. They are certainly useful in macrosociological analyses and in comparisons because of their quantitative character and because they can be easily observed. The problem of their validity remains open, nevertheless, meaning their connection or validity in relation to the phenomena being studied. We are confronting a theoretical problem, since we are attempting to define the concept of what is urban and to examine to what extent, among the many possible manifest indicators which can be used to isolate empirically the concrete reality corresponding to this concept, which, among these will be the most convenient for purposes of study.

A sociological definition of the concept should be based on data specifically associated with the particular social structure which characterizes urban society, in contrast with the non-urban or rural social structure. If a universally valid definition is being proposed in addition, these data should be general enough to cover very different types of societies. This is the principal difficulty: the nature of the urban and the non-urban vary fundamentally according to the kind of society in question. The concept of the urban, to a greater extent than other sociological concepts, has a historical character, which implies that a definition should have enough content in order to isolate concrete phenomena. A universal definition of urban, although possible, would not be sufficient for analytical purposes: for this a level of concreteness would be required and its applicability would necessarily remain restricted to a determined type of society. It is obvious that different levels of abstraction (or of concreteness) can be considered simultaneously, but it would be dangerous to extend definitions which are valid in a determined context, or on one level of applicability, to another context or to a different level. Many of the discussions on the urban have remained sterile precisely because of a lack of clarity in relation to these restrictions on the use of these diverse concepts.

One of the most successful attempts to define the city in terms of a sociological theory, Wirth's, presents precisely this defect: he extends the applicability of the concept further than the limits of its historical validity. Wirth defines the city as "a permanent settlement, relatively large and dense, of socially heterogeneous individuals." This definition provides the variables which, in Wirth's judgment, characterize urban social structure and at the same time, condition many of its cultural and psychological features.[2] The influence of Durkheim and Simmel is recognized here, especially in Wirth's description of urbanism "as a way of life." Volume, density and heterogeneity are the characteristics of urban society, and from these flow other features: predominance of secondary relations, individualism, tolerance, segmentary roles, propensity to change, social mobility, abstract thought, along with many elements which are considered to be pathological, subsumed under the rubrics of anomie and of social disorganization. Then, this notion of the urban, as has been pointed out many times, is most appropriate to a determined historical phase of the city, and to a given type of society. Many of the features indicated by Wirth are the same as those assigned to "industrial society," in the dichotomies which oppose this type of structure to the "preindustrial" or "traditional" type. The city is perceived as a secularized society par excellence, and in addition, urbanization is converted into a synonym for modernization and secularization. Analogous criticisms can be directed to other theoretical schemes, for example, to the idea of the folk-urban continuum. Another of the negative elements which usually characterize the city as a secularized society is its assimilation to the so-called "mass society," to which it attributes all the negative connotations of this concept.[3] Tte restriction of the validity of a definition to the given historical context is perfectly legitimate. Weber's idea that the city should be considered above all as a political community made up of equals, endowed with sovereignty and with the military means corresponding to this is undoubtedly very fertile when explaining the role of the Western city in the rise of modern society, and as such is contrasted with the Eastern city, site of autocratic bureaucracies, deprived of power and characterized by a system of castes which establishes insuperable barriers between its inhabitants.[4] But the phenomenon of the urban and of urbanization in an epoch of rapid technological and social transformation requires other conceptual instruments.

Primary Urbanization, Secondary Urbanization and Secularization

Redfield and Singer[5] have attempted to formulate a scheme to differentiate conceptually folk society and two types of cities: the city which promotes "orthogenetic change" and the city which promotes "heterogenetic" change. Redfield conceives of the city as playing an important role in cultural change, but with the distinction indicated, intends to demarcate clearly a separation between the preindustrial city and that corresponding to "secularized" societies. In the first case, the city does not deny or destroy the ancient folk culture but develops it, within the same values, systematizing it, giving it a "cultured" expression (in the sense of higher culture) in art, philosophy, and letters.

In the second case, the situs of heterogeneous change, the urban is a creator of a new cultural form which denies folk culture and replaces it with values of rationality, predominance of the technical and scientific, secondary relations, and other characteristics which are usually employed to define secularized societies. In connection with this typology two types of urbanization are defined: primary urbanization and secondary urbanization. Primary urbanization does not lead to a sharp contrast between rural and urban culture, since it feeds on the former and represents a sublimation, and a "cultured" articulation of traditions.

Secondary urbanization, on the contrary, supposes the rise of values and of a social structure which substantially modifies the rural and traditional culture. It deals precisely with the process of secularization, which, as was seen in the first chapter, constitutes the basic change, the necessary (although not sufficient) condition, of the rise of "modern-industrial" society. Redfield and Singer's definition can doubtless contribute to clarifying part of the confusion which still exists about urbanization. If the present process is doubtless "secondary urbanization," the fact that the same can occur in areas where primary urbanization took place previously, and that modernization takes place in extremely complex circumstances, obliges us to keep the distinction clear. Among other things, the rise of a "national identity" in the new countries can give new meanings to the cultural products of "primary urbanization." We are dealing with forms of "ideological traditionalism."[6] Contents of the "preindustrial" culture are transformed into elements of the new national consciousness which the intellectuals and the political leaders of the ex-colonial countries try to promote among the masses. Structures corresponding to primary urbanization can continue to exist with those produced by secondary urbanization, and this is a phenomenom which can have significant consequences.

It is important to consider the works of Sjoberg, destined to provide generalizations about the "preindustrial city," especially the preindustrial city of our times,[7] which is to say it is a social structure in rapid transition towards other forms, to which not only the schemes constructed on the basis of social types corresponding to previous stages at the beginning of the process of transition are not entirely applicable, or of those which have achieved more advanced stages of the process, but also cannot be analyzed in the same terms used for the transition which took place in countries which initiated "the great transformation" early, especially England, the United States and other nations of Western Europe.

Certainly, as has been shown by Weber and others, the Western city played a central role in the creation of the cultural preconditions which made the coming of industrial society possible. From there arose the values, attitudes, forms of thought, the human groups, and the cultural works on which this new type of society was constructed. The Western city played an essential role in the process of secularization which finally, through its association with the change in economic attitudes and the use of technology and energetic forms of high potential, began the rise of the "modern cultural industrial complex."

Demographic Urbanization and Economic Development in the Countries of Early Development

On the other hand, even in Europe, we should clearly distinguish the role of the city as a cradle of the modern world, with its impact on the great historical processes of the Renaissance or the Reformation, the rise of science and secularization in politics and economics and the role and the location of the city in relation to the universal conditions which required a certain level of urban concentration so that industrialization (in a strict sense) was possible. We are dealing then, with the connection between urbanization on the one hand and economic development on the other. Here urban concentration is a necessary functional requirement, given a certain level of technical and scientific development, and certain features of the social structure (certain "preconditions" for the rise of the industrial "type"). But once the principle of instrumental rationality is diffused, it can be shown how the necessities of economic rationalization, even on the level of "spontaneous action" of enterprises in a liberal regime, tend to promote the ecological concentration of the population. Lampard[8] has summarized in a very clear scheme the mechanisms which have given rise to urban concentration upon the rise of the "first" industrial society and its diffusion in the Western world.

The specialization of functions and the resulting interdependence lead to the necessity for integration, and from here, given certain conditions, to ecological concentration. The location and the size of the city will result from a balance of different elements: the cost of the transportations, availability of raw materials and of labor and the location with respect to consuming markets. The so-called "external economies" of the concentration will result from the reduction of costs originated by these considerations. It is necessary to add the reduction of the cost of investments relative to the economic infrastructure (such as provision of water and energy, administrative services, cleanliness, urban transport and others), or in "social" investments (housing, sanitary services, education, protection). Among this type of "economies" Lampard also points out (quoting Marshall), the psychological climate created by the concentration of industrial activity: a climate especially favorable for innovation, where intellectual stimulation for change would find optimum conditions. Certain organizational and material advantages of concentration in the scientific and intellectual fields should not be forgotten: for example, libraries and laboratories. To these "external" economies are added obviously the "internal" ones: reductions in cost derived from the increase in "scale" of the economic operations.

If these, and other purely technical-economic requirements of industrial development, are present which lead to urban concentration, this same effect becomes a cause of further concentration, not only because it increases the forces of attraction to the existing concentration, but new necessities also arise, derived from the change in scale of the urban entity: for example, the growth of the necessities of coordination and organization (the appearance of new services). To this process is added another which also contributes powerfully to increase "urban concentration." The increase of the tertiary sector, not only through the above-mentioned necessity in relation to the functions of organization but also by the increase in all services and the appearance of new forms. This fact is related, on the other hand, to greater industrial productivity, since the personnel dedicated to the production of material goods is considerably reduced and on the other hand, to the continual innovations and the growing expansion of consumption in ever-widening sectors of the population.

As has already been indicated, one of the essential conditions of the process of urban concentration, although not the only one, is the level of technology. Changes in this tend to produce (if the other conditions remain constant) changes in the type and degree of concentration. This is what has happened with the appearance of new classes of energy after the steam engine. If this was the most powerful factor for urban concentration, the use of the internal combustion motor or electricity has originated new conditions which favor what we could call "urban dispersion," the appearance of the great metropolitan areas, of a continuous system of urban agglomerations which cover entire regions and can include tens of millions of inhabitants. This new process, caused not only by technological innovations but also by substantial modifications of the social structure of the countries of more advanced development, is substantially altering the city and at the same time, gives new meanings to the term "urbanization." The technological changes on the one hand (revolution in the transportation system and in the means of mass communication), united to the process of "growing participation" and of "self-sustained mobility"[9] which characterizes the most advanced phases of industrial society, lead, in effect, to a homogenization of society, tending to erase differences between city and country. The process implies that the style of life, cultural forms and the type of social structure which distinguished the city from the country and which (to follow the terminology of Redfield) in "secondary" urbanization tended to oppose city and country as two well differentiated societies, is now extended to all of society. The consequences of this tendency would be the definite erasure of many or all the differences between "urban" and "rural" society through the absorption of the latter by the former. The process will assume three principle forms.

First, the spectacular reduction of distances in terms of cost and time (the so-called "space friction") tends to decrease, which enlarges enormously the geographical radius of the unitary organization of functions, influencing the limitations of social character more than those of a spatial or physical order. The area of "functional" organization, open to redistribution and optimal differentiation of activities, persons, and "material culture," tends now to extend itself through the entire nation (and even to transcend it to the extent that the removal of social obstacles permits it and is widened by means of supranational planning; for example, "common markets"). This process implies a strong intensification of the contacts and of the ecological interdependence between the diverse regions of the country. The result is, as has been observed,[10] a change in the scale of the society and the great metropolitan areas. The cities and smaller centers, as well as other areas, tend to be integrated intimately in a national system, which provokes, for example, an extraordinary ecological mobility on the part of the inhabitants which tends to cover the national territory in its totality.

The second aspect is that the change in scale is united to the growing importance of the great organizations — whether these be private or public enterprises, syndicates or other forms of association — which cover the national territory and exercise their influence on the inhabitants over and above their location in one or another city, in the urban or in the rural zones. They thus tend to construct a system of roles "oriented towards an organization on a national scale, industries on a national scale, occupational groups on a national scale," because, regardless of the physical location of residence, the members consider as their natural place the organizational net which covers the nation, or even transcends it. They are "citizens of the nation," with equal or greater right than members of the urban community, where they live "accidentally."

The third aspect of the process is associated with the above-mentioned revolution in the means of mass communication (film, press, TV, radio), the profound changes in the system of stratification, and the effects of the growing participation in consumption, education, politics, recreation, with all that this implies in relation to norms of thought and attitudes.

All three aspects of the process point out a potential disappearance of the country-city dichotomy; at least in the stages of growth of maturation of industrial society, urban society tends increasingly to coincide with the nation. It has been said, paradoxically, that with the universal advance of urbanization, the city disappears as a historical entity (at least in the Weberian sense) and is replaced by the nation.[12] On the other hand, "urbanism as a way of life" tends to be transformed into the universal way of life, independently of the ecological location of human groups. With these last considerations, we arrive at another meaning which can be given to the term urbanization, a meaning which resembles the classic definition of Wirth. The difference is that it does not try to point out universal data about the urban phenomenom but rather a certain specific form which it adopts in the countries in which two other characteristics are also present: a high degree of economic development and historical membership in a determined cultural circle — that of the West.

Theoretical and Methodological Problems in the Study of the Correlations Between Urbanization and Other Processes

It was indicated that the growing demographic concentration in the cities can be considered as one of the subprocesses of social modernization. The historical experience of the countries of "first transition" reveals a determined form of connection between urbanization and other component processes, in particular, economic development (above all, industrial development), and the extension of secularization to different areas of behavior. The preceding paragraph alluded to this kind of connection. To what extent can we expect that this will repeat itself, or, on the contrary, undergo substantial modifications in the countries which have initiated the transition much later? On the other hand to what is the process of secondary urbanization, as it has taken place and is occurring in the West, connected not only with universal requirements of modernization but also with special and and nontransferable cultural forms of the Western countries themselves?

It would only be possible to answer these questions partially. What seems unquestionable is that the speed and sequence in which the process of growing urban concentration is taking place varies in notable ways when the historical circumstances on the international as well as on the national level vary. With the term "historical circumstances," we indicate a set of conditions of every type, enumerated briefly in the first chapter.[13]

In a first approximation we can attempt to verify the existence (or nonexistence) of a degree of relatively high correlation between urbanization (defined as urban demographic concentration) and a variety of other component processes of the transition. As we know, the usual procedure for this kind of verification is to find some means of correlation between indicators of the processes whose association is being formulated as a hypothesis.

The construction, selection, and use of these indicators obviously presents a series of very complex problems of a theoretical order and conceptual order, as well as that of mere accessibility of information; and it cannot be affirmed that these problems now have a satisfactory solution, despite considerable theoretical and empirical work which has been carried out for many years.[14] Its use is now well diffused and despite the great limitations offers at least a point of departure. In this section we will limit ourselves to giving some examples of the indicators which can be used to attempt to measure the degree of correlation between demographic urbanization and other subprocesses.

The construction of indicators of urbanization, in the strictly demographic sense of the term, is relatively easy in comparison with the difficulties presented by the measurement of other processes. As was indicated at the beginning, the most common indicator of urbanization is the proportion of the population in urban centers defined on the basis of a determined size. Taking off from this base, different kinds of rates of urbanization can be constructed, in a dynamic and statistical sense.

Much more complex is the problem which the indicators of social, economic and political modernization present — not only through the practical and conceptual difficulties already mentioned, but also because of their almost inexhaustible variety. Terminology and concepts vary considerably; for example, the United Nations, in a study on the interrelation of processes of modernization, grouping them under the concept of "social development" (as distinct from "economic development") uses a series of demographic (life expectancy at birth, infant mortality), educational (proportion of children going to school, within groups of corresponding ages, rate of illiteracy), occupational (proportion of unemployed in the active population) and consumption indicators (calories, carbohydrates, other "personal" consumption). But here "social development" is a different concept from social modernization. The indicators selected by the United Nations imply a determined aim: to measure the "quality of life," an aspect of the process of transition, seen from the point of view of the "well-being" of the populations to which the same indicators refer. The point of departure is the idea that "economic development" should present only a means for improving the "quality of life" of individuals, and not as an end in itself. This deals with an aim which is not only legitimate, but essential. But, undoubtedly, from the practical and conceptual point of view, this definition presents difficulties.[15] The concept of "social modernization" which we have been using, points to another theoretical orientation. Its purpose is to provide an analytical scheme for historical and causal study of the process of global transition. The selections of indicators should satisfy this requirement.

Many attempts exist to operationalize the subprocesses included in social modernization. We should remember in the first place one of the best known, that of Karl Deutsch. This author has classified his set of indicators under the concept of "social mobilization."[16] He deals, nevertheless, with a rather different notion than was analyzed in a preceding chapter. According to the terminology used here, we can speak of a set of indicators referring to the three aspects of modernization: social, political and economic. Deutsch recognizes the existence of a great number of possible indicators, but, given the hypothesis of their interrelation and their relative interchangeability, he selects among them seven which correspond to the underlying process of what we call social mobilization, especially in connection with political behavior. These indicators are: the percentage of persons exposed to an important degree to one or more meaningful aspects of the modern way of life (use of machines, buildings, consumer goods and; exposure to governmental practices); percentages exposed to the mass means of communication (the "public means" of the press, radio, TV, films); percentage of persons who have changed residence; percentage of persons who live in urban centers; percentage of persons occupied in non-agricultural activities, in respect to the active population; percentage illiterate; and national product (net or gross) per capita.

All these indicators can be constructed on the basis of preexisting information, which presents considerable practical advantages. It should be recognized, however, that it also has great limitations. On the one hand, data is being dealt with on the national level, which usually hides internal discontinuities, especially important in the less developed countries.[17] Besides, many aspects of social modernization cannot be expressed through the information which public or private entities compile with different ends. For this reason, various scholars have proposed and used in some cases other types of indicators which they find to be more valid.[18] Lerner, for example, has suggested some definitions of indicators which can be more directly related to changes in personality and could detect the transition from the situation of "nonparticipation" (traditional) to that of "participation" (industrial or modern). Such index indicators are: (a) empathy defined as the capacity to place oneself in the position of another — the capacity of "identification with new aspects of the environment"; this capacity will depend on mechanisms of projection (attribution to others the attributes of oneself) and of introspection (attribution to oneself the attributes of others); in both cases "oneself" incorporates "others" (or rather because one wishes to be like others, or rather because one feels that others are like oneself); (b) the capacity to judge; defined as the propensity to give opinions on questions, that, from the traditional viewpoint, completely escape the competence of an individual. Lerner tries to show how these phenomena are connected with other aspects of the process of modernization, and in particular, in what manner some indicators like illiteracy, urban residence, participation in means of mass communication, political participation, form a "system" related to the two above mentioned indicators.

There is no doubt that empathy, as well as the propensity to judge, represent important symptoms of the process of secularization as it has been previously defined. Both point to psychological changes necessary for voluntary action to replace prescriptive action and implicitly reflect the degree of propensity to change. But, contrary to the other indicators recorded until now, all these require the use of special investigations and obviously present the problem of its translation into operational terms of concrete instruments of observation (problems that were not overcome entirely by Lerner). Another very interesting suggestion for the construction of indicators referring to the processes of social modernization analytically distinguishing their aspects, is that of W. Moore.[19] However we are confronted here with the fact that in the majority of the cases, investigations, inferential and indirect observations are needed, and that at any rate, the translation of this to operational terms (not attempted by the author) may not always be possible with the means available. A global indicator of the process of secularization not always used in an explicit manner is the reference to the birth rate, or another demographic index capable of detecting the path of conscious planning (or of voluntary action) in the sphere of matrimonial relations. Although here we are also dealing with only one aspect of the process, which can take place in some cases relatively independently of others, it would seem that, as long as the effects of some deliberate and massive attempt to introduce birth control to a traditional population (as happened in Japan) are not dealt with, the planning of births, deliberate but not induced by external means, on the individual level, should imply a degree of secularization in family relations which is fairly advanced and which at the same time should have some probability of being accompanied by other aspects of secularization, at least in relation to "electiveness" of action, stratification (aspirations of mobility), and others. The advantage of this indicator would be its easy access. In relation to the limits and convenience of its use as an indicator of "secularization" it would be necessary to analyze its validity in relation to various aspects of the global process which it is designed to detect.[20] To this end, the limitations derived from the lack or inaccuracy of the data and the fact that in general it deals with gross rates should be indicated, and also that in the secularized countries of very advanced economic development an increase is birth is taking place, an increase which does not imply a relapse to unplanned birth, but probably a change in the ideal size of the family. In these cases the rates of birth can become very sensitive to changes in the economy, children being now a form of "consumption." This implies that at certain periods, in some countries of high development, the birth rate can remain relatively high and coexist with a high degree of secularization in family relations.

In a more recent epoch other important attempts at the construction and application of ad hoc indicators of modernization constructed have been made. This is the case of the scale of modernization elaborated by A. Inkeles and applied in a comparative study of various countries[21] or the questionnaires used by J. Kahl in his investigation on modern attitudes in Mexico and Brazil.[22]

TABLE 1
Correlations between an indicator of urbanization (percentage of the population living in centers of 20,000 or more) and indicators of economic development, social modernization (approx. 1955-1960)[23]

Variable	Coefficient of Corr.	Number of Countries
Economic Development		
1. Gross National Product (GNP) per person	0.71	110
2. Gross Internal Investment, as percent of GNP	0.42	72
3. Percentage of GNP generated by agriculture	0.67	73
4. Consumption of energy per person	0.84	72
5. Percentage of population economically active (PEA) in agriculture	0.72	92
6. Percentage of PEA in nonagricultural activities	0.78	75
7. Percentage of the population of working age occupied in industry	0.67	41
8. Index of industrial diversification	0.87	41
9. Index of external dispersion relative to imports	0.80	22
Social Modernization		
A) *Demographic Transition*		
10. Gross birth rate	0.50	80
11. Gross mortality rate	0.33	54
12. Life expectancy at birth (women)	0.71	69
13. Infant mortality rate	0.69	74
14. Rate of dependency (proportion of population from 15 to 64 years, over total population in percentage)	0.56	62
B) *Social Stratification*		
15. Percentage of dependent workers (employees and workers, over total population of working age)	0.69	76
16. Distribution of income (index of inequality)	0.39	20
C) *Consumption and Health*		
17. Motor vehicles registered, per person	0.74	67
18. Calorie consumption, per person	0.69	40
19. Percentage of consumption of carbohydrates over total consumption	0.66	40
20. Number of inhabitants per doctor	0.69	114
21. Number of inhabitants per hospital bed	0.62	117
D) *Education*		
22. Percentage of literates in population of 15 years or more	0.66	109
23. Percentage of secondary school students and primary students over total population of 15 years	0.71	74
24. Number of university students or equivalent per 100,000 inhabitants	0.56	100

TABLE 1 (Continued)

E) *Mass Communications and Interchange*

25. Circulation of newspapers, per 1,000 inhabitants	0.69	115
26. Radios per 1,000 inhabitants	0.68	115
27. TV per 1,000 inhabitants	0.54	67
28. Film attendance, per person	0.62	96
29. Combined index of mass communications (newspapers, publications, telephones, circulation of pieces by internal mail)	0.82	73
30. Number of pieces sent by internal mail, per person	0.65	68
31. Number of pieces sent by international mail per person	0.54	66

Political Modernization

32. Percentage of GNP spent by government (social security included and public enterprises)	0.47	41
33. Percentage of public employees, (same inclusions), over total population of working age	0.56	21
34. Percentage of voters over population of voting age	0.38	90
35. Cutright index of functioning of representative democracy	0.69	77
36. Percentage of persons speaking dominant language, over total of the population	0.54	61

In Table 1[23] a certain number of correlations have been united between an indicator of urbanization and indicators of economic, social and political modernization, which have been classified in subgroups whenever possible. It deals with aggregate data, on the national level. As may be seen, all these indicators are found to be related to urbanization (positively or negatively according to the form assumed by each indicator of modernization), but as can be expected, these correlations, although "high" in many cases, are very far from being "perfect"; there exist "relapses" or "advances" in urbanization in relation to the other process in a considerable number of cases. All that can be affirmed on the basis of these correlations is the existence of a generic "tendency" for the process of urbanization to be associated with other component processes of transition. In reality, all these processes are associated, and the application of statistical techniques, factor analysis, for example, can show that these indicators behave as if a structure composed of a few factors or independent "dimensions," or even only one factor, operates above the many component subprocess. For example, in one of the first attempts of this type, Cattell and others isolated twelve underlying factors in the intercorrelations of some seventy indicators of modernization belonging to forty "modern industrial" countries.[24] Berry carried out an analogous work using forty-three indicators of economic development and modernization (for ninety-three countries), finding four basic factors underlying the forty-three indicators." Among these, one stands out, called by this author the "technological factor," of greater importance than the other three.[25] More favorable conclusions to the "one-dimensionality" of the process were reached by Schnore, in a study directed precisely at analyzing the relation between urbanization and economic development (including in its definition, social modernization). In his analysis (in which twelve indicators were used) urbanization appeared as one of diverse aspects of a single process. If many processes can be distinguished on the conceptual level, all these appear extremely interrelated on the empirical plane.[26] Correlations on the international level, like those realized by Dillon Soares for Venezuela, Brazil, Chile and Japan, also produced similar results.[27]

These and other similar results are certainly useful insofar as they represent a point of departure for analysis. They confirm the hypothesis that the transition can be perceived as a global process and that all the various component subprocesses are interrelated. At the same time, they indicate that there exist considerable variations in the form adopted by the transition in each country. They confirm what was suggested in the first chapter about the considerable variations in the rhythms or rates of change, and in the sequences of the subproducts in the peculiar conditions (internal or external) which characterize the different societies in transition. The next step would then be a theory or system of hypotheses referring to the possible forms of transition and to the conditions and factors that in each case determine them. The hypotheses concerning the process of urbanization in relation to the other component processes should be part of this general theory. As had been said, this theory does not now exist and the preliminary attempts to arrive at it can take different paths, perhaps complementary ones, starting from theory, with the construction of models, or from empirical generalization. An illustration of the latter has been seen in the scheme of stages referring to Latin America, a scheme of limited validity to a region which is relatively homogeneous and to a determined historical period. The comparison of this scheme with others corresponding to other regions can perhaps provide a first approximation to isolate the conditions and determining factors of the different forms assumed by the transition. Another procedure could be to compare the "profiles" of development and modernization reached in a given moment by a great number of countries, and to try to extract from this a typology of such "profiles." This is the procedure used in the United Nations' study, in which indicators of economic development were compared with indicators of "social development." They proceeded to classify all the countries in relation to each one of the selected indicators, on a scale of six categories in order of growing economic and social development. In this way the development of those countries could be defined as "even" which remained in the same category for all the indicators, or which had reached the same relative degree of development in each one of the aspects considered. In the study it was seen that in the more advanced countries the indicators of social development and economic development tended to form a more "even" configuration than that of the less advanced countries in transition.[28]

A very serious limitation of this procedure, which also can be applied to the correlations and to the factor analyses already mentioned, is that they compare countries whose transition began in different epochs, in a set of very different historical circumstances on the international level (with its impact on the national level). As has been shown, these circumstances vary continuously and in this way alter very significantly forms adopted by the transition in the countries which initiated it at different times. This effect can be clearly seen in the case of the process of urbanization.

Urbanization and Industrialization

We know that the level of urbanization of the less developed countries is in actuality more elevated than could be expected, given their degree of economic development, when they are compared with the level of urbanization the more advanced countries had reached in correspondence with a similar degree of development. In accordance with this criterion, "over-urbanization" has been spoken of for the majority of the underdeveloped or developing countries, and this is especially applicable to Latin America, whose urbanization is the highest of all the regions of the Third World. Already at the beginning of the decade 1950-60 Davis and Goldsen observed that, with few exceptions, all the less developed countries were characterized by an accelerated process of urbanization.[29] The historical data confirm this impression. For example, the most urbanized group of countries in 1890, with a proportion of population in urban centers (of 20,-000 or more inhabitants) of 33.8 percent reached in terms of "real product" per person an average index of 869 (in "international entities" of Colin Clark). In 1950 a group of Latin American countries, with an average of similar urbanization 32.5 percent reached only an average index of "real product" per person less by a fourth (624 U/I) with respect to the former.[30]

In the experience of the first country to industrialize, England, the process of urban concentration advanced almost pari passu, with industrial growth. At the same time there occurred a profound transformation of the rural sector, resulting in the expulsion (or "liberation") of peasants, expanding rapidly the demand created by modern industry.[31] If the process of industrialization is taken as a key aspect of economic development (according to the definition suggested in a previous chapter) a more appropriate way to analyze urban growth in relation to industrial growth is to utilize an index which relates these two processes. In Table 2 an index of this type has been used.[32] Its application to data from twenty-five countries is hardly an illustration of the process, much less than a verification. As can be seen, the less the economic development (measured in GNP per person), the less the urbanization-industrial occupation relation is. The correlation between GNP per person, and urbanization-industrial occupation index is negative (-0.74). It is also interesting to observe that this inverse correlation tends to be greater on the lower levels of urbanization (and of economic development). Starting from more advanced stages of the transition, the urbanization-industrial occupation relation becomes relatively more independent of the degree of economic development. On the other hand, it can be noted that when the countries are separated in two groups, of earlier transition and more recent transition, the first group registers an urbanization-industrial occupation index fifty percent less than that of the second; in other words, greater urbanization in relation to the degree of industrialization takes place in the countries which started their transition more recently. In the historical circumstances (social, cultural, political and economic) of the past century and the beginning of this one, the process or urban growth tended to be slower and later in comparison with economic development. See Table 2.

TABLE 2

The urbanization-industrialization relation (U/I index) and the degree of economic development (GNP) on different levels of urbanization (1950-1955)[33]

Urbanization (percentage of population in cities of 20,000 or more inhabitants	No. of countries	GNP per Person (Average in U.S.A. Dollars	Index of urbanization/industrialization (U/I) Averages	Correlations Between GNP and U/I
Less than 25 percent	8	247	300	0.91
26 percent to 40 percent	9	900	237	0.87
41 percent or more	7	1219	200	0.68
The 24 countries	24	—	—	0.74
Most developed 13 countries in 1913	13	—	177	—
Least developed 11 countries in 1913	11	—	336	—

The observation of this contrast between the countries of early transition and of recent transition has suggested the notion of "over-urbanization." The countries which are now least developed will be affected according to this thesis by an abnormal or pathological process of urbanization, as long as the process does not remain within the correct proportions functionally required for its degree of industrialization. Some authors have rejected this position since it adopts as a universal model what occurred historically in the countries most advanced in the transition today.[34] Taking into account the examples of this historical experience, the causes as well as the effects of the process of urbanization in the countries in development should be analyzed in relation to the circumstances in which their development is taking place, circumstances which certainly differ from those of the past century.

The growth of the urban population on a larger scale than the growth of the proportion employed in industry has occurred in all countries. A glance at Table 3 shows that the urbanization-occupation relation in the secondary sector has continually increased. The urban population has grown much more than the proportion of people occupied in industry and other activities of the "secondary" sector (classification of Colin Clark). See Table 3.[35]

TABLE 3
Urbanization-Occupation Relation in the Secondary Sector for a Group of Countries (1840-1950)[35]

Countries	(Approx) 1840	(Approx) 1870	(Approx) 1890	(Approx) 1910	(Approx) 1950
G. Britain	67	—	112	145	150
France	—	36	50	80	93
United States	59	—	92	107	119
Australia	—	—	126	127	150
Sweden	—	—	59	60	130
Russia	—	—	—	100	113
Argentina	—	45	96	106	141
Chile	—	—	—	93	133
Cuba	—	—	—	115	172
18 Latin American Countries (Average)	—	—	—	—	137

The urban explosion in the countries of "early transition" has been produced by various successive phases, which occurred at different times in different countries. In relative terms, the great urban growth occurred in the most advanced countries of Europe euring the nineteenth entery, although recently, after World War II, we have seen a new intensification of this growth, especially in countries like Italy, Spain and others, that is still characterized by the subsistence of a very extensive rural sector.[36] In Europe and in the other developed countries urban growth occurred in part through vegetative growth (in the nineteenth century), but especially through rural-urban internal and international migration. In general terms, the same scheme of analysis of this process suggested in the preceding chapter is applicable to the countries of "early" transition and to those of recent transition.

On the objective or environmental level[37] the factors of "expulsion from the country" originated in the modernization of agriculture, which permitted the "liberation" of an enormous number of people and the drastic reduction of employment in the primary sector. A second cause of "expulsion" from the country was demographic growth. In addition, the same economic and technological transformation affected the urban sector simultaneously. The growth of the population employed in industry stimulated only a first phase of urban expansion. The technological changes and the consequent growth of productivity put a brake on the increase of the population absorbed by industry. In reality, the whole secondary sector stabilized itself or even tended to decrease in terms of percentages. Nevertheless at the same time, the rise of new necessities — health, education, social services, recreation, and free time, organization and administration — greatly encouraged the service sectors. In this way, it was the intense increase of productivity in agriculture and industry which permitted the growth of the tertiary sector. Such have been the environmental changes which generated the objective factors of "attraction to the city." In economic terms, while the agricultural demand diminished, the urban demand grew, a demand that in the more advanced phases was not based on the necessities of industry, but on the appearance of new necessities.

On the "normative" and "psychosocial" levels, the rupture of the traditional order tended to occur with a certain slowness for great sectors of the population, in comparison with the analogous process in many countries actually in development. The fact that in the nineteenth century there did not exist effective means of mass communication was perhaps one of the factors which maintained the isolation of the "peripheral" sectors within the societies whose bourgeoisie, in the central zones, were vigorously encouraged by capitalist development. In Russia, a basically similar process occurred since the great majority of the population, still a rural one, tended to remain in traditional ways of life and it was only in the course of socialist construction that its mobilization towards modern ways was encouraged. This process was to a considerable extent subject to a central planning which was as much economic as social and psychological. Displacement from the rural to the urban zones, and from preindustrial to industrial ways, originated profound and long lasting conflicts in all the countries. It is notable, that in various European nations migration from the country had very different characteristics in the past century and until World War I, in comparison with the migrations of the post-World War II period. In the first case migration did not imply a definitive rupture with the traditional order; in terms of the intentions of the migrants it was a transitory migration, carried out with the intention of procuring the means to acquire land in their native home and reestablishing "normal" conditions in terms of expectations and typically traditional aspirations. In the migrations of the second post-war period, the central motivation was the definitive abandonment of rural life and the decision to adapt to the ways of urban industry permanently.[38]

The phenomenom of "marginality" in economic, political, social and cultural terms took place in those countries and affected large proportions of the population, but their entrance into the modern sector was not only relatively slow but took place through their partial incorporation into determined spheres of activity, while in others, the norms and traditional attitudes were still maintained. At least, incorporation into industrial work, like manual labor, tended to precede changes on the psychosocial and normative level in regard to attitudes, expectations and interpersonal relations. Throughout the process urban unemployment was a constant fact,[39] reaching in cyclical crises menacing levels. Economic development (and the draining of the great migration to overseas, especially in the nineteenth century and the beginning of the twentieth century, as much as this draining, caused the decrease in vegetative growth) finally permitted the population of working age to be absorbed into modern economic activities of greater productivity. Although this absorption was far from complete, at least in the market economies, it is sufficient to remember the persistence of considerable sectors economically and socially segregated, like the Negroes and other minorities in the United States, and the persistence of underdeveloped areas in many advanced countries. The process of mobilization in its different objective and subjective aspects, took place in these countries in a discontinuous manner, in great successive "waves" separated at times by lapses of more than a generation. In reality, the entire urban working class remained relatively isolated or segregated from national society and from various spheres of modern culture until very late, since their incorporation and (relative) integration into the national system only began to take place in the last two decades, at the achievement of greater maturity of the economies of the respective countries. Besides, the discontinuities in the process and the occasional phases of accelerated mobilization did not prevent very sharp conflicts and tensions, which in some cases jeopardized the system.[40]

The process in the countries in the course of development differs from what was previously described in three principal aspects: (a) the internal and external situation in the origin of urbanization; (b) the sequence in which different subprocesses have taken place; (c) the intensity and speed of them. We refer only to three aspects, since other details will be included in the examination of the Latin American case.

With the exception of some new countries in which an urban preindustrial structure did not exist, the process of "modern" urbanization took place usually on the basis of the preexisting urban structure, or preindustrial type. In the countries developing today this structure is in great part mo'lded by the situation of economic and political dependence of the country in question in respect to the metropolis or industrialized countries. The political-administrative necessities during the colonial epoch, as well as the economic necessities derived from the export of raw materials and the import of manufactured products (which constitutes the most common form of incorporation of the country to the world market and modern economy), profoundly affected the urban structure. In this way, beginning already from the point of departure, there is a difference between the countries in which the step from preindustrial urbanization to industrial urbanization took place because of more endogenous than exogenous factors.

The sequence in which the subprocesses took place was altered for different reasons. In the first place, the industrialization proper was retarded or even impeded by a conjunction of internal and external factors. Among the former, the type of culture and the dominant attitudes, the lack of capital, internal market, and organized infrastructure, basic investments, were influential; among the latter, the very situation of a country exporting raw materials and the complex of local and foreign interests favorable to the maintenance of this situation were influential. The retardation or the lack of industrial development did not prevent the unfolding of other processes of social modernization, especially those which arose from the diffusion of scientific and technological innovations not directly dependent on the degree of industrialization. Such is the case in the drastic reduction of the mortality rates, which together with the maintenance (or the increase) of the "traditional" birth rate, led to the demographic explosion or in the diffusion of means of mass communication, which implied the introduction of powerful or subjective mobilization. The persistence of an extremely unfavorable agrarian structure in the majority of the less developed countries, the enormous increase of demographic pressure and the acceleration of the processes of subjective mobilization, constitute important factors which explain in part rural-urban migration, without the existence at the same time of an increase in the demand for urban employment, on an equivalent level. In addition, although to a much lesser degree than the available work force, there was a certain transformation of the traditional structure which required an increase in urban employment. We are referring especially to the "modernizing effects" of the primary economy of export alluded to in another chapter. For example, the organization of the state, the establishment of social services of all kinds, commercial and financial activity, the growth of the internal market and the beginnings of industrialization (although limited to the production of nondurable consumer goods, or for the sectors of small resources) required without doubt a new demand for labor in the cities. It is important to note here that the expansion of the public and private bureaucracy and of services was much greater than in corresponding stages of development in countries of early transition. An important cause of this was that the "model" of the state and of society, and the type and level of necessities which the new developing institutions were trying to serve, were not those that had characterized the countries of early development in the past century, but were those of these same societies but in their present already advanced structure. The functions of the state had tended to grow continuously, whatever the type of the dominant economic system. The same occurred with services. It was not possible to ignore the requirements of organization and services on a more modern level, once that these had appeared and the consciousness of their necessity had been diffused. Certainly, this possibility of expansion of services and of public and private organization was limited by the available resources in each country. But in many of them "economic expansion" on the basis of the primary economy of export[41] provided relatively abundant means. In many cases it was carried out at the expense of directly productive investments. For all these reasons in most of the countries of more recent transition the structure and volume of urban employment were influenced by conditions not directly connected with economic development and industrialization proper. It is obvious that a certain proportion of the population of working age which lives in the cities of these countries is not absorbed by services of the "modern" type and should be considered as marginal, or relatively marginal to modern forms of economy. This is the type of "pseudo-tertiary" which inflates the occupational statistics of the underdeveloped countries. But, at the same time, there is a real tertiary sector which is larger than that which corresponded to equivalent degrees of economic development, according to the experience of the past. And this greater size is explained on the basis of the quoted "modernizing effects" of the type which exercises great influence on the present. Finally, the introduction of modern means of transport, in great part oriented to the necessities of the primary economy of export, contributed powerfully to break the isolation of many zones of the national territory, favoring contact with urban centers and migration to them, particularly towards those expanding because of their economic and political function in this type of economy.

The speed and volume of some of these causal processes of urban growth were much greater in the countries in development today than in the countries of earlier development. For example, the growth of the population never reached in European countries the rate of three percent annually which characterizes today certain regions of the Third World. With a growth which did not go over half of the quoted rates, the European countries needed to send more than sixty million people overseas. In a considerable proportion, the present rural "exodus" to the cities is the substitute in the developing countries for the great European migration of the past century. To this should be added as another accelerating factor, the introduction of means of mass communication and the facilities for modern transportation which eliminated or drastically reduced, the psychological and material isolation of great sectors of the population and consequently facilitated their material mobilization to the only focus of attraction available in present conditions: the cities.

Urbanization without industrialization or with retarded industrialization is then, the result of the set of external and internal conditions which characterize the transition in countries which have initiated it in more recent times. What will be the consequences of this on the other processes, and especially on economic development, is a very complex problem which cannot be resolved by qualifying it simply as "over-urbanization" or abnormal urbanization. For now, the commonly observed fact should be recognized that in these countries, a part of the urban population is marginal from the point of view of their economic activity, as well as in relation to the forms of consumption and other aspects of modern culture. The fact is usually emphasized that the occupational structure produced by urban expansion, and not accompanied by structural changes in the economy, produces a distribution of the active population which, although nominally it seems to approach that of the developed countries, presents substantial differences. What stands out is that in these cases the service sector does not correspond to modern occupations but to traditional forms, for example, domestic services (that tend to disappear in the countries of more mature economy) and other nonmodern activities of low or no productivity. In this sense these occupations are only a type of disguised unemployment, moved from the country to the city.[42] This is what we have called "pseudo-tertiary": persons in this situation not only do not carry out proper activities of a modern tertiary sector, but their consumption and way of life (although not necessarily their aspirations) remain in great part marginal in respect to modern society. Analogous reasoning can be applied to a certain proportion of the population who figure in the occupational statistics as working in the secondary sector. Not only does this include artisan activities of a preindustrial type[43], but other activities of very low yield which also constitute disguised unemployment and father a social sector pyschologically different from the modern industrial proletariat. To these "marginal" or "semimarginal" people can be added the unemployed that represent a considerable proportion in some cities. The presence of the "pseudo-tertiary" and of other marginal categories should not make us forget the expansion of the tertiary to which we have already referred, which, although it has gone beyond the "historic" level expected in a given degree of economic development, still constitutes a sector of the population who, from the social and psychological point of view, is incorporated into modern forms of urban life. For this it is necessary to distinguish between the "pseudo-teritiary" (and if one wishes, the "pseudo-secondary") and the socially and psychologically real tertiary, although expanded in greater proportions than the level of economic development, according to strictly "historic" criteria.

To what extent does this "excess" of urban population become a negative factor for economic development? According to some, "overurbanization" acts directly on economic development, diminishing the propensity to save, discouraging agricultural production and diverting the scarce resources from investment of high productivity to low yield investment.[44] It has also been shown that urban concentration, especially concentration in "primate" cities is an unfavorable factor for even development on the geographic level, and thus is an obstacle for national integration. The phenomenom of the primacy of the cities is connected in the peripheral countries with an economic structure dependent on international commerce. These cities function as a point of contact between land transport (from the interior) and maritime transport (to the exterior), of primary production. Their location and growth responds to needs of international commerce (of "outward" development) and not integrated development on the national level. The transport system serves the same ends and tends to multiply the deforming effects of the "syndrome of the primary economy of export." The primate city and its immediate hinterland with its great concentration of wealth, its modern culture and its disproportionate economic expansion, has been a negative factor for the development of other regions and of the nation as a whole. The material and human resources have been concentrated disproportionately in these areas, to the detriment of other regions of the country. Even in the beginning of the process of industrialization, the preexisting urban structure tends to determine the location of new activities, adding new factors of disequilibrium and a spatial distribution of industry which is unfavorable for future development.[45]

Although few dare to deny the existence of these negative conditions, some authors point out that urban concentration can also have favorable effects. For example, the very notion of "over-urbanization" has been questioned: the concentration of scarce resources in a few urban centers may be more efficient than if they were disseminated in a great territory; the positive function of the city as a dynamic center for education and technical and social innovation can compensate for the costs, economic and social, of "over-urbanization." And this can be a factor for economic development and industrialization in the underdeveloped regions. In any case, the function of the city in developing societies is different than the historical function that they played in the first industrialized countries. Finally, the desirability of integrated modernization and development has been questioned. Perhaps the conditions in which both processes occur make such an integration impossible. Or perhaps the internal geographic discontinuities can represent a factor which accelerates the process as a whole, at least in certain stages of transition.[46] At any rate, as Hoselitz pointed out, the "generative" function or, on the contrary, the "parasitic" dysfunction of the cities, especially the "primate" cities depends on a very complex series of economic and noneconomic factors which can intervene in any case. Unfortunately, we must conclude with the same words written by Hoselitz fifteen years ago, in the sense that the determination of these factors and their interrelationships still are one of the principal labors in the study of the connection between urbanization and other processes which intervene in the transition.[47]

Notes

1. United Nations, "Étude sur les données relatives à la population urbaine, et à la population rurale dans les récensements récents," *Études Démograhiques*, 8, (New York, Lake Success; 1950) Chapter 1.
Additional problems in relation to the delimitation of the "center" of "urban agglomeration" are evident. The well known dichotomy between administrative limits and areas actually urbanized, and the lack of coincidence between both can assume different forms. In Argentina, The Directory of Statistics recognizes the urban parties agglomeration of greater Buenos Aires, made up of the federal capital and eighteen parties of the province. But until the present, the censuses have not given information tabulated in relation to the zone which includes areas which are still not urbanized (a small percentage of the population which does not live in agglomerations of 2,000 or more, according to the official definition accepted in Argentina). In addition, there are in the country other agglomerations which include more than one administrative division (parties or departments).
On the identification of the urban agglomeration and urban center, see the first three chapters of J. P. Gibbs (ed.), *Urban Research Methods* (New York: Van Nostrand, 1961).
2. L. Wirth, "Urbanism as a Way of Life" in P.K. Hatt and A.J. Reiss, *Cities and Society* (Glencoe, Ill.: The Free Press, 1957).
3. The valuational character of the dichotomies "secular-accessible, urban-rural, community-society" have been observed. Another ideological infiltration is the concept of mass society often attributed to the city as such. To remember that the analysis of the pathological — social disorganization — is historically connected, very closely, with urban sociology, and reflects above all, the circumstances in Chicago in the decade of 1920-30.
4. M. Weber, *Economía y Sociedad,* Mexico, F.C.E., (1944), V III, Chapter VIII.
5. R. Redfield and M.B. Singer, "The Cultural Role of the Cities," in *Economic Development and Cultural Change*, III (1954), 53-73.
6. G. Germani, *Política y Sociedad, op. cit.,* Chapt. III.
7. G. Soberg, *The Preindustrial City* (Glencoe, Ill.: Free Press, 1960).
8. E.E. Lampard, "The History of cities in economically advanced areas," in *Economic Development and Cultural Change,* III (1954), 81-136.

9. Cf. Chapter III and *Política y Sociedad, op. cit.*, Chapt. VI.

10. S. Greer, The Emerging City (Glencoe, Ill.; Free Press, 1962), p. p. 33 ff.

11. *Loc. cit.*, pp. 43-48.

12. D. Martindale in his preface to the English translation of *La Ciudad*, by Max Weber; *The City* (Glencoe, Ill.: Free Press, 1958).

13. See tables.

14. Since Alfredo Niceforo published one of the first (or perhaps the first) texts on indicators of modernization at the beginning of this century, the bibliography on indicators of modernization has multiplied. Cf. Alfredo Niceforo, *Les indicateurs numériques de la civilisation et du progrès,* (Paris: Flammarion 1921). Also, the availability of the data has continually increased, which is in itself an indicator of modernization. Besides, the compilations designed ad hoc have been added to annual national and international publications. The best example is that of B. Russet, K. Deutsch and others, *World Handbook of Political and Social Indicators* (New Haven and London: Yale University Press, 1964). Another example of the same kind, but limited especially to data on economic development is the *Atlas of Economic Development*, prepared by Norton Ginsburg (Chicago: University of Chicago Press, 1961), (Spanish translation: Buenos Aires, EUDEBA). Other projects which use a number of indicators are described and analyzed in Richard J. Merrit and Stein Rokkan (eds.), *Comparing Nations* (New Haven and London: Yale University Press, 1966). In the indicated references numerical data only are used, but there are other attempts at using also a type of nonstatistical information. An example of this is the work of A.S. Banks and Robert B. Textor, *A Cross-Polity Survey* (Cambridge: MIT, 1963), in which all the variables of the "nominal" or the "ordinal" type and dichotomies are used.

15. United Nations, *Report on the World Social Situation* (New York, 1961), Part II. J. Drewcowski and W. Scott, for their part have constructed an index of standard of living, directed precisely at measuring the "quality of life" in countries with different cultures: *The Level of Living Index* (Geneva: United Nations Research Institute, 1966).

16. K. Deutsch, "Social Mobilization . . . ," *op. cit.*

17. On this problem see Merrit and Rokkan, *op. cit.* Kingsley Davis has formed serious criticisms on the use of indicators which have not been generated by a theory. See his article, "Problems and Solutions in International Comparisons for Social Science Purposes," Spanish version in *American Latina*, 1, (1965), pp. 61-76.

18. D. Lerner, *The Passing of Traditional Society* (Glencoe, Ill.: Free Press, 1958), Chapters II and III.

19. W. Moore tried to formulate a methodology for the measurement of the social consequences of technological change, without implying in it any kind of determinism in the manner of Ogburn. It is an interesting theoretical scheme which distinguishes three levels of connections between technical change and social change (material products, work roles, and that of the "rational spirit") and various entities of observation. He proposed a series of indicators, the majority of which require special investigations or indirect observations and inferential ones (and obviously their operational translation into adequate instruments); see his work, "measurement of organization and institutional implications of changes in productive technology," in Bureau International de recherches sur les implications sociales du progres technique: *Changements techniques, économiques et sociaux* (Paris, 1958).

20. A well known use of this index — or of the vegetative growth rate — to charcterize in a global manner the transition of traditional society to industrial is by D. Riesman and others in *The Lonely Crowd* (New Haven, Conn.: Yale University Press, 1960), Spanish version: *La muchedumbre solitaria* (Buenos Aires: Paidos, 1968), 2nd ed. The greater part of the demographic literature shows the social factors related to demographic transition, and a very brief synthesis can be found in the article of N.B. Ryder on fertility in P. Hauser and O.D. Duncan (eds.), *The Study of Population,* (Chicago: The University of Chicago Press, 1959); another ample summary can be found in the book published by the United Nations, *The Determinants and Consequences of Population Trends* (New York, 1953).

Some examples seem to show that the birth rate can function as an indicator of traditionalism (or secularization) independently of other processes (for example: degree of urbanization, industrial development or economic development in a strict sense). Such would be the case of Brazil or Mexico (as an example of backwardness in the path of deliberate control in the more urban and industrialized areas) or of France (as an example of progress in relation to the transportation in a technical-economic sense). Cf. considerations on the cases of Brazil and France in F. Lorimer, *Culture and Human Fertility* (Paris: UNESCO, 1954). With all, it is possible that this deals with indicators which are not very sensitive to the intitial changes towards greater secularization; R. Klineberg found that only starting from a level of illiteracy greater than eighty percent, is a radical change produced in the birth rate, while advances of ten to sixty percent of literates do not seem to be associated with appreciable modifications; (unpublished study quoted by K. Deutsch, in *op. cit.*, note 16).

21. Alex Inkeles and David H. Smith, "The OM Scale: A comparative Socio-Psychological Measure of Individual Modernity", *Sociometry*, 29, (1966), 353-77.

22. Joseph A. Kahl, *The Measurement of Modernism* (Austin, Texas: the University of Texas Press, 1968).

23. Except for the variables that will be indicated, the correlations have been taken from Russet and Deutsch, *op. cit.* In these cases the indicator of urbanization is the percentage of the population which lives in centers of 20,000 inhabitants or more. The coefficient of correlation is Pearson's.

The variables 3, 17 and 14 correspond to the study of Leo F. Schnore, "The Statistical Measurement of Urbanization and Economic Development" in *Land Economics,* August, (1961). The variables 8, 9, 27 and 33 belong to the study published by Philip Cutright, "National Political Development: Measurement and Analysis" in *American Sociological Review,* 28, (1968), 253-64. The variables 4, 13, 18 and 19 have been taken from the United Nations Study, *op. cit.* For all the correlations, the coefficient employed in the above-mentioned cases is Spearman's.

24. Raymond B. Cattell and others, "An Attempt at More Refined Definitions of the Cultural Dimensions of Syntality in Modern Nations," in *American Sociological Review,* 17, (1951), 408-21.

25. N. Ginsburg, *op. cit.*

26. L. Schnore, *op. cit.*

27. Gláucio Ary Dillon Soares, "Congruency and Incongruency among Indicators of Economic Development, An Exploratory Study," work presented at the International Conference of Comparative Social Investigation, Buenos Aires, 1964.

28. United Nations Report, 1961, *op. cit.*

29. Kinglsey Davis and Hilda Hertz Goldsen, "Urbanization and the Develop-

ment of Preindustrial Areas," in *Economic Development and Cultural Change, III*, (1954), 6-2.

30. The data for this computation have been taken from A. F. Weber, *The Growth of The Cities in the Nineteenth Century* (new edition, Cornell U. Press, 1963), pp. 144-45 and Colin Clark, *The Conditions of Economic Progress* (London: MacMillan, 1957), Chapter III. See G. Germani, "La Ciudad como mechanismo integrado," in *Revista Mexicana de Sociologia, XXIX*, (1967), 387-406.

31. Eric E. Lampard, "The History of Cities in the Economically Advanced Areas," *op. cit.*

32. Rate of urbanization (percentage of population in cities of 20,000 and more inhabitants) over rate of industrialization (percentage of economically active population working in manufacturing) per 100. The smaller the index, the less the urbanization in relation to industrial employment. Cf. Germani, *op. cit.*

33. Compiled on the basis of data from: United Nations, *Report on the World Social Situation*, (New York: 1957), p. 127; J.D. Durand, "Patterns of Urbanization in Latin America" in *Milbank Memorial Fund Quarterly, XLIII*, 4. (1965), The correlations are computed on the basis of Spearman's index. The eight countries with less than twenty-five percent urbanization are Pakistan, Bolivia, India, Haiti, Phillipines, Mexico, Costa Rica, Finland; the countries with a level of twenty-six to forty percent: Egypt, Chile, Puerto Rico, Venezuela, Austria, France, Sweden, Switzerland, Canada: with forty one percent or more: Argentina, Holland, W. Germany, England, Belgium, Australia. The classification of the thirteen most developed countries and the least developed countries in 1913 was made on the basis of data included in C. Clark, *op. cit.*

34. See V.N. Sovani, "The Analysis of Overurbanization," in *Economic Development and Cultural Change, XII*, (1964), 113-22.

35. Data from United Nations, *Report on the World Social Situation*, 1957, *op. cit.;* Adna F. Weber, *op. cit.;* C. Clark, *op. cit.* The index has been computed by dividing the percentage of inhabitants in cities of 20,000 or more, by the percentage of the economically active population which works in the secondary sector (construction, manufacture, electricity).

36. It should be remembered that in the period between the two World Wars, in various countries of Europe, antiurban ideologies predominated. Especially in the Fascist countries, the "return" to the land constituted one of the principal objectives of the totalitarian state. After 1945, especially with the Common Market, the movements of population from the country to the city assumed the volume of a real "exodus." Nevertheless, in 1960 it was estimated that only for these six countries rural-urban movement will affect many millions of people in the immediate future. See G. Beyer, *Rural Migrants, op. cit.* On the migrations in the nineteenth century, see A. F. Weber, *op. cit.*

37. Omitted

38. See for example, F. Alberoni, *op. cit.*

39. The Marxist notion of "reserve army" was founded on this fact.

40. In the second and third chapters it was mentioned how the totalitarian movements and rightist regimes can be interpreted as forms of demobilization forced on the popular sectors in a phase of rapid primary mobilization.

41. Omitted

42. Peter T. Bauer and Basil S. Yamey, *The Economics of Underdeveloped Countries* (Chicago, Ill.: University of Chicago Press, 1957), Chapter III.

43. Artisan activities and other activities of the secondary sector based on technologies which absorb more labor than capital can be useful or even necessary in determined conditions or in certain stages of development.

44. These considerations of J. Friedmann and T. Lackington about Chile constitute a common opinion applicable to other analogous situations. See "Hyperurbanization and National Development in Chile" in *Urban Affairs Quarterly, II,* (June, 1967).

45. Gunnar Myrdal, *Economic Theory and Underdeveloped Regions* (London: Duckworth & Co., 1957), Chapter III; Bert F. Hoselitz, "Generative and Parasitic Cities" in *Economic Development and Cultural Change, 3,* (1955), pp. 287-94; Wilber R. Thomson, "Urban Economic Growth and Development in a National System of Cities" in P. M. Hauser and Leo F. Schnore (eds.), *The Study of Urbanization* (New York: John Wiley, 1956); P.M. Hauser, "The Social Economic and Technological Problems of Rapid Urbanization" in Bert F. Hoselitz and Wilbert Moore, (eds.), *Industrialization and Society* (UNESCO, Mouton, 1962); Philip M. Hauser, (ed.), *Urbanization in Latin America,* (Paris: UNESCO, 1961); Philip M. Hauser (ed.), *Urbanization in Asia and the Far East,* (Calcutta: UNESCO, 1957); International African Institutes, London, *Social Implications of Industrialization and Urbanization in Africa South of the Sahara* (Paris: UNESCO,1957); Office of Social Affairs of the U.N., *Report on the World Social Situation* N.Y., U.N. (1957), Chapters VIII, IX and X. See also the bibliographies in R.M. Morse, "Latin American Cities: Aspects of Function and Structure" in *Comparative Studies in Society and History, IV,* (1962): pp. 473-493, and "Recent Research on Latin American Urbanization: A Selective Survey with Commentary" in *Latin American Research Review,* I, (1965), pp. 35-74.

46. R. M. Morse, *op. cit;* Albert O. Hirschmann, *The Strategy of Economic Growth* (New Haven: Yale University Press, 1958); Benjamin Higgins, "An Economist's View" in Jose Medina Echavarria and Egbert De Vries (eds.), *Social Aspects of Economic Development in Latin America* (Paris,: UNESCO, 1963), V. 2, part II; N.V. Sovani, "The Analysis of Overurbanization," *op. cit.*

47. B. F. Hoselitz, *op. cit.*

10.

Urbanization in Latin America

The Growth of Urban Concentration

Morse, in suggesting a scheme for the two principal stages of urban history of Latin America emphasizes the differences between the cities of Western Europe and the colonial cities of the region: "Whereas the Western European city represented a movement of economic energies away from extractive pursuits towards those of processing and distribution, the Latin American city was the source of energy and organization for the exploitation of natural resources."[1] The city was essentially the point of departure for the settlement of the soil. Accordingly, this author characterizes the first stage by a centrifugal trend, a tendency towards decentralization. The central ecological unit, the site of power and social organization, tended to be the large estate, the autonomous and self-sufficient "hacienda." If the city represented the power of the state, the hacienda expressed another power, that of the great landowners "whose de facto authority could be measured by the number of workers and dependents they controlled and by the extent of the land which represented their property."[2] Left to itself, in the absence of opposing forces, the centrifugal tendency would have prevailed. But Latin America was not isolated. It depended on the colonial power, and the city represented precisely this power in its administrative, political and economic aspects. What Morse calls "the second stage" of urban development, characterized by centripetal tendencies radiating from the city through the power of the metropolis, is founded on this dependence. The cities then, did not disappear, but their location and growth were determined above all by the requirements of the administrative and political powers, and by the necessities of an economy almost exclusively oriented towards the export of natural resources (primary goods). This second stage did not end with independence; instead it was intensified with the growing integration of the region into the world market. The characteristics of the urban net, such as the configuration assumed by the transportation system (especially the railroads), were shaped above all by the necessities of the kind of economy which was dominant. In general, according to the geographical peculiarities of each country, the railroads tended to radiate from the embarkation points of the exports towards the locations of primary production, neglecting to secure direct connections between other areas of the national territory. This exerted a determining influence on further development, including the location and ecological concentration of industry and, in an accumulative way, urban centers and the rural zones. The great cities, points of contact with the outside and above all with the hegemonic countries, were transformed into "islands" in which modernity and wealth tended to remain encapsulated or segregated, while their influence on the rest of the country was "parasitic" rather than "generative." Although this pessimistic picture was relieved in some countries in which the "modernizing effects" of economic expansion caused greater diffusion in the society and population, the "dual" character of the economy and of the social structure and its tendency to persist and even be strengthened with time, were without doubt typical features of this centrifugal type of urbanization. Self-sustained structural dualism, over-urbanization and urban primacy, are all integrating elements of the syndrome of the primary economy of export.

It can be said that in Latin America "modern" urbanization, or the component process of social modernization, began with the third stage of the scheme suggested in the first chapter with the economic expansion "outwards" based on the great development of the primary economy of export and the consequent attenuation of structural dualism. The expression "modern urbanization" should be understood in a special sense and with the restrictions which have been shown in the preceding chapter on analyzing the contrasts between the process of urbanization in the countries of earlier development (which are also central countries, some of them in hegemonic positions) and those of later development (frequently colonial or ex-colonial).

As has already been shown, preindustrial or premodern industrialization in the region was strongly marked by this same orientation which became more accentuated from the beginning of the second half of the nineteenth century.

During this stage, the process of urban concentration was slow, with the exception of a few countries. It was in the next stage, approximately at the beginning of the third decade, when a very strong acceleration of the process took place in all countries of the region. Two phases of urban growth can be distinguished here. In the first one, the few countries in which strong urban growth took place, tended to be those in which the modernizing effects were more diffused, and also were accompanied by foreign immigration from overseas on a large scale. Towards 1890 three Latin American countries were among the twelve most urbanized countries in the world, in a series of fifty-nine nations. At this date Uruguay, Argentina, and Cuba occupied respectively the ninth, twelfth and fourteenth places. Another three countries, Chile, Ecuador and Venezuela were urbanizing more slowly than the rest, but figured in the top half of the above quoted list.[3] Towards 1950 Latin America had become the most urbanized region of the Third World with a level of urban concentration

TABLE 1
Percentage of the total population living in cities of 20,000 or more inhabitants*

Countries	1890	1900	1910	1920	1930	1940	1950	1960
Argentina	23		36				48	58
Uruguay	30							
Chile	14		28	28	33	36	43	55
Cuba	29			24	28	31	36	
Venezuela	8				9	18	32	47
Panama					23	27	27	33
Mexico	10					18	24	30
Puerto Rico		6		9	14	19	27	28
Costa Rica		7			19		22	24
Colombia	7					13	22	
Brazil	9			11		15	20	28
Peru	8					14		29
Bolivia	4	9					20	
Ecuador	12						18	27
Paraguay	4						17	
Nicaragua				4		8	15	23
Salvador					9		13	18
Guatemala							11	
Dominican Republic				4	7		11	19
Honduras						6	7	12
Haiti							5	

*Adapted from John D. Durand and Cesar A. Pelaez, "Patterns of Urbanization in Latin America" in *The Milbank Memorial Fund Quarterly XLIII* (1965) No. 4, part 2. The data for 1890 are from Adna Weber, *The Growth of the Cities in the Nineteenth Century* (Ithaca, Cornell U. Press, 1963).

The dates do not always correspond to those indicated in the headings of the columns. They have been classified in the nearest year indicated in the table.

approaching that of the developed areas (see Table 2). This situation is, in part, a consequence of the fact that various Latin American nations have achieved a degree of greater modernization than other underdeveloped regions of the world. But it is also the effect of an acceleration of urbanization, unaccompanied by an equally rapid advance in industrialization and economic development. When Latin American is compared with the United States in respect to "equivalent" epochs of its transition, it is seen that though the process follows the same pattern, there is a notable acceleration in the rate of urbanization of the region, especially since 1950. The distribution of the urban population shows the pattern of "primacy," typical of less developed regions. In 1960, Montevideo absorbed 45.9 percent of the total population, Buenos Aires 33.8 percent and Santiago de Chile 25.9 percent. Venezuela and Cuba (1953) followed with something less than 18 percent each, and Peru almost reached 15 percent. In sixteen countries out of twenty, more than one-half of the urban population was concentrated in only one city and similar situations could be observed in many other countries, to an even more marked degree. The great density of certain zones of high urbanization contrasted with large empty spaces; the populated centers concentrating around the "primate" cities and constitutes a kind of "island" in the middle of immense and almost unpopulated territories.[4]

TABLE 2
Percentage of population in cities of 20,000
or more inhabitants 1950-1960.

Regions	Estimations	
	1950	1960
World	21	24-25
More developed regions:	37	41
North America	43	46
Europe (without Russia)	37	40
Soviet Union	31	36
Oceania	58	65
Less developed regions:		
Africa	10	13
Asia	14	16-18
Latin America		
(Argentina, Chile, and Uruguay)	47	56
(Rest of the region)	21	28

(Adapted from Durand and Pelaez, see Table I, p. 3)

It is possible that this situation of accentuated "primacy" and of concentration of the urban population in limited areas of the national territory constitutes a transitory phase of the process, and upon achieving a greater degree of modernization and development, the lesser centers may tend to grow more rapidly, reestablishing an equilibrium. Although it is not probable that this would occur spontaneously, in the last decade (1950-60) a relatively larger growth of tte intermediate cities could be observed. The urban population seemed to decrease its tendency to concentrate into only one city. The cause of this seems to have been in some cases a change in the orientation of the internal migrations towards intermediate cities.[5] It is possible that a certain redistribution of the urban population may start to occur when alternative poles of growth in other zones of the country have been created, limiting the exclusive attraction of the "primate" city.

Internal migrations played and still play a central role in the acceleration of urbanization during this fourth stage, in addition to the natural growth of the urban population, which in the majority of the region's countries is considerable. This contrasts notably with the acceleration which occurred during the third stage, previous to the First World War, which took place as a function above all of foreign migration. This occurred in countries like Argentina, Uruguay or in the south of Brazil; and especially in the first two, internal migration until the 1930s was rather small. Although to a lesser extent, this can be affirmed also in respect to the other countries. For this reason, where migration from overseas was lacking, the rhythm of urbanization was slower than in the preceding decades.

Determining Factors of Urbanization

The characteristics of urbanization, as well as its changing rhythms and its sequence in relation to the other component processes of the transition, can be explained as a function of the form assumed by social modernization and economic development. In general terms, the causes of accelerated urbanization ahead of industrialization are applicable to Latin America and are similar to the dependent countries of retarded transition, already described in a preceding chapter. Applying the generalizations already suggested to the Latin American case, the principal structural factors of urbanization can be synthesized in the following points:

- Primary economy of export
- Modernizing effects of the resulting economic expansion.
- A certain degree of industrialization
- Accelerated demographic growth
- Concentration of land ownership and low productivity of agriculture

These objective factors at the same time operate as functions of normative and psychosocial factors, according to the theoretical scheme presented in another part of this book.

Since the second half of the last century, with the development of industrialization in the West, especially in England, the technological innovations in transportation and communications, and the increase of the necessity for primary goods in the already industrialized countries, the primary economy of export achieved a rhythm of accelerated expansion. At the same time, large foreign investments were made, largely dedicated to creating the infrastructure required for the development of the export of primary goods and to assure the import of manufactured products from England and other industrialized countries. In this way the centripetal tendencies of the preexisting urban structure were intensified by the economic expansion from the second half of the century. At the same time, many of the countries of the region achieved more advanced stages in the making of a modern state; from this came another factor of concentration in the capital cities, and also, where a federal system existed, in the heads of the states or provinces.

These factors of urbanization are characteristic of the first phase of urban growth in all countries of the region. Where the modernizing effects were more pronounced and accompanied by foreign immigration, the beginnings of industrialization and the increase in services (in the modern sense), there was an acceleration of the urban concentration; in the others, urbanization followed a much slower rhythm. The attraction of the external immigrants to the cities is a universal phenomenom of the migrations from overseas of the past century and the beginning of the present one. But its accentuation in Argentina, Uruguay and other countries of the region was not only due to the actual demand generated by modernization, but also to a considerable extent, to the fact that land was monopolized by the great landowners. Despite a certain number of immigrants who were able to settle in the rural zones, the majority was obliged to remain in the cities.

The second phase of "modern" urbanization occurring from the beginning of 1930 and even after the Second World War obeyed four principal factors:

- Beginning of industrialization in many countries or its intensification where it had already begun in preceding decades
- Growth of modern services, (the diffusion of the new necessities of state, education, health, etcs. as they were occurring or had occurred in the modernized countries)
- Demographic explosion
- Reigning conditions in the rural zones

Factors one and two correspond to the universal and normal causes of urbanization. In this case the increase is accompanied by a greater demand for urban work. This "actual" increase in demand took place to a different extent in all the countries and should be mentioned as one of the aspects of the process. But the last two factors, growth of the population and conditions in the rural areas, arise from particular conditions of the region. In respect to demographic growth, we have seen that its acceleration occurred with some exceptions at the beginning of the 1930s and was intensified afterwards (with the exception of the countries already at the phase of decreasing birthrate). While in the period 1920-30 the natural growth in the region as a whole was from 1.8 percent annually, it is presently up to 2.9 percent. These rates are an average and include the rural areas as well as urban. Although these have a lower natural growth rate than the former, a part of the increase in the urban population is due to this natural growth. But the major contribution is the migrations, especially the rural-urban migrations. It is here where the fourth factor operates: the social and economic conditions of the rural zones (unemployment, low salaries, poverty and hunger, lack of opportunities for improvement, lack of sanitary facilities, educational facilities, and others). The structure of land ownership with its high concentration of property or rather its opposite, the *minifundio*, constitutes in the majority of the countries one of the principal causes of expulsion. The great concentration of landownership in Latin America is well known. This is a continuation on a higher scale of a historic tendency which originated in the colonial period under the hacienda system, although in the majority of the countries the appropriation of land by a few families or individuals continued during the entire nineteenth century. According to some estimations for the whole region, 1.4 percent of agricultural or livestock landholdings take up sixty-five percent of the arable land. Combined with the latifundium is the minifundio — the proliferation of farming units below the economic minimum. Both extremes make the introduction of better techniques and investments which could affect the level of productivity, difficult in different ways. According to some studies[7] the diffusion and the application of more appropriate technology in the countryside face four principal obstacles: first, insufficient services of agricultural extension; second, the structure of the ownership of land; third, a low level of education of the peasantry; and fourth, other institutional factors, for example, lack of credit and an efficient system of commercialization. It could be said that the process of expulsion from the country also can be a result of better techniques and economies so that, in increasing the productivity of agricultural work, an excess of the work force remains which must move to another sector of the economy. This last case is not common in Latin American, given the situation of technical and economic backwardness in the agricultural sector. In the post-war period, agricultural and livestock productivity has not grown.[8] This is connected not only to the state of underdevelopment in which the rural populations have been maintained, but also to the lack of adequate agrarian policies and insufficient investment. All of this is related in great part to the persistence of the latifundia, and the set of archaic attitudes which generally characterize the landholding sector. In part for these reasons, and in part because of other factors, another factor of expulsion should be noted: the progressive and "alarming" (according to CEPAL's report) deterioration of the fertility of the soil in the Latin American countries. The destruction of natural resources contributes to a considerable extent to the rural exodus. In this context and given the technical economic stagnation of agriculture, the growth of population pressure created by the high rate of growth of the population necessarily causes the displacement of the excess towards the cities.

Given the great inequality in the distribution of income in the rural zones, including current low productivity, the revenue extracted by the large landholders would be sufficient for important investments in agriculture and in industry. It has been estimated, for example, that if the proportion of revenues consumed by the landholders in Chile were the same as in Great Britain (for an equivalent sector), the personal expenses of consumption of this group would be lowered from 21.1 percent to 10.3 percent of the national revenue. This availability of capital would be sufficient to double the investments in fixed and circulating capital. This would mean that the net investment would be raised from 2 percent to 14 percent of the net national revenue.[9] These considerations can be extended to the rest of the region. The persistence of the latifundia is also responsible for the fact that only a part of the arable land is really used. In a study of landholdings in seven countries it was observed that one-sixth of the land belonging to the large properties was cultivated. Nevertheless, these proprietors controlled the best lands, located in the most favorable zones, and also had easy access to technical aid and credit.[10] At the other extreme of the scale, the low productivity of the minifundio is also a consequence of the structure of property and of the kind of dominant social relations. The possibility of introducing better techniques in agriculture was annihilated by the low level of education, lack of access to information, lack of means and other causes.

Given the complex of unfavorable conditions in which the rural population finds itself, and under growing demographic pressure, the only escape is migration to the cities.

To these factors of expulsion from the countryside, the factors of attraction to the city should be added. If the demand for industrial work of modern service is very much less than the influx of workers who migrate to the urban zones, and in general, the degree of urbanization is much more advanced than economic development, it is still certain that economic opportunities in the city are better than in the country, although in the activities of low productivity of the "pseudo-tertiary" or the "pseudo-secondary," even for the unemployed.

Although the distribution of income is extremely uneven, in agriculture as well as in other activities, agriculture is where the most unfavorable situation is registered. In Chile, for example, the average income of the proprietors (12.4 percent of the population active in agriculture), was fourteen times greater than that of the agricultural workers without land. In 1956 in Cuba before the revolution, when the average income of families was 370 dollars per year, the peasant family only earned 92 dollars per year. In Brazil the national average (per person in the active population) was 440 dollars, while in the rural zones of that country the level was much lower than the national level of 110 dollars per year. In the peripheral zones of that country the level was even lower: in the northeast 85 dollars and in the sugar plantations, 50 dollars annually.[11] The disparity between average income in agriculture and other activities is illustrated by the estimates presented in Table 3.

In all of Latin America, although in differing degree according to country, the living conditions, nutrition, health, education and even housing and personal safety are much worse in rural zones than in urban. Types of consumption, like the use of shoes or wheat bread, are distributed very unequally between the city and the country. The same occurs with the different types of cultural integration, literacy, use of the national language, participation in politics, exposure to the means of mass communication.

TABLE 3
Gross Income Per Person Occupied in Various Activities
(approx. in 1950) Latin America

Activities (in dollars, 1950)	Raw income per year, per person
All activities	689
Agriculture	308
Manufacturing industry	1,078
Mining	3,206
Transport and other public services	1,206
Commerce and other public services	1,229

Panamerican Union, *Estudio Económico y Social de América Latina,* 1961, Washington, D.C., General Secretariat of the Panamerican Union, V. 2, p. 250.

The divergence between activities would be even more pronounced if the distribution in income between enterprises and workers and employers and workers were taken into account. This distribution is much more unfavorable in agricultural activities.

The combination of factors of expulsion from the country and the attraction to the city acts through changes on the normative and psychosocial plane. The great internal migrations are not only an effect of the structural and environmental circumstances but also of the deterioration of the traditional normative order and the rise of new activities. This is to say that in one form or another and with different degrees of intensity, the great internal migrations represent an aspect of the process of social mobilization. In effect, although the conditions of actual life in the agrarian zones in many cases have not improved in relation with the past, they also have not deteriorated. But these conditions cannot be accepted any longer, at least by a part of the rural population. All the studies on internal migrations show economic motivations — lack of work, low salaries, precarious level of life — as the principal motivations for migration. Nevertheless, there are also other causes: desire for education, aspirations of mobility, "desire for change," and other analogous reasons. But in "economic motivation," the basic fact of rejection of the inhuman conditions in the rural zones is found. It is true that this motivational set can vary from individual to individual, and according to region. For example, where migration is proportionally less, it is probable that selective factors operate in the decision to migrate (for example, the more dynamic, intelligent or educated, the ones who have greater or clearer aspirations of mobility). But in zones where migration assumes a massive character these selective features can be lacking and migration can represent a displacement in which the moment of conscious election and deliberation is less important. In any case, migration can be preceded by a considerable degree of psychological mobilization, in the form of exodus from the rural zones with a low degree of deliberate motivation on the individual, but always constitutes in one way or another, a certain degree of rupture with the traditional pattern and a "displacement" not only physical but also psychological, which can originate "availability" and the successive psychological mobilization, with various possible consequences.

On Some Consequences of Urbanization in Latin America: The Accelerated Growth of the Middle Urban Strata

In Latin America, as in other regions of the Third World, the notion of overurbanization can be applied, in terms of degree of industrialization and of economic development. In all the countries of the area the industrial-urbanization-occupation relation tends to be high, and the expansion of the tertiary sector is not in proportion to the degree of advancement in the economic structure. Nevertheless, it is also necessary to emphasize that movement to the cities and the reduction of the rural population constitute an irreversible fact and form part of the process of modernization. Although this may have produced a drastic change in the rural structure, with a large increase of productivity and the concomitant social changes, a large proportion of the inhabitants of the rural zones will have been displaced to the cities. Given the high rate of growth, the growing urban concentration was inevitable. The real problem is not in overurbanization, but in underindustrialization and in underdevelopment, in the primary activities as well as in industry. Urban marginality in its different forms, the sanitary problems, housing, education and other services in the cities have not been created by excessive concentration in the cities, since these same services should have been provided in the rural areas and at a higher cost. Naturally, this does not mean that urban concentration accompanied by the pattern of "primacy" of a few great agglomerates is not highly irrational. A more equilibrated urban net, based on a hierarchy of different size, distributed adequately through the territory of the country in combination with various "poles" of development, would be much more rational and certainly capable of providing a more solid ecological base for integrated national development. But these problems escape the more restricted guidelines used here.

A balance also should be made here between the negative and positive consequences of advanced and accelerated urbanization on economic development. References will be limited to some aspects of the process which refer to the modifications experienced in social stratification in concommitance with urban expansion, and especially, what can be called the "overexpansion" of the middle urban strata. It is clear that "concomitance" and not "determination" is being referred to here, insofar as the phenomenon is part of the process of social modernization, in terms of the scheme being followed, of the "modernizing effects" occurring during the third and fourth stages. It should be remembered also, that the expansion of the middle strata is not the only change produced in the nature, composition and volume of the urban classes. The appearance and the growth of a modern proletariat and a marginal urban sector, as well as changes in the composition and nature of the sectors of the upper classes are processes which are no less important. The limitation of these observations to the expansion of the middle sectors is due more to the fact that a good example of an "effect of modernization" is being offered, which is transformed under certain circumstances into a mechanism of stabilization of the status quo or an obstacle for further change.

"Overexpansion" is being spoken of here in relative terms, which is to say, in relation to the degree of economic development, taking once more as a base of comparison the developed countries and the more advanced global transition of earlier development. The problems, inherent in this type of comparison, should also be remembered.

TABLE 4
Profile of Urban Stratification in Argentina and
in the United States of America (middle occupational
strata and lower strata in the secondary and tertiary activities)

United States				Argentina		
Years	Middle Strata	Lower Strata		Years	Middle Strata	Lower Strata
1870	33.5	66.5		1869	8.7	91.3
---	---	---		1895	24.0	76.0
1910	34.2	65.8		1914	30.7	69.3
1940	38.3	61.7		1947	41.4	58.6
1960	46.9	53.1		1957	48.4	51.6

G. Germani, "La ciudad como mecanismo integrador", *Revista Mexicana de Sociología*, XXIX, 1967: 387-406).

The first case of what has been "overexpansion" of the urban strata can be seen by comparing the same process in Argentina and in the United States. Naturally, a comparison of the profiles of the primary sector would present very different features, since the latter country, different from Argentina, had a large rural middle class in the past century. But the rural sector in total tended to lessen while urban society gradually was transformed into a middle class society. This occurred through the expansion of the "nonmanual" urban sector, and because of the approach of at least one part of the popular sector to the type of work and market situation which characterizes the middle class. In Argentina, also, the rural sector had diminished considerably, but today includes more than one-fifth of the total active population. But, although a lower-middle class in the primary sector has been achieved, its proportion to the national level was always considerably reduced.

Historic data can only be found for a few Latin American countries[12] and it is not possible to make a comparison of the type utilized in Table 4. Besides, with the exception of Argentina, Uruguay and partially, of Chile, this expansion is very recent—at the maximum, in the last two or three decades (or rather, corresponding to the fourth stage of the scheme.) But the profile of stratification existing in 1950 and the tendencies which show estimations based on the data from the census of 1960 compared with the current profile of some advanced countries, seem to confirm the idea that in Latin America the middle urban strata are expanding more than could be expected taking into account the historic experience of the more modernized countries.

In 1960 various countries approached or even were above the level of thirty percent of nonmanual categories in secondary and tertiary activities in total (besides Argentina, Chile, Costa Rica, Cuba, Brazil, Colombia, and Panama were also in this situation).

TABLE 5
Profiles of Urban and Rural Stratification
(1950 approx.)

Countries	Secondary and tertiary activities Urban			Primary activities Rural		
	Middle		Lower	Middle		Lower
		Self-employed	workers		Self-employed	Peons
Argentina	41.4	5.5	53.1	32.1	4.7	63.2
Chile	29.4	10.6	60.0	2.3	28.3	69.4
Costa Rica	31.0	9.8	59.2	15.0	25.6	59.4
Cuba	35.9	12.4	51.7	1.4	36.1	62.5
Venezuela	26.8	17.5	55.7	4.8	58.2	37.0
Colombia	28.1	16.6	55.3	17.0	39.9	43.1
Brazil	31.9	13.3	51.5	3.2	62.5	34.3
Panama	31.9	14.1	54.0	1.1	89.6	9.3
Paraguay	26.8	24.4	48.8	3.8	86.0	10.2
Ecuador	20.1	19.1	60.8	1.5	58.5	40.0
Salvador	24.2	18.3	57.5	2.9	47.6	49.5
Guatemala	16.2	41.9	41.9	2.7	64.8	32.5
Bolivia	25.6	24.4	50.0	1.0	59.8	39.2
Haiti	12.6	46.2	41.2	1.3	92.2	6.5

(G. Germani, "La ciudad como mecanismo integrador").

Some data from 1960 that can be used here show that the same tendencies towards expansion continued: Venezuela registered 31.5 percent nonmanual; Panama 36.8 percent, and El Salvador 21.4 percent (always on the tertiary and secondary level). For Mexico (not included in the table) there are various estimations but all these show that no less than one-third or more of the urban strata are composed of nonmanual categories, and this level will have increased since 1940.[13] Although systematic comparisons cannot be made, some relative data from advanced countries suggests the same impressions as those suggested by the comparison with the urban profile of stratification in the United States. For example, in 1960 Norway had a 39.3 percent of secondary and tertiary nonmanual; Sweden 33.0 percent; Australia 41.0 percent, and England (in 1951) 34.3 percent.[14]

The causes of this advanced (and also accelerated) expansion of the urban strata in Latin America should be found in part in the advanced growth of the tertiary sector and in the bureaucratization of industry. To this should be added others which derive from the characteristics which transition has assumed in Latin America, characteristics to which some allusions have been made in preceding chapters. To these aspects, and also to some of the consequences of the phenomenon, the context of the last section of this chapter will be dedicated.

The Evolution of the Urban Middle Classes in Europe and in Latin America

The theme of the urban middle classes, their existence, nature, importance, and meaning, (especially political), has occupied the attention of many students in the last two decades. The publication of the series of monographs organized by the Panamerican Union at the beginning of the 1950s[15] revealed that for the first time in the majority of the countries of the region there were nuclei of middle classes of increasing importance. But many authors, including those who participated in the monograph series, expressed doubts about the nature of these sectors. In general, it was observed that these were not differentiated from the traditional upper strata by an adequate class identification. "The members of the so-called middle classes," John Gillin wrote in the middle of the 1950s, "make every effort not to identify with the middle class itself, but with the upper classes, or to the contrary, with the proletariat intellectuals."[16] Another amply diffused point of view sees in the existent social stratification in the region until the middle of the twentieth century, the coexistence of two class systems: the old "feudal" pattern, of two classes (a traditional upper and a lower class) separated by a rigid division, in terms of social distance, lack of mobility and hierarchical personal relations. Ralph Beals, on systematizing his general conclusions, based especially on the monographs on the middle classes published by the Panamerican Union, arrived precisely at this type of conclusion:

> Until better instruments of measurement are available, the situation in the majority of the countries can be described above all as characterized by a system of three classes, each one differentiated internally into a series of stratified groups of different status. Nevertheless, from the point of view of cultural behavior and self-identification, the feudal system of two classes persists, in spite of growth in the majority of the countries of intermediate groups from the point of view of their economic situation. The values and typical attitudes of the upper class towards manual work and the lower class are fully accepted by the majority of the members of the middle classes. In some countries the upper class and the middle class tend to appear from the economic point of view; in others, the economic divisions are superimposed on social position."[17]

According to Beals, the only countries where a certain lessening in the degree or disappearance of the "feudal" system of two classes and the corresponding attitudes can be mentioned were the predominantly European countries, or of predominant European orientation (Argentina, Chile, Uruguay, Costa Rica and Mexico). The same author recognized that the system of stratification was submitted to strong tensions and was experiencing rapid changes. On the one hand, he observed, the old upper class was becoming poorer or was becoming oriented, at least in part, to investment in urban property, industry or commerce, in place of remaining restricted to the old forms of latifundia ownership. At the same time, conflicts were encountered within the same class, through internal conflict or external attacks on the part of the lower and middle classes. The process of industrialization, besides, sustained in part by itself, should be considered as the most grave menace to their political and social hegemony, already serious threatened. Perhaps one of the important conclusions of this analysis was that the growth of the middle classes did not represent by itself a guarantee of stability. To the degree that these strata are permeated by values similar to those of the upper class, the menace originated by the popular classes can be transformed into a repressive force against the advances of the popular sectors.[18]

The advance of the middle classes acquired even greater importance in later years, especially since the publication of Johnson's book on the political transformation of Latin America[19]. Although this author has exercised considerable influence in suggesting an optimistic perspective about progressive action, he neglected to utilize the term "middle classes" for motives analogous to those indicated already:

> Arriving at a decision as to what terms to use to identify the middle urban groups was a difficult task, and the result was not completely satisfactory. In

the first place, it appeared necessary to avoid the terms "class" or "strata" which have connotations essentially economic for the peoples of Western Europe and the United States, while in Latin America only in the last years income and wealth have been added to education, prejudices, behavior, ways of life, antecedents and religious and aesthetic sentiments, as determinants of social position. Today (in Latin America) some of these cultural determinants continue to still exercise in the assignment of social status a much more important role than they play in the United States.[20]

Despite the fact that the character of the middle strata is not completely "modern," and its internal heterogeneity is well-known, Johnson decided that they would play a preponderant and positive role in political development and the stability of Latin American societies, within representative democratic forms and the market system. This interpretation and similar others were then seriously questioned by various authors. The phases through which political movements based on the middle classes appear to have passed are as follows: from revolutionary ardor or advanced reformism, to the acceptance of the status quo or of conservative tendencies, the alliance with the upper bourgeoisie or even with the remains of the traditional oligarchy, or in any case, a high degree of internal fragmentation, changes of orientation, and ambiguity.[21] But it is not our purpose to analyze in detail this process. The work of Graciarena should be consulted, which presents an analysis of the political trajectory of the middle classes in Latin America.[22] We will complement this analysis by suggesting some comparisons with the "middle sectors" of the advanced European societies of the capitalist type and their political evolution. These comparisons, made with more rigor than is possible here, could make obvious differences and similarities of great interest for the understanding of the process of the transformation of the urban middle classes in Latin America.

In the first place, the popular idea, especially among foreign observers, of the supposed "cultural components" and the lack of class identification of the middle urban groups seems surprising. These observations repeat almost textually the analyses and the descriptions that can be collected through one-and-a-half centuries or more of theoretical speculations and empirical studies on the European middle classes. Also, many of the theoretical and empirical studies about North American society emphasize "cultural" components such as prestige, family origin, manners, education, ethnic origin, attributing to them an importance which does not appear to be less than what is expected of Latin American society, although it can be admitted that a system of stratification is being dealt with, characterized by an ideology (and by a reality) more egalitarian than the one predominating in the class systems of European societies.[23] At any rate, the dichotomy between manual and nonmanual work, with all its connotations, has existed in the entire cultural area of the modernized

West, and only upon reaching the most advanced stage of the society of mass consumption, with the appearance of the "new working class," does there seem to have been (according to some) a "convergence," resulting from the embourgeoisement of growing sectors of the proletariat, and on the other hand, by the adoption of less individualistic and more collectivistic manners (for example, unionization), by sectors of the middle classes.[24] If both these are debatable (convergence and embourgeoisement), it can be accepted that now there is much less resistance by a part of vast sectors of the lower middle classes to accept a greater participation of the working sectors in certain types of consumption that before were peculiar to "nonmanual" workers. This is to say, there is in the advanced industrial societies (of private enterprise economy), less fear of the "invasion" of status by part of the lower strata. But this is a new occurrence and marks a profound difference with the "status" panic manifested by the petite bourgeoisie and the European middle class in the period between the two wars. This new fact could be the symptom of certain changes in the system of stratification. Let us examine the changes experienced by the stratification system under the impact of the increase on various forms of mobility in arriving at a phase of "self-sustained mobility." Here a scheme of analysis can be introduced based on three successive phases or types of society, through which the Western countries of early transition and capitalist development have passed. These three phases can be called "paleocapitalist," "transitional," and "neocapitalist."

Before very briefly characterizing these phases, it is necessary to clarify some suppositions of the present analysis. In the first place, we believe that what some observers of the Latin American middle classes call "cultural components," the elements of status, exist in one or another form in every system of social stratification. The explanatory model used is not important (Marxist, structural-functionalist, or purely psychological, which is to say, tending to reduce the existence of class or states to purely psychic "une chose d'opinion"); upon describing a system of stratification, components of status will always be found and these should be considered as determinants of the empirical behavior of individuals, at any rate, on a short-term basis.[25]

This position is not original since it reflects explicitly or implicitly the "multidimensionalist" positions which seem to predominate in contemporary sociology, especially since Weber. What is strange is that many Latin Americanists have considered the cultural components of greater prestige assigned to nonmanual functions in the middle classes of the region as "archaic"[26]. The second point refers to the idea that "structural dualism" is a universal fact of social change and is not found only in countries of later development. This means that in the history of the presently advanced countries, a phase of structural dualism has been experienced, that this dualism can have diminished or disappeared in later phases and that, finally, it could reappear under new forms in the future. For this motive, notions similar to those of the "declining" or "archaic" classes and "new," "modern" or "emerging" classes (so common in Latin America) have been used currently (with the same or other terms), in the analyses of the transformations of the presently advanced societies.

Some clarifications should be added to this. In the first place, the term "dualism" should be understood in a broad sense, as coexistence of two or more structural forms (strata, characteristics of the system, such as norms or values) which correspond to classes of different "ideal-typical" societies. Usually this differentiation is given by virtue of the asynchronism in social change; for this reason "archaic" (declining) forms are spoken of, in contrast to "modern" (emerging) forms. Nevertheless, it can be convenient to introduce a tripartite classification: "declining" forms, "basic" forms, and "emerging" forms. Within a scheme of analysis which supposes asynchronism, permanent change and rapidity of the change, we have three coexisting forms which can correspond to states ("societies" or "structural configurations") of different "ideal-typical" types; the declining forms correspond to the remaining archaic or traditional society, the basic form to "modern society" as it can be defined in a given moment of the transition (in the present), and the "emerging" form to the society to which present society seems to be orienting itself in its following stage (the "future" modern society). This terminology supposes the presence of the contemporaneity of the past, the present, and the future. In the second place, we should show that the terms "declining," "basic," and "emerging" do not necessarily refer to decline, or emergence, in terms of numerical volume proportional and placed in the various dimensions of stratification (power, wealth and prestige). Fundamentally, it is used here to indicate an orientation of the historical course, an orientation in the sense of transformations which the society (and the stratification system) are experiencing. This orientation is deduced or inferred by means of a model (or system of hypotheses), "constructed" by the observer (the social scientist), who is carrying out the analysis. Its pertinence, "realism" and predictive capacity are in great part determined by the general state of theory and the quality and quantity of the data used at the time of formulation, which is to say by the "historic level" achieved by the discipline at the time.[27] For this reason the situation of the observer is different when he analyzes a process which has already taken place and when he is confronting one which is occurring: in the first case, in attempting to explain what happened he already knows what specific orientation the transformation assumed. He can identify more clearly, for example, an "emerging" class if it has come to affirm itself in successive epochs. His predictions about the future are more uncertain than his "retrospective" predictions. In referring to the meaning of the terms "class," "declining" sector, "basic" or "emerging" sector, these, according to the case, can include estimations in regard to future growth or decline, in number, position of power, wealth, or prestige, or several of these attributes at one time. A "declining" upper class can have been the "basic" class in a previous phase, but can maintain great power for a long time in its declining phase, including a hegemonic power which in the declining phase is seriously threatened. In the future, nevertheless, continuing the distinction which has been formulated between basic upper class and declining upper class, this latter should experience a lessening or even disappearance, through fusion with the basic class, because of processes of descreasing mobility, individually, or of the entire strata. Analogously, an emerging class can grow in number and/or power (prestige or wealth) and eventually be transformed into the basic class, in a successive stage, to the extent that the forseen tendency is effectively realized.[28] It is also certain, in the second place, that the distinction between basic, emerging, or declining classes tends to disappear, and there is a tendency which can be of a general nature, towards the fusion of these groupings. Fusion means here loss of identity, or sufficient loss so that it is unimportant from the analytical point of view.[29] It is also certain, in the second place, that the distinction, although it has no concrete or empirical referents, should be utilized as an instrument of analysis, in the sense that for certain ends it is convenient to ignore the distinction between emerging, basic or declining classes at the same level. Taking into account these two observations — that of substantive order, and that of methodological order — we will speak of declining, basic or emerging "sectors," within each class, leaving open the possibility of its concrete fusion or its identification in certain aspects or in some circumstances, and remembering at the same time the analytical convenience of maintaining the distinction or not.

We will now describe the three phases from the point of view of the stratification system. The occupational structure in the three phases can be described in accordance with the classic model suggested by Colin Clark.[30] In the paleocapitalist phase the "primary" sector is declining but still involves an important proportion of the active population. For example, England in 1841 still had more than one-fourth of the economically active population occupied in agriculture and mining; in 1870 the United States recorded more than fifty-two percent in these primary activities. The "secondary" sector, industry, can be considered "basic" for this phase, insofar as it represents the central element of the economic-industrial system. Statistically it is growing, and in addition, it is in the same sector (and in its corresponding social sectors in which the technical-economic transformations are operating, which will produce the fundamental characteristics of paleoindustrial society. This society or phase of industrial development can be called "secondary" and applies also the socialist type of industrial development. In the transitional phase, the primary sector has decreased statistically, but still has a certain importance, as in the case of the United States in 1920, when it included one-third of the active population, a little more than one-fifth in Germany (between 1910 and 1930), or can even reach major proportions in the European countries which are developing under the capitalist system but are of later or slower transition (for example, in France we find nearly thirty percent in the 1920s, in Italy from forty to forty-six percent in the same period, despite the heavy industry which had developed before the turn of the century). In this phase, the secondary sector has already reached its peak and tends to stabilize itself. But it has experienced (and continues to experience) strong internal transformations following the same basic tendency observable in the paleocapitalist base, which is to say, a tendency towards a greater technical-economic concentration. Finally, the phase of "transition" registers a notable increase in the tertiary sector. For example, England had in 1871 almost thirty-six percent working in commerce, transportation, and various services, while thirty years later this proportion barely surpassed thirty percent. In the United States, the difference is more pronounced, from 23.3 percent in 1870 to 37.7 percent in 1920. Besides, the internal composition of the sector was fully transformed: accelerated reduction of "traditional" services (domestic and others) and increase of "modern" services. In the neocapitalist phase the primary sector was reduced to the minimum, the secondary sector had diminished or rather had been stabilized at the level it had achieved in the preceding phase, and the tertiary sector had expanded until it represented the sector of the greatest size in the composition of the active population. Production of goods as well as the production of services have followed the tendency towards high technical-economic concentration and financial concentration. It is the epoch of the great corporations and "conglomerates."[31]

The stratification system in its three phases, in respect to the general characteristics of the system as well as the nature and composition of its strata, has been experiencing a parallel evolution. In the paleocapitalist phase we find in the upper class, on the one hand, the "declining" sector, connected with primary production, and the preexisting system (the "aristocracy"). It is considered "declining" in relation to its historical destiny, although it can continue to exert considerable economic and political power during this phase and following phases, and can enjoy a still predominant prestige. But sharing this hegemonic position, we find the bourgeoisie as the "basic" sector in the same sense of historical future, which is to say, as a protagonist of the industrial transformation of the economy and of society. At the other extreme of the system, in the lower positions, we observe on the one hand a rural, declining sector (but which can still be preponderant in numerical volume, composed of small tenants, poor proprietors, peasants without land, as well as surviving "pockets" of the subsistence economy, which have still not been integrated into the national market or are partially connected with it). In some countries there can be sectors radically excluded from national society, as in the case of the Negroes (during the slave-owning regime), very marginal sectors, and as occurred with other ethnic minorities. The "basic" sector of the lower class is formed by this urban proletariat. But, and this is of great importance, their degree of social and political mobilization is low and partial. A characteristic, on which we have insisted various times in this and in other works, is that if industry and the new modern services have already created an occupational sector (also "modern"), numerically important in many spheres of life, its members continue to be traditional. Whatever violence or intensity of social protest has taken place at certain times, the politically mobilized or unionized sector of the working class is still very small. We can consider it as the "emerging" sector of the lower strata in paleocapitalist society, a sector which will grow and become "basic" in the following phase (of "transition"). Finally, in the paleocapitalist phase, in the intermediate sector, it is possible to show with certainty a declining sector and an emerging sector, but less easy to identify the basic sector. Declining certainly in numerical volume and power, is the segment of the middle strata connected to primary production (where it exists). This is certain even where, as in the United States, the rural middle class represented one of the most powerful sectors of the political structure at the beginning of the process of industrialization; also there, its decline will be inevitable. Also declining are the intermediate sectors connected with archaic forms of production of smaller middle-sized business. In the "emerging" sector we find categories of public and private functionaries, employees of offices and dependent professionals, who will then be united under the term of "new middle class." This segment of the active population, still very small in the paleocapitalist phase, is destined to grow incessantly through three phases. "Old middle class" will be precisely the name it will receive in following epochs and it will represent the basic sector of the intermediate strata in paleocapitalist society. In reality, they belong to the same occupational categories of the bourgeoisie: they are industrial contractors, businessmen, professionals. They are classified as belonging to the basic sector when their activity is oriented in the "modern" sense. Thus, the small and middle industrial promoters constitute a typical element of this group. There are two other characteristics which are of interest. On the one hand, we are dealing with individuals (or families) of descending or ascending mobility. The great industrial, commercial, and financial bourgeoisie will find in this sector one of its most important bases of recruitment. But at the same time, they occupy a social place which is seriously menaced; they also can become proletarianized.

In reference to the profile of stratification, it can be said that a great part of the population is located in the lower strata. A conjectural distribution which is "typical," carried out based on various historical studies,[32] assigns to the upper class four percent of the total, eleven percent to the urban middle class (secondary and tertiary), and thirty-five percent to the lower urban strata. The other fifty percent is rural, and on the structure of this sector will depend the existence and the size of a middle rural class. The system is characterized also by high degrees of discontinuity between the strata, of ranking of interpersonal relations, and consequently of institutionalization of the "image" of the stratification system. The manual/ nonmanual line is profoundly marked, and the restricted middle urban class "old" and "new" tends to identify itself with the upper classes. (This is the "false consciousness" which Marxism attributes to it, especially to the dependent middle class.) Although the possibilities of actual mobility are now considerable (also because of structural changes), the norms of mobility of ascriptive type and the attitudes and aspirations corresponding, continue to be diffused in a great part of the society and, in any case, coexist with emerging norms and attitudes which are favorable to mobility and to the criteria of success. Among the most significant changes which mark the phase of transition we observe a subsequent diminution of all the rural strata; but it is in this phase that the great landowning interests can, in certain countries, continue to share the power with the bourgeoisie (in a situation of partial fusion, of alliance, of conflict). And, at the same time, the intermediate rural strata (where they exist) can still play a significant role in national politics, and typically, display reactive or defensive actions of sectors in retreat. The basic sector of the upper classes continues to be the same as in the preceding phase but now the directorial and bureaucratic element begins to be important. At the same time, the process of concentration continues. More important changes can be found in the lower and middle classes. In the first, the urban proletariat has been consolidated, and now is completely mobilized and organized and has increased in power; it can now be identified as a new "emerging" sector of a "working aristocracy," which through its income, level of consumption, and integration in national life, announces the "new working class" which is characteristic of the neocapitalist phase. While from the point of view of numbers, the lower class has decreased (nevertheless changing its composition — less rural and more secondary and tertiary), the middle class as a whole has increased considerably. But the entire change corresponds to the "new middle class" to the "dependent" bureaucratic, professional, and technical sector, while the urban independents of the "old middle class" have decreased in proportion and inside the economic structure are located in positions of growing dependency in respect to the large enterprises and the public sector of the economy. The general characteristics of the system continue to be the same as in the paleocapitalist phase, which is to say, with features of "high" stratification and profound cleavages, especially in the manual/nonmanual line, but with two important modifications. The first is related to the profile of stratification, which now registers a considerable expansion of the middle strata. The second is the increase in the proportion of persons of incongruent status, which is a consequence of the fact that mobility has increased considerably (individual, structural, and "by growing participation").[33] The norms and attitudes referring to mobility on the middle and upper levels are still oriented to more archaic patterns. It is precisely the intermediate strata, in all its sectors, which is most affected. Threatened from above by the growing concentration of economic and political power, and from below by the advances of the organized working classes, close to becoming proletarianized in relative and absolute terms, and maintaining still the old aspirations and "cultural components," it is particularly exposed in this phase to the "panic faced with privation of status." This was intensified by particular situations of "displacement",[34] produced by strongly traumatic processes, like the World War I, the great inflation of the first post-war period, or the Great Depression.

In the third phase, neocapitalism, the manifest tendencies in the transitional period arrive at their maximum expression. Besides the processes already indicated, referring to the drastic reduction of the primary sector (in some countries, under three or four percent), and the lessening or the stabilization of the secondary sector, the changes in the upper class can be shown, with the extension of so-called separation of property and control, the accentuated concentration and the following advance of the technocratic element (civil and public and private military). There are other modifications, nevertheless, which are interesting to the present analysis. In the first place, the nonmanual strata are now half or more of the total active population; the internal heterogeneity of the strata has increased considerably in occupational terms as well as in terms of social and ecological origins (with a great increase of incongruence of status, which is now transformed into a characteristic of the system); the manual/nonmanual cleavage tends to lose importance or at least "visibility" and the whole system of stratification now tends to be perceived as a "continuum" rather than a hierarchy of well-differentiated and distant strata. Although the underlying reality can be different, this is the image which predominates in the "consumption," or neocapitalist society, as it is called here. Finally, the whole system is dominated by what we have called "self-sustained mobility" through the continuous circulation of status symbols from above to below (in respect to occupational symbols as well as symbols of consumption). While all these changes have the effect of increasing consensus and social integration, they tend to stabilize the middle classes. In reality, all the strata, propelled by the mechanism of self-sustained mobility, perceive themselves as in a "forward" movement; or with more precision, this collective process is lived as if it were an individual ascent. It is possible that at the same time a real decrease in inequality is taking place, especially in the middle zones of the profile of stratification, which now includes the majority of individuals; but this is not as important as the fact of self-sustained mobility. It is this movement "forward" which gives stability to the middle strata. The continual "invasion of status" on the part of the lower strata ceases to generate "status panic" since the middle strata is compensated by its own ascent. Besides, two other components contribute to the same stabilizing effect: (1) the changes already shown, the decrease of visible cleavages in the "great gray zone" of urban society, and as a result of the generalization of the incongruence of status and of the experience of mobility, the diffusion of ideologies and more egalitarian attitudes; (2) the fact that in this phase the situation of real dependence has been institutionalized, tends to be more a guarantee than a menace to its security. In effect, the middle class on the other hand is composed in great part of salaried workers and these dispose differently of the means of defending their interests (in particular, trade unions, for the lower levels). On the other hand, the surviving sector of businessmen and "independent" professionals have found subsidiary roles in an economy dominated by great conglomerates, which permit them to subsist, although dependent on them. This very dependence has been transformed into a mechanism of security.

The stability of the middle class in the neocapitalist phase depends on the stability of the stratification system, and obviously, on the global social system. A first menace for the system of stratification resides in the persistence and actual or potential importance of the marginal sectors which have remained marginal to the system itself, and to national society — which is to say, in the existence and importance of surviving zones and peripheral populations within the country or of ethnic minorities. The most typical example is that of the United States with a sector of its population below the "poverty line," and its Negro, Puerto Rican and other sectors, mostly enclosed in the cities. Another example is in the surviving underdeveloped zones which exist in various European countries, or in the foreign population, which in certain countries like Switzerland, is replacing the national working class. In all these cases, the marginal sectors are to be incorporated, but in certain circumstances, the process can be full of conflict. Much more decisive for the stability of the stratification system is the maintenance of the process of self-sustained mobility and the possibility of continuing indefinitely the "forward" movement. Both processes are conditioned by the capacity of the global social system to follow, without appreciable interruptions, a continual process of technological innovation and growth of production. We are not dealing only with the viability on the long range of the economic neocapitalist system, but with a set of economic, social, and political circumstances on the national level and no less, on the international level. The existence of an "external proletariat," which takes in the great majority of the population of the planet, is one of the significant elements of this configuration of factors. (In this analysis we have omitted all reference to the socialist systems.) Their trajectory and present situation is obviously different, but it seems to us that also with respect to these, it is possible to distinguish different successive phases and that its future stability depends as well on the capacity of the global system to secure processes of self-sustained mobility and an uninterrupted movement "forward." Finally, this movement, in the socialist societies as well as in the neocapitalist, should not take place only in terms of goods and economic services, but also in terms of the satisfaction of preexisting necessities and the creation and satisfaction of new ones; in the socialist societies, and in a different form also in the neocapitalist ones, the problem of liberty and the meaning of the individual, and creativity and self-realization seem to be assuming a central importance.

According to this analysis, it is in the second transitional phase of development in capitalism that the middle classes go through their greatest period of instability. It is the epoch in which, especially in Europe, the "crisis of the middle classes" is spoken of (from the beginning of the century until World War II). If in all countries this crisis has originated important political-social movements, it is only in some that it is expressed in "classical" fascist forms. In these countries, besides producing the massive phenomenons of "displacement" and "secondary mobilization" of the middle classes which make up the human base of the revolutions and the fascist regimes, a particular constellation of contemporary and historic factors condition the action of the different sectors of the upper class towards solutions, which in one manner or another reestablish in its favor the equilibrium of power. Among these factors should be noted: (a) a retreat in national integration (the case in Italy, Germany, Spain and countries of Eastern Europe); (b) the fact that the process of modernization, and especially, the development in capitalist form, are realized more through "a revolution from the top," carried out by a directing upper class, than on the base of conditions created by a revolution "from below"; (c) the fight between the declining sectors (agrarian) and basic (industrial) of the upper class, and its solution in terms of a compromise between both. This comes at the expense of the lower urban and rural strata, and gradually at the cost of stagnation of the class struggles originated by the advancement and rapidity of primary mobilization of the lower strata, especially urban, which pushes the aligned sectors of the upper class to procure forced demobilization, utilizing for this the massive support provided by the middle classes.[35]

After this rather long excursion on the evolution of the European middle classes, we can return to the consideration of the processes which affect the Latin American middle classes, considering in the light of the European experience what Graciarena very properly calls the "crisis of the middle classes" in Latin America.[36] We are dealing precisely with this. These sectors are experiencing a process similar to that experienced in Europe during the phase that we have called transitional. This does not mean that in this field, no less than in other aspects of transition, there do not exist great differences between the Latin American experience and that of the Western countries of earlier development. But there are some common elements which derive above all from the similarity of their location in the global social structure, and in stratification. The differences, which are many, arise from the external and internal factors as shown repeated times. Also, within the limits of comparison permitted by these contrasts, certain equivalences can be found. In particular, we suggest that from the point of view of the situation of the middle strata, the third stage of the process of modernization in Latin America should be compared with the paleocapitalist phase, and the fourth stage with the transitional phase. Some of the differential features are obvious. The paleocapitalism of Latin America was not founded on industrial development but on the primary economy of export. As a direct consequence of this fact the process of industrialization was held back in respect to many of the stimulated modernizing consequences, or at least, facilitated by the economic expansion originated in this type of economy. Although conditioned by other factors, the accelerated urbanization, the growth of the tertiary, and the overexpansion of the middle urban strata pushed forward economic development and industrialization. When this process gathered strength in the stage of internal growth, these aspects of the social structure had reached comparable levels with the transitional phase of European capitalism (although many other aspects and areas were backward, at levels even prior to the paleocapitalist phase). In general terms, it can be affirmed that transition towards modernity was not preceded in Latin America by revolutions "from below" or it occurred in only a partial manner. The revolutions which achieved independence did not imply an essential change in the structure of society nor in the type of upper class. Although in formally independent countries (even in the exceptional case of the Mexican revolution, which most approaches the revolutions "from below" which are generators of modernization) these movements were inconclusive or were reabsorbed by some kind of compromise.

To a considerable extent, the transition to modernity was initiated under the protection of modernizing oligarchies, in the form of autocracy or of restricted democracy (as in the European case), but always within the rigid limits of their class horizon. And these limits were to a considerable extent determined not only by their own position as the monopolizer of power and the necessity of maintaining themselves as such, but also by a form of development based on the primary economy of export and not on industry. This is an almost complete inversion of the European situation. We are also dealing with a bourgeoisie whose interests were closely tied in a relationship of dependence to the interests of the industrial bourgeoisie of the central countries. Although their desires of political and social modernization were generally more sincere, they inevitably had to experience the double limitation of their position in the social structure and in the historical situation on the international level. The Latin American middle class rises in the first place as a type of subproduct of this special type of modernization and is based, no less than the prosperity of the upper classes, on the fruits of the primary economy of export. As a group situated in a determined position inside society and within a determined (and dated) historical situation, their horizons were equally limited. They fought with the oligarchy to widen the base of political participation, and with ideological expressions that did not differ substantially from those manifestly professed by the oligarchy itself; and especially, during the phase of the primary economy of export it only proposed to transform into reality the constitutional projects formulated by the oligarchy. They lead multiclass movements of the populist type; but this was possible only because they did not have an organized proletariat under them. It was easy for them to function as a progressive sector of society. From this purely political point of view, the Latin American middle class was perhaps more democratic and progressive than its European counterpart (above all in the Latin countries). Although this furnished many of the leaders of the new working class movement in the paleocapitalist phase, it did not create a widespread populism, only the extension of the "progressive-democratic" orientation that it could generate in many Latin American countries. The middle class also limited itself in Latin America to the affirmation of formal democracy, but never lacked components of "social justice" — although these tended to become accentuated towards the end of the third stage and were affirmed above all during the fourth, characterized precisely by the mobilization of the masses. But in the same way as the modernizing oligarchical elites, the middle class never perceived clearly as a class the limits of the economic structure that facilitated their existence and expansion until this structure collapsed under outside impacts. The industrializing impulse was generated from outside and a great part of the middle class participated, but elements of the old oligarchy were not lacking which did the same.

Even the old oligarchy presided in some countries over the first phases of the process of substitution of imports. During the stage of outward expansion or in the terms of the comparison that we are following, during the primary paleocapitalism, the middle classes in Latin America were an "emerging" class that was rapidly transformed into a "basic" class. A declining intermediate strata was not lacking, particularly the old artisans replaced by the importing of manufactured goods from the industrialized countries, and the declining sector of the upper class, such as the marginalized sectors of the latifundistas who could not adapt themselves to the new mode of export economy or who remained on the margin of the changes, in precapitalist or "feudal" conditions (as at times they are called, using the term feudal in a loose manner).[37] Apart from this declining sector, the Latin American middle class was a class in ascent during primary paleocapitalism — ascent in political social terms and in terms of numerical expansion. There was not in this stage a "problem of the middle classes" in Latin America, and their position can appear as firmer and less ambiguous than in Europe, where, even in the paleocapitalist phase, within and outside of Marxism, these strata were discussed as essentially problematical and of ambiguous and contradictory political behavior. This does not imply that in Latin America, their identification as a class was not strongly influenced by the "cultural components" of prestige and identification (as aspiration) with the upper class, as occurred with the European middle class. Another hypothesis which should be considered is that the stratification system in Latin America approximates that of the European (especially in central and southern Europe) in regard to the degree of hierarchization and distance or cleavages between the classes. But these elitist features of the system did not necessarily limit the "progressive" political orientation of the Latin American middle class, since in its confrontation with the ruling elite it could make use of the support of the popular urban classes. Such support was possible since, at this time, the industrial proletariat was still in a process of formation and constituted an even less mobilized and organized sector than its European counterpart during the phase of industrial paleocapitalism; for this reason, it was not in a condition to organize itself into a party composed exclusively of workers. It is during this phase that the urban middle class began to overexpand itself in Latin America; a process that continued and was accentuated during the following stage of industrial development. This overexpansion, as was indicated, obeyed in part general factors which affected countries of later transition: increase of services, of the necessities of organization, public and private bureaucracy, and technocracy, to an extent unknown in the history of European paleocapitalism. But at the same time, expansion, according to the certain judgment of many observers, also obeyed other causes. In part, it was a consequence of its own success in incorporating itself to national life; recent power was used in not small measure to favor its own quantitative expansion and also to open new channels of mobility especially through secondary and higher education. In part, it was a result of the flexibility shown by the oligarchical upper class; it was a form of cooptation, in part not deliberate and perhaps in many cases not desired, but also in some form more or less clearly perceived by some of the most foresighted and realistic groups of this sector. This cooptation paid off through the reformist moderation of the movements and regimes of the middle class.

The crisis of the middle classes in Latin America began to be manifest with the crisis of the economic-social and political system during the third stage, with the crisis of the primary economy of export, and was accentuated later in the problems of a different type which accompany the process of industrialization and the mobilization of masses which characterize the fourth stage.

The middle class, certainly, also benefits from the "new course" which the economy assumes with industrialization. On the one hand it provides at least a part of the new industrial managerial class, and a great part of the executive, bureaucratic and administrative sector that industrial activity requires, even in its first phase of substitution of imports. And this demand, it should be remembered, is not limited to the historical level existing in the first phases of industrialization in Europe, but is closer to the structure of bureaucratized industrial enterprise of today. On the other hand, the process of industrialization, accelerated urbanization, and other changes accentuate the necessity for services, and in this way contribute even more to the expansion of the middle class, increasing their possibilities of mobility and their participation in consumption. But at the same time, this stage produces new causes of tension, internal conflicts within the class and conflicts external to it, insecurity, and threats from above and below.

In the stage of the primary export economy, the middle class was not more homogeneous than its European counterpart. It was a conglomerate of heterogeneous sectors whose economic interests contrasted between themselves. Nevertheless, perhaps even to a greater extent than in various European countries, the middle classes of many Latin American countries showed a certain political coherence. It was not only a community of "intermediate" situation; it had not only "cultural components" in common, aspirations, orientation of identification and separation from the lower strata, but also its capacity to grasp from the ruling class a significant participation in national life. But the heterogeneity and the contrasts which could remain partially latent during the epoch of ascent tended to manifest themselves effectively in times of crisis. And even during the growth produced by industrial development, to these old divisive factors were added others. Thus, the entrepreneurial-industrial function of a certain part of the middle class had to confront the syndically organized bureaucracy; chronic inflation produced transferences of income from one sector to another of the middle classes, although the syndicalized sectors could defend themselves much better in these circumstances than their European counterpart between the two wars. An important reason for this fact is that in this epoch, the degree of syndicalization between the "white collar workers" in Europe was much less than the massive syndicalization characteristic of these categories in many countries of Latin America (although with exceptions).

To all this is added the threatening pressures from above and below, in a very similar form to what was observed in the transitional phase of European capitalism. Certainly, at both extremes, the composition and nature of the upper and lower strata in Latin America present different aspects. But the structural situation of the middle classes was still analogous, with this double pressure of groups whose power is growing. During the fourth stage, the upper class in Latin America was a conglomerate formed by the old landholding bourgeoisie, the old established industrial bourgeoisie (to the extent that it was connected with primary production), and the new bourgeoisie, risen from the recent industrialization. But the possible internal cleavages of this class were not necessarily favorable for the no less fragmented middle classes, in the same way that they were not favorable in the European situation. Besides, in Latin America there is a component of great importance, which acts as a pressure: a considerable part of the larger, more modernized industries are under foreign control, and this is a current and potentially menacing circumstance for the middle national sectors. At the other extreme, the urban working class (which has grown extraordinarily), although it has not been able to form yet working-class parties, has acquired considerable strength, not only through its unions but also through the new populist formations of "national-popular" type which, if they include nuclei of the middle class, are much more affected by the influence of the working element than the preceding populist parties, where the lower strata formed a smaller proportion and were much more subordinated to the middle-class elements.

To this should be added what can be called a constitutional problem of the middle classes in Latin America. The fact that to a certain extent their existence and expansion is due to a policy of compromise with the existing order. This policy under certain circumstances can be convenient and favorable for ordered change, but in the long run diminishes the potential for change in the sectors who practice this for too long or in less appropriate conditions. All these factors and others not mentioned here, seem to form the actual "crisis of the middle classes" in Latin America. Their contradictions, ambiguity, backslidings, and more generally in recent times, reactions in the sense of apathy and alienation, are the expression of such a crisis.

In Europe during the transitional phase, the conjunction of various circumstances — stagnation of the economy, struggles between sectors of the upper class, mobilization of the working class and highly traumatic events which led to the displacement and the secondary mobilization of the middle classes — originated the Fascist regimes and other authoritarian escapes from the situation of impasse created by the many groups in conflict. In Latin America, since the crisis of the export economy destroyed the bases of the old equilibrium, there have been attempts at "classic" Fascist solutions. But all these have failed until the present, due to various factors. In the first place, the international climate is no longer favorable to this type of solution, and the corresponding ideologies have ceased to be viable. In the second place, as we saw, the Latin American middle class, despite its seeming paradoxicality nature, is still permeated with democratic beliefs. In the third place, and this is very important, in Latin America, traumatic collisions capable of producing displacements and processes of mobilization of the middle classes, as occurred in certain European countries, have not taken place. The deterioration has been slow. Besides, it has been interrupted by periods of growth. In effect, the crisis produced by the collapse of the primary economy of export, which did not lack Fascist attempts in Argentina, Uruguay, Chile and Brazil, was compensated to a great extent by industrial growth in the phase of substitution of imports. Despite the national-popular movements which the confrontation of the middle class against the first mass movements of a working-class base produced, (although of multiclass composition), the whole urban population, especially at the poles of industrial development, could in some manner benefit by growth. Especially in the more industrialized areas of the larger countries, an effect of self-sustained mobility was produced. This effect, although on a much lower level than in the neocapitalist societies, had similar psychosocial consequences, since it started from the lowest levels.[38] Later, stagnation set in, and undoubtedly the continuation of a situation of this type raises the most serious questions for the future. But if the crisis of the Latin American middle class has not been expressed in a classic fascism, it is not due only to the absence of conditions which could have permitted its mobilization. In effect, there have been, and are in the present phase of transition in Latin America, a configuration of features which produced conflicts which are difficult to solve at a particularly decisive time for the execution of economic development. The confrontation between sectors of the ruling class and between these and the lower classes, have already led to different types of "syncratic" agreements, according to the formula of Organsky.[39] But its significance, in a comparative view and in relation to the current stage of the transition, is that of playing the role of functional substitute for fascism. This is certain, independent of the intentions, purposes, and manifest and conscious ends generated by many of these military interventions. Besides, these processes take place in a peripheral area, which is to say, in an area dependent on the decisions of the hegemonic powers. The internal politics of these countries are not separable from the orientations and decisions of such powers. To a considerable extent the "functional substitute" of fascism tends to act in consonance with such orientations and interests (or more precisely, with the orientations and interests of certain power groups within the hegemonic nations). This need not necessarily be. But it seems to have been, until the present, the preponderant tendency.[40]

The considerations made until now only touch superficially upon the problem at hand. But perhaps a point of departure can be offered for a deeper consideration of the contradictory role that the urban middle classes presently play in Latin America.

At any rate, an adequate consideration of this role cannot be realized, without analyzing at the same time and with equal care the popular and upper classes.[41] Both, as we have indicated, have experienced major changes during the fourth stage of the process of modernization. And everything indicates that from the viewpoint of economic development as well as other changes in the social structure and political aspects, a new configuration of features is emerging and crystallizing; which is to say, we are at the beginning of a new, the fifth, stage of the process. Unfortunately, its beginnings seem to point to a stage of economic stagnation and political authoritarianism, perhaps not very different from the processes which took place between the two wars in Europe.

Notes

1. Richard M. Morse, "Latin American Cities, Aspects of Function and Structure" in *Comparative Studies in Society and Politics, IV*, (1961-62), 474.

2. United Nations, Economic Commission for Latin America, *Social Development in Latin America in the Post-War Period* (Santiago de Chile, 1964/Dec. E/CN/12/660), 34.

3. A.F. Weber, *The Growth of the Cities in the Nineteenth Century* (new edition, Ithaca, N.Y.: Cornell Univ., 1963).

4. United Nations, Economic Commission for Latin America, *Social Development, op.cit.*

5. Adapted from John D. Durand and César A. Peláez, "Patterns of Urbanization in Latin America," from the *Milbank Memorial Fund Quarterly XLIII* (1965), No. 4, part 2.

6. Jacques Chonchol, "Land Tenure and Development in Latin America," in Claudio Veliz (ed.), *Obstacles to Change in Latin America*, (London: Oxford University, 1965). Also see an analysis of the results of a study on landholdings in

Latin America: Solon L. Barraclough and Arthur L. Domike, "Agrarian Structure in Seven Latin American Countries," in *Land Economics, XLII*, (1966), 391-424.

7. United Nations, CEPAL, *Problemas y perspectivas de la agricultura latinoamericana*, (Buenos Aires: Solar-Hachette, 1965), part 1.

8. United Nations, CEPAL. *op.cit.*

9. Barraclough and Domike, *op. cit.*

10. Ibid.

11. United Nations, CEPAL, *Problemas y perspectivas, op. cit.*

12. *Política y Sociedad*, Gino Germani (Paidós, Buenos Aires, 1968), Chapter VI.

13. See the estimates of J. Kahl, *The Measurement of Modernism* (Austin, Texas: University of Texas Press, 1968).

14. Data computed from the *Demographic Yearbook* of the United Nations for 1964. The data from Australia is from Kurt B. Mayer, "Social Stratification in Two Egalitarian Societies" in R. Bendix and S.M. Lipset (eds.), *Status, Class and Power* (New York, N.Y.: Free Press, 1966). Data from England from G.D.H. Cole, *Studies in Class Structure* (London: Routledge and Kegan Paul, 1955), Chapter VI.

15. T. Crevenna (ed.) *Materiales para el Estudio de las Clases Medias en América*, (Washington,: Union Panamericana, 1952), 6 volumes.

16. John Gillin, "Ethos Components in Modern Latin American Culture," in D.B. Heath and Richard N. Adams, (eds.), *Contemporary Cultures and Societies of Latin America*, (New York: Random House, 1965).

17. Ralph Beals, "Social Stratification in Latin America" in *American Journal of Sociology, LVIII*, (1953), 327-39.

18. R. Beals, *op.cit.*

19. John J. Johnson, *Political Change in Latin America, (Palo Alto, Calif.: Stanford University Press, 1958).*

20. *Loc. cit.*, p. viii.

21. Omitted.

22. J. Graciarena, *Poder y clases sociales en el desarrollo de América latina*, (Buenos Aires: Paidós, 1967).

23. The literature on this theme is enormous. For a fairly complete revision of the theories of the middle classes from the middle of the 18th century until the present, see Roger Girod, *Etudes sociologiques sur les couches salariées: Ouvriers et employés* (Paris: Marcel Rivière, 1961), Chapters I to IV. On the persistence and importance of the motivational level and political behavior of the components of prestige in the middle classes of Europe between the two wars, see R. Aron and others, *Inventaire III, Classes Moyennes* (Paris: Alcan, 1939). For the United States, see Milton M. Gordon, *Social Class in American Sociology* (Durham, N.C.: Duke University Press, 1958).

24. See the articles of D. Lockwood, Goldthorpe and others in the book compiled by Joseph Kahl, *Comparative Perspectives in Stratification*, (Boston, Mass.: Little, Brown, 1968). See also the references in Chapter III, *Sociologia de la Modernizacion.*

25. In the text, two types of viewpoints in the study of social stratification are referred to: a purely descriptive view, which is only occupied with analyzing the features of the system of stratification as it appears to the observer in terms of indicators (objective and subjective), including elements such as prestige of occupation,

type and amount of income, life style, consumption and attitudes; and an explanatory view in which these characteristics are placed in a causal relation with other aspects of the social structure (productive system or relations of production, values system central to the society, functions in relation to parts or the whole of the social system) or including, as in the viewpoint of Warner, the whole system as purely dependent on oneself, which is to say, on people's subjective states.

26. This is partly due to the particular characteristics of the country of origin of many Latin Americanists (the United States), where effectively egalitarian values are stronger and more visible than in Europe, and in part to the fact that neocapitalism is taken as a base of comparison, which has been experiencing a transformation in regards to the visibility of the importance of "cultural components."

27. G. Germani, *La sociología en América Latina* (Eudeba, 1964) last chapter.

28. The distinction between sectors of a class, in function of its historical future, is partly inspired by the principle of "fundamental stratification" of Theodor Geiger; see Paolo Farneti, *Theodor Geiger e la conscienza della societa industriale,* (Torino: Giappichelli, 1966), 76 ff.

29. On this fusion effect, see *Política y sociedad, op. cit,* Chapter 3, Section 10.

30. C. Clark, *The Conditions of Economic Progress,* (London, England: MacMillan, 1957).

31. All the data preceding are taken from C. Clark, *op. cit.,* and R. Girod, *op. cit.* According to Girod, in the middle of the nineteenth century (in correspondence with the phase we have called paleocapitalist), the distribution in the three sectors was the following: fifty percent primary, and the other half secondary and tertiary (but with the strong predomination of the former).

32. R. Girod, *op.cit,* p. 102; (the estimates of Girod are only applicable to the paelocapitalist and neocapitalist phases).

33. See a definition of this concept in *Política y Sociedad, op.cit.,* Chapter VI, section 4.

34. See Chapter II, *Sociologia de la Modernizacion.*

35. In the recent interpretations of fascism, which have suggested some of these factors, the following are noted: Barrington Moore, Jr., *Social Origins of Dictatorship and Democracy* (Boston, Mass.: Beacon Press, 1966); A.F.K. Organsky, *The Stages of Political Development* (New York, N.Y.: A. Knopf, 1965); G. Germani, "Mass Society, Social Class and the Emergence of Fascism," *Studies in Comparative International Development IV,* (1968). According to the theory of "syncratic development" formulated by Organsky, fascism is one of the possible forms that the political-social system can assume in a determined stage of transition, a stage that grosso modo corresponds to the "transitional" phase of the scheme used in the text. According to him, it is in this stage when crises can occur between various conflicts: between agrarian elites and industrial elites, between the elites (as a whole) and workers, and between industrial workers and agricultural workers. Of all, the most significant is the conflict between agrarian elite and industrial elite, and the (transitory) resolution of this conflict is the syncratic regime, a form of fascism in which the industrial component is reduced, (see *op.cit.,* Chapter V).

36. Graciarena, *op.cit.*

37. Torcuato S. di Tella, *La teoría del primer impacto del crecimiento económico* (Rosario: Instituto de Sociología, Facultad de Filosofía, Universidad del Litoral, 1965).

38. See Chapter III, *Sociología de la Modernización.*

39. See Note 36; which is to say, some form of compromise between sectors of

the upper class, accompanied by the demobilization of the popular classes. The mechanism for this is the military government. It is possible due to the deeply rooted pattern in the Latin American political culture, which makes military intervention a legitimate recourse in political life.

40. For the case of Brazil, Hélio Jaguaribe suggests the hypothesis of a fascism based on military support in combination with foreign interests. See his "Stabilité Sociale par le 'Colonial Fascism'," in *Les Temps Modernes*, (October, 1967).

41. An analysis of the transformation of the landholding oligarchy to an internally differentiated elite, with different intermediate types, has been carried out by J. Graciarena, in *op.cit.*, Chapter II).

Index